Maria Luisa Josgun

Beside
Still
Waters

MARIA
LUISA
FARGION

translated
by
Iole
Fiorillo
Magri

PAIDEIA PUBLISHERS
ASHFIELD, MASSACHUSETTS

Library of Congress Cataloging-in-Publication Data

Fargion, Maria Luisa.
[Lungo le acque tranquille. English]
Beside Still Waters/ by Maria Luisa Fargion; translated by Iole Fiorillo Magri.
    p.   cm.
Translation of: Lungo le acque tranquille.
ISBN 0-913993-15-8
1. Jews—Italy—Tuscany—Persecutions. 2. Holocaust, Jewish (1939-1945)—Italy—
Tuscany—Personal narratives. 3. Fargion, Maria Luisa. 4. Fargion, Lina. 5. Tuscany
(Italy)—Ethnic relations.
I. Title.
DS135.I85T88413 1992
940.53'18'09455—dc20
                                                        91-47653
                                                          CIP

CONTENTS

Notes

1. A collection of stories about St. Francis.
2. A female character in Dante's "Purgatory," exiled by her husband to Maremma, where she died.
3. In Boccaccio's *Decameron*.
4. Friar Cipolla, the main character of Boccaccio's tenth Novella of the sixth day in the *Decameron*.
5. *The Devil's Brother*," an opera by Auber.
6. November 11, a day that is traditionally warm, similar to a day in Indian Summer in the United States.
7. Benedetto Croce (1866-1952), a great Italian philosopher, historian, critic, and an anti-fascist.
8. From Leopardi's "Le vaghe stelle dell'Orsa."
9. From Dante's *Vita Nuova*, song 23, ll.
10. Dante's *Inferno*, c. IV, l.

English Translation Dedicated to Pina

L'ora del tempo e la dolce stagione
Dante, *Inferno I, 43*

The hour of the day and the sweet season

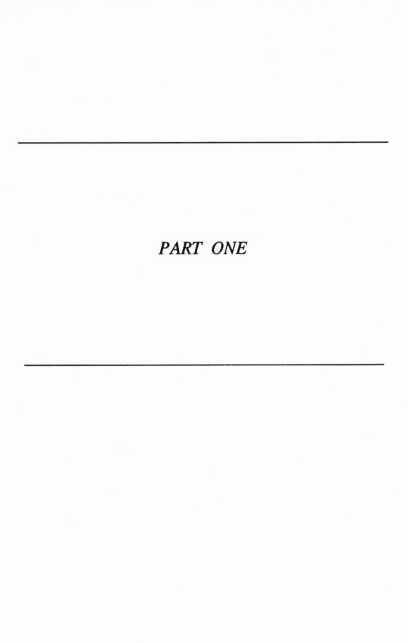

PART ONE

"At five? Are you crazy? Why should we get up so early? It would be different if we were going by train...but not by car!" After a little give and take, my cousin Annalena and I agreed on six o'clock. I was impatient to get to Poggio. I was anxious to see my mother, my sister, and my cousin Uccio. Besides, I enjoyed early morning trips.

The evening before, the downpour had kept us stranded in town. The one and only driver was not to be found until later, and in that kind of weather no one would take us there by carriage.

It was seven in the evening. In the lobby of the inn the doorway framed a pale rectangle of light lined with rain. Irritated by the gloomy day, the last summer flies were beating against the window panes.

It was dark inside. A boy wearing an apron, who was both scullery boy and waiter, decided to turn on the three lights. Attracted by the lights, the flies were now flying around the door toward the hot bulbs. They kept buzzing between the tables, on the plates and glasses, on the grapes and figs in the cupboard. Luckily, the tablecloth was clean, a sign that there was hope for clean sheets. As for the supper, after so many watery soups – white, yellow, greenish – it seemed too good to be true for my cousin and me once again to savor the red and white Tuscan salami, so aromatic and peppery, the bread, Chianti wine and the sweet figs.

We had enjoyed the downpour. Beyond the glass door, we took pleasure watching the green umbrellas pass by now and then, glistening in the rain like big wet leaves.

We went up to our room at eight o'clock. In the room were two iron cots with white cotton fringed spreads and flaxen sheets, homespun, but clean, as we had hoped. No closet, only a bureau made of dark wood with a thick white marble top. A small oval mirror, slightly clouded, hung so high that we could barely see ourselves in it, even on tip-toes. In a corner was the washstand with a jug and a porcelain basin, and two chairs for our clothes. Because of the storm the window blinds and shutters were already shut.

While we were still in our slips, a violent streak of lightning suddenly lit up our room, followed by a crash. The lights went out. In the dark we could hear the rain beating against the wooden shutters as if whipping them. Then pelting rain poured on the window pane, and then stopped.

Someone knocked at the door. I grabbed my robe, hastily covering myself. It was the landlady bringing us a candlestick with a lighted candle. I thanked her and she replied in her country dialect, "Poor souls! It could be worse! I brought you this little light. From now on we'll all be in the dark."

The candlelight was reflected in the mirror. Annalena was combing her beautiful light chestnut hair which sparkled in the wavering candle light. It cascaded along both sides of her slender neck in two thick shining waves.

I looked at myself for a moment, as if at a stranger or as if seeing myself for the first time. I was a brunette, with large dark eyes. My darkness was now enhanced by the contrast of my cousin's lighter coloring.

In the wood framed oval mirror, our two faces seemed as if caught in a medallion. Annalena whimsically swept up her hair and pinned it. The dim light of the room reflected in the mirror, slightly highlighting her image on a hazel-colored background, as in a faded old photograph.

Where had I seen that face before? Suddenly, for the first time, I saw a resemblance to our maternal grandmother, who had been my cousin's age – eighteen years old – when she got married. I looked a bit like her, too, in spite of being dark-haired. Or perhaps it was because all youths look a bit alike. Diffused on their skin is an aura that softens and refines their appearance.

I kept looking in the mirror, fascinated. How long would we continue to look like this? Was the time of our youth perhaps lost? The landlady's words echoed in my mind: "From now on, we shall all be in the dark!"

One cloudy morning in 1938, those of us who read at the newsstand the announcement of the doubtful privilege of being part of "the race" thought we were either only half awake or had not slept well. Three days later we were applying for our passports.

We had no intention of emigrating to Siam, the Congo or Greenland – all names that up to that time had resided quietly inside the De Agostini Atlas. However, those names now began to jump out of the Atlas with welcoming smiles from yellow, red, or black faces. Just the opposite of Italy, our country, our homeland, so beautiful yet so foreboding. This was our land, where people just like us, with the same white skin, speaking the same dear, delightful tongue, did not want us anymore.

The longer the list of places, the more exciting and reassuring the effect was. Italy does not want us, perhaps the Dakotas in the United States will, or Venezuela, or the Philippines. Surely we didn't want to leave out the Philippines.

We were like starving people – starving for love, understanding, and human sympathy. But getting away was something else. First of all, since visas were required, we began to hunt for them.

At the French Consulate, the consul would shake his head saying, "Oh, France? France?" and it sounded as if we would not be allowed to cast our eyes on "France," as if France were forbidden fruit. "To Palestine, *voilà... Pourquoi non? Il faut se mêler avec la terre, savez.*" "Mix with your land." We understood its meaning in later years; those words echoed inside us for a long time. However, in 1938 nothing was farther from our thoughts than the idea of "mixing with the land," and above all with Jews. German Jews, Russian Jews, or Polish Jews emigrated to Palestine. For us, they were Germans, Russians, or Polish! We had nothing in common with them!

We thought we would leave Italy as expatriates from our own land; we could not imagine ourselves as wandering Jews, but rather as Italian exiles. We would be Italians abroad, exiles persecuted by an unjust regime, even as others had been persecuted long before us. Wasn't Petrarch's passionate cry still valid for us?

> Is this not the dear soil for which I pined
> Is this not my own nest
> Where I was nourished and was given life?
> Is this not the dear land in which I trust,
> Kind and loving mother...

Our motherland had suddenly turned into a mean stepmother, yet we had never loved her so much, with such intense and desperate feeling. Rejected by our homeland, our love for the people and things that had remained true to us grew stronger...a few friends whom we loved so intensely and desperately, as do those approaching their final farewell, and the things that had become closest to our hearts and brought back memories. Not abstract things, but animated beings, live, concrete, loved and loving. Concentric circles, created by a welling up from our hearts embracing our home, our city, our region, all of Italy and her language.

Then I dreamed of teaching Italian abroad. I looked for catalogues from universities all over the world. (Others were doing the same thing.) I would choose names of full professors and address to them awkward letters, almost like S.O.S. messages launched into the void, through space, from sky to sky, from sea to sea.

I wrote to the City of San Paulo in Brazil: "October, 1938: I am a graduate with a degree in humanities and I would like..." Then I would erase the "I would like." What on earth would I get by using a weak conditional tense? So I would start all over again: "I am a university graduate with a degree in humanities...in humanities...in humanities." And I couldn't think of anything else to say and I repeated myself like a broken record. That was it, I had a degree in humanities, in Italian literature, and here in Italy I was not allowed to teach Italian!

Perhaps we needed to be more practical, make a clean break from the past. What use is a degree for us? For the first time we got together with other young people like us. We all agreed on a clean break! Many things were spoken of, and one idea came through that stuck in our minds and enthused us. We felt intoxicated with an unfamiliar cheerfulness. We listened to ourselves talking, hardly recognizing our old selves, the bourgeois young ladies, living a tranquil life that would turn into a drowsy sweet boredom. Up until then, time had passed slowly, in the library, in our rooms, with open books in front of us. Now we, the same young ladies, were speaking strange phrases, like "burning bridges," "separating from the family," "declaring our independence," even "living with a lover," since legal marriage was forbidden to us. Suddenly our horizons had broadened!

Trained only to overcome common little obstacles within the limited area of family and school, we were now like wild colts, dreaming of running over prairies, jumping over cliffs, ravines, torrents.

Who said we must be only teachers? We felt sorry for our classmates, doomed to teach Latin declensions, "*rosa, rosae*" to young students for all their lives.

If we had been asked to leave for Alaska as gold miners, we would probably have taken such a proposal quite seriously, thus discovering unsuspected talents within us.

Even the most modest job fascinated us...dishwashing in America! We could already imagine ourselves as dishwashers, with a clean apron under which beat a clean and fearless heart.

We all began to study languages, modern languages, of course, not Latin. English was number one, (well...the United States!) "The book, give me the book." We would chant these sentences over and over again with enthusiasm and boredom simultaneously.

We were also discovering a new dimension of friendship, that of real friends, bosom buddies and not that of classmates to whom we were tied by homework done together in the same room.

Bicycle riding was a fad at that time. We would go for long rides away from the city, experiencing a newly found freedom. Our bicycles had several different speeds, and we managed to pump up hills all the way to the top without ever getting off. Bicycling up hills made our hearts beat fast. The wind blew our hair over our burning foreheads, but we went on, sustained by a kind of commitment, a promise to ourselves: "If I make it up to there where the road turns, I shall also make it to..." Where did we want to go? "There," where the unknown was. Any obstacle overcome became a good omen that gave us secret joy. Once again we could savor the joy of living, a feeling that had seemed lost forever.

At the time a popular tune sounded particularly delightful and relevant:

> ...if the tune
> of the old organ grinder
> will change,
> our destinies may too.

At the end of May it looked as if the "tune of the old organ grinder" was indeed going to change for me. A letter arrived from Pisa. It was from my professor of Italian literature with whom I had discussed my dissertation and who now asked to see me. My heart jumped with excitement at his mysterious message. What would he want from me?

There I was, strolling under the archway of my university, La Sapienza, trying to keep in step with of my imposing professor. From the large hall a sudden gust of wind almost blew off his big, wide-brimmed hat. He stopped and pressed it down in a fit of rage. For a brief moment he stared at me, frowning as if my being there provoked him. His big dark Sicilian eyes flashed. In vain he held back his rage, his thundering voice exploding at intervals with a fearful crescendo, and began to spit out curses and invectives against the one who had permitted "*such torture that was a wound and a shame for all Italians.*" His words are still vivid in my mind. Then the volcano subsided, and he gave me some good news. There was a request for teachers willing to emigrate to the United States. I thanked him, stuttering with emotion. Back home I immediately wrote him a long letter expressing my deep gratitude.

A few days later I was back in Pisa, hoping if only to see him pass by under the arcades. He did pass me, but greeted me hurriedly with no mention of my warm letter. I felt embarrassed and ashamed.

At home the exciting news had been received in a way that I had not expected. Papa shook his head, clearly showing his incredulity, indicating that he did not consider it important. He said, "You don't even speak English! Besides, there is a vast distance between saying and doing." He chuckled, adding, "and with you, there is an ocean!" At a time like that I couldn't stand his turning everything into a joke.

Mother, evidently, was not pleased, and said nothing. Only my sister begged me not to forget her. With tears and hugs I assured her. She thanked me and asked me to bring her to America, too, as soon as an affidavit of support could be arranged. Together we dreamt of our Eldorado, imagining ourselves with a small group of Italians and with many American friends, of course. We were no longer the incurably timid young girls. On the contrary, we fancied ourselves as being bold, fearless, and even a little adventurous.

Meanwhile I was getting ready for my departure by learning both English and typing. I asked Mama to make sure my wardrobe was ready, especially for the winter. Winters are cold in the United States. Besides the raincoat, I would need a heavy coat and a loden cloth coat.

It was May and already hot, but I kept trying on my new "loden" in front of the mirror, caressing its short soft texture so like that of a small colt.

Little by little my room would get bigger and bigger, the mirror would disappear. In my fantasy, the familiar streets of my small city became big avenues of an unknown metropolis, all lit up with many signs, while our palaces turned into skyscrapers. I was walking on 57th street in New York. Usually I feel intimidated in a crowd, but not now, in my "loden." In fact I felt like a fish in its element.

The whole month of May passed by, and also June. Day after day, but nothing new happened.

Early in July a note from Pisa reached me. It was very brief. My professor informed me that a rejection had unfortunately arrived from America. A few kind words ended his letter.

The summer of '39 was approaching. My sister, luckily, was wrapped up in her work, "Cattaneo and the United States of Europe," a wonderful subject and a comforting one!

The United States of Europe... It was still a long way off, just as more than a century before, when those poor disillusioned writers of the nineteenth century were dreaming of it. Nevertheless, I was being careful not to disturb my sister, and simply left her in the midst of all those papers.

As for me, the idea of returning to the beach, the idea of the usual swims that I hated, among hateful people, was unbearable.

And there I was, dusting off my passport. To go to Switzerland there was no need for a *visa* or an *affidavit*. Yet, Switzerland was "abroad"! It could mean a way, a first way, a stepping stone.

I needed a companion though. Unfortunately, my sister was busy with her dissertation, and could not come with me. So I chose my cousin. Annalena had just finished high school. She was available, completely free. Although she didn't show the enthusiasm I had anticipated, she did not refuse to join me.

"Better than nothing," she said with the apathetic acquiescence which sometimes exasperated me.

There we were, in Switzerland, sitting around the dinner table at Madame Hemlère's *pension*. There we were, wondering about those next to us at the table.

We discovered shortly that the girl from Trieste with the long, very blond hair was also of "the race."

Madame Hemlère spoke of her in a low voice, cautiously, as one who confides in someone on a delicate subject. This caution astonished us, for we had just told her candidly of our identity.

Weren't we in Switzerland? In a free country, the one always friendly to political refugees?

To be a part of the persecuted group seemed to us to be far from a dishonor. Rather it gave us a sense of pride. We felt that people were in agreement with us. It seemed to us that all honest people would have supported us.

And it had been so with Madame Hemlère. She showed kindness to me right away, perhaps because that's how I felt toward her right away.

An old lady, tiny as a sparrow, she reminded me of a little bird, slightly defeathered, with her thin flyaway grey hair and eyes lovely as peppercorns.

I told her about us, of my desire to teach. Now, in Switzerland, I felt this desire reborn, like a tiny green leaf on a branch after an energetic pruning. I spoke to her about my plans. Perhaps if I could find a teaching position in a boarding school I could enter the University. I was interested in the French language and in French literature, and could very well get another degree.

Madame Hemlère listened to me.

The girl from Trieste lived in the room next to the one that Annalena and I occupied.

On one occasion we spoke to her. Since she was about our age and, moreover, of our same country and religion, it seemed to us more than natural that there should be a little confidence and perhaps friendship among us. But we were immediately disillusioned.

To start with, she told us that it was not at all necessary to throw to the four winds that "lovely" piece of news: the fact that we were Jewish. Did we want to be considered for a medal of honor?

She had no such intention, all the more so that her physical type was completely "Aryan," meanwhile shaking her long, blond hair with obvious pleasure. Besides, did we ignore the fact that right there at the *pension*, the German student was a Hitler fanatic?

"You ignore all these things; you are so naïve," she concluded with obvious scorn.

As for the young German woman, a florid girl with cheeks colored like a baby's, her blue eyes gazing at us seriously, it seemed only proper to detest her since she was a Hitler fanatic.

During the first days at the *pension*, however, we had treated her cordially, dreaming, with Cattaneo (the nineteenth-century writer) of the United States of Europe... But now? Did she know who we were?

Once, at the table, after someone mentioned Hitler, she sighed as if wounded, while her cheeks suddenly lost their florid color.

"*C'est un homme très malade, très malade,*" she said. She spoke like a mother who was speaking sadly of a son she fears losing.

The sentence was ambiguous in any case. Could she also have meant that Hitler was *très malade*, mentally ill, perhaps a madman?

No one pursued it further. No one asked any questions.

The young German lady continued to be kind to us. Whenever I arrived at the table a bit late, she always pulled up a chair for me, or eagerly handed me the bread or the drinking water.

We never came to really hate her.

This young German lady and many others were attending *les cours de vacances.* My cousin and I were completely free. We alternated between "tourist" walks in the woods and at the lake, and walks with a purpose, like going to the office in order to obtain permission to lengthen our stay, or to the boarding schools looking for a teaching job.

Boarding schools were abundant in Switzerland. But how long would my sojourn permit last? When I asked for renewal, the clerk looked at me with a suspiciousness that turned into hostility when I said I wanted to teach.

"To teach? *Travailler? Oh non!*" The Swiss would welcome any foreigner as student or tourist, but work was only for the Swiss. "*Comprenez-vous? Ne vous mettez pas dans la tête de rester en Suisse!*" he concluded, looking at me severely.

I was falling in love with Lausanne and confess that I was actually setting "*dans ma tête*" the idea of remaining there at least one or two years. As a university student, everything would have been all right.

With a year ahead of me it would have been like having an enormous bonus..., being able to study again, to know people in that enchanting city, and snow in winter...

How happy the Swiss looked, the legitimate citizens of Lausanne, "*les enfants du pays*," who could live there in their own country, in their own homes, carefree, without needing to ask for sojourn permits that were granted to us almost with an "eye-dropper."

I did go to the University once to ask for information. I thought I was addressing a clerk from the registrar's office. Instead, I was introduced directly to Monsieur Le Doyen, Dean of the School of Humanities.

I was not ready for this meeting. I was suddenly caught by that old feeling of anguish, a sudden weakness, and I had butterflies in my stomach as when one enters an examination room. I was also conscious of my poor French.

"*C'est vous la demoiselle Italienne?*"

In the spacious room, the walls covered with books, the old gentleman invited me to sit down. He took off his glasses and then looked at me from the other side of the table, with his clear, kind eyes. Unexpectedly, I felt at peace.

That air was familiar and healthy. It was the breath from books, and from the tranquil and quiet attitude of a person who has the taste for and the habit of studying. I felt at ease, and a little of that calm, of that serenity, permeated me pleasantly.

I don't remember how much I said, as I was mixing French phrases with longer and longer ones in Italian.

Le Doyen listened to me, full of benevolence and without showing the least inclination of impatience.

At one point, I said how much I desired to register at the University and to stay at Lausanne for a year. I liked the city and praised it passionately. He interrupted me.

"Il n'y a pas les trésors d'art qui se trouvent à Pisa..."

He spoke exceptionally slowly, as if isolating the words among long pauses of silence, as if his voice found repose and also support on the "esses" that he pronounced charmingly – *"trésors, Pisa."*

The words arranged themselves as if they were lines of a lullaby that soothed me.

He said that I might include Italian in my course of study, which was also a part of the foreign language department. *"Car vous devez le savoir merveilleusement bien,"* he concluded with a smile.

When I left the room I was radiant. I thought I would obtain the sojourn permit, and remain for at least one year in that enchanting Lausanne where there was an enchanting university and inside the university an enchanting old man with whom I would be doing enchanting studies.

Three days later a paper arrived for me with the order to leave Lausanne, and even worse, all of French-speaking Switzerland, within a week.

Why was I being expelled like this?

One word buzzed in my head. Perhaps I was one of the "undesirable" people? But "race" had nothing to do with it since the order was solely for me and not for my cousin Annalena.

When I went to the clerk to ask for an explanation, the same one of *"ne vous mettez pas dans la tête,"* it seemed to me that he approved of the wicked verdict even spitefully.

What was the reason for it? I already had a degree, while my cousin did not. In my case I was no longer the age of an *étudiant,"* what I actually wanted was to teach, to *"travailler."*

Oh, how I regretted that I had mentioned it to him the previous time. It turned out to be completely useless to insist upon admission to the University where people are completely free to get even three or four degrees at any age. For this insensitive Swiss, such a goal of knowledge was unthinkable.

I don't know how I got the idea of confiding in and revealing my case to the English *demoiselle* employed at the United Nations in Geneva; she was now on vacation in Lausanne, at our *pension.* It seemed to me that, as a representative of free England, she should have hated any tyranny; and the fact that she was a part of the UN seemed to me a good omen, as if she could have the full authority and arbitrate the fate of all people in general, and (a little) of my fate in particular.

Very tall and angular, of uncertain age, between thirty and forty, with hair in flat waves that perfectly framed her triangular face, the *demoiselle* sat with great dignity at the table every day, eating in silence or exchanging only a few courteous words about the weather or some other banality.

At my story she blushed lightly as if she were insulted, but I soon realized that her indignation was not for what I was telling her, but for my unheard-of lack of reserve, for my impropriety in looking to her as a confidante. She regarded me with such an icy look that any desire to continue my story disappeared for good.

And so, a separation from my cousin was being forced on us.

She had not been expelled and was not obliged to leave. As a matter of fact, for several days she had been employed as a baby-sitter in a kindergarten.

She was not enthusiastic about her job. "To comb a baby's hair is easy," she told me, "but forty babies every morning? You simply go crazy. A bow for this one, bangs for another, curls for a third child...and trouble if on Sundays their mothers find them without the 'banana,' or with one braid instead of two – it's the end of the world! And then, lunch outside. Even that seems like a game, eh? But the children smear butter all over their faces, and worse yet is what they do with the blackberry jam. To top it off, there are bees and wasps that make them scream when stung, and that continually fall into their glasses. It drives you crazy, I'll tell you!"

My cousin Annalena has always been easy-going. She had no enthusiasm for that hectic life. Were I to return to Italy, she would leave with me. And without scenes such as I was making. Luckily she had been the one to insist on dragging me on outings; otherwise I would have spent my time between the Consulate, the *bureau des étrangers* and the University, only to get the same result, "being expelled from Switzerland." Certainly, my head was always in the clouds dreaming dreams. On the contrary, she, Annalena, had succeeded in getting a job in the kindergarten.

I looked at her with admiration. It was true that with all my enthusiasm I had accomplished nothing. Dreams, dreams, and still more dreams; in Switzerland even as in Italy.

My cousin wasn't like that.

Maybe, to offset her constitutional laziness, she possessed a stubborn tenacity in reaching a goal, an inner force, an instinct that pushed her forward, much like big ants that, taking hold of a grain, carry it laboriously, never letting go, until it is concealed in their nest.

At times her persistence annoyed me.

When we went into the city, she would stop every few steps, at elegant stores in the center, at dark shops on the outskirts, and at every stand in the market, invariably daring to ask in her poor French and rhythmical monotone the price of every object.

"*Combien coûte ça ? Quel est le prix?*" she would ask, from the most expensive jewels to a kitchen spoon.

I was ashamed, but it was impossible to keep her from making these inquiries. "What does it matter to you?" I would ask, "We're not going to buy anything."

But she didn't budge, she never changed. Finally in our last days, she decided to buy some souvenirs within reach of her pocketbook.

When we were far from the city, stretched out under the sweetly rustling trees, looking at the sky while a weightless leaf detached itself from a branch, I would forget everything, and just dream. I would not move from there.

I would lie there without any sense of time.

A part of me seemed to be detached like one of those leaves. It would fly away like a feathery and shiny star, one of those winged, changing seeds that are in fact called "luck." Like "luck," they touch us lightly, flying higher and higher, while the few times we succeed in catching them, they break apart in our greedy fingers in small impalpable silk strands...

After awhile, I realized that Annalena's voice was awakening me, "Isa, what are you doing? Are you sleeping? Let's eat; we must reach Chillon. It takes at least two hours," she said to me as she unfolded the map that she always brought along.

Truly, I didn't bear a grudge toward my cousin for this.

I owed it to her for discovering the most beautiful places around Lausanne: a swim in the lake, and a ride on the small lighted steamboat in the dark tranquil water barely lighted by colored lanterns. Together we visited churches, castles, exhibits; we went to the cinema, delighted to learn that Greta Garbo spoke French.

We would put napkins on the grass. We would then eat sandwiches that Mme. Hemlère had prepared for us, and drink the tart grapefruit juice.

And now we were obliged to say farewell to Switzerland: to the woods and to the lake, to the University, to Mme. Hemlère and to the round table.

I was envious of everyone who was staying. More than anyone else, I envied the two Danish girls. They were two very young sisters who looked like two peas in a pod. Always together, always a pair, they almost seemed to fly, their steps dancing, their short hair bouncing. They ate in a hurry, like little birds that lightly stop to peck a seed and fly away.

They were constantly flying off to parties and balls, on trips...

So it was, for them, one day after another, every day, as if "the hands on the face of their youth" had stopped with joyous enchantment at the same hour.

Someone advised me to get in touch with the Political Refugee Committee for help.

In the waiting room were people speaking in all the languages of the world, a sort of tower of Babel.

Some were dressed oddly, in between tourist and beggar; under an almost new sport coat, original in its cut and color, would appear a pair of worn pants. People wearing overcoats or ski jackets mingled with others in shorts and sport shirts. Many were equipped with luggage: back packs, plaid throws of lively colors, and swollen suitcases tied with string, all with tags from many different places. Men and women seemed to know one another; they spoke excitedly. It was clear that they were used to coming here often, and to the long waits.

I spoke to no one and no one spoke to me.

The stench of sweat and smoke hung in the room. The crowd engulfed me. I lacked air, I was suffocating. I had flaming cheeks and a sense of chill on the back of my neck, a dry throat, and burning eyes.

Suddenly I felt uneasy and dismayed, a feeling that increased unbearably, like nausea. It was no longer a physical sensation, but something worse, like something that I had never experienced before.

I was one of them. I was a foreigner, without any rights. I was in that office to beg a sojourn permit.

No one knew me.

It was not like in Italy, where it was always possible to give an address, a place where I could be found, to give the name of somebody I knew; even without an identity card, I felt secure, tranquil. Not now. I clung desperately to my purse containing my passport, my sojourn permit, still valid for another week, a few Swiss francs, just enough to buy a return ticket: all my riches!

Had even one of these things been lost, these objects of little value, it would have been enough to be mistaken for someone else.

Who knows you? Anyone can distrust you, and rightly so. And what about the language? With that little bit of French!

It seemed that suddenly I began to stammer, it seemed I would never stop stammering, I would no longer be myself. I would no longer be anything at all.

A person without a country perhaps?

How dreadful this world is! I started to panic. I still clutched my purse desperately.

Finally I heard my name.

It was my turn.

I went into the next room. There was a long line of people standing before a window. I took my place in the line.

Ahead of me I could see only gesticulating arms and hands, one after the other. All the right hands were waving documents: cards, identity cards, passports, permits, booklets and papers of all colors, with signatures, visas, stamps, seals from over half the world.

As I was pushed by the tide, I eventually found myself in front of the window, face to face with the clerk, an elderly woman, gruff, and with no expression. I handed my appeal to her.

Her eyes, behind light blue glasses, scanned my petition, written in the French I had learned at school.

The language was all right: "*rien a corriger.*" I smiled then, like a schoolgirl who had received a good grade for her composition, but my smile faded quickly at her next words. My petition was to no avail. "*Rien du tout.*"

I had not much confidence in petitions so I answered that, in fact, I had not entertained much hope. I would certainly leave. In a few days I would return home, to Italy.

At my words, pronounced rather calmly, she gave a start as if she had been stung by a wasp, and her blue eyes looked at me as if in shock, curious, as if she were in the presence of a phenomenon.

"*Vous, vous voulez rentrer en Italie!*"

Return to Italy? Was I crazy? I, who had fled to Switzerland successfully, would now want to return to Italy? Didn't I realize what could happen to me back in Italy? With Hitler and Mussolini? Never mind the stay permit. Far better to pretend sickness and have myself placed in a concentration camp right there in Switzerland. Better to be killed.

Her cheeks burning with anger, she continued to speak, heedless of the long line of petitioners behind me.

All the same, I left Switzerland before the end of the week.

Nothing was farther from my mind than the idea of living outside the law, without proper documents, just leaving everything to chance.

I thought of life like a tranquil river running between two banks: between a birth certificate that you collect on one side, and the other inevitable certificate drawn by others, on the opposite side.

The river seemed to be strewn with a series of floating corks, marking the unchanging milestones that one must reach, places that strengthen one and keep one afloat: vaccination certificate...grammar school diploma...junior high school...high school diploma...a degree. All those floating corks seemed to me indispensable and very important.

At the beginning of our train trip my cousin and I were the only Italians. All the others were foreigners, mostly French. But on reaching the border, the French got off a few at a time at different stations, while Italians began to come aboard, like when one pours milk in a demitasse of coffee, diluting it a bit. The language also became mixed, and little by little the French chatter was superseded by the Italian. The flowing words, open and closed vowels, each with its special tone, its clear color, without all the "eau," "oe," "eu..." without the spicy sauce of the French "r" which, although it enhances, hides all other tastes.

By now in our compartment, only a tiny French child was left, very small, three or four years old, accompanied by his mother.

It was already the end of September and it was no longer hot, but the little child had little on, no socks, just small white sandals, wearing a skimpy blue jumper with straps.

His nudity was particularly striking, usually so natural in children who, although bare, look beautiful dressed in their silky skin. But the little French child's flesh was pale, bloodless, and contrasted greatly with the blue jumper.

Also his little face seemed almost wrinkled and a little worn, with his brilliant black eyes, as if he were a kind of *viveur* in miniature.

Perhaps it was the French language sounding on those childish lips that contributed to my absurd impression. Such an esoteric language...

Unfit for a child! I was surprised to think this, as if French children should speak a language different from their mother tongue!

"Maman, donne moi d'autres bonbons."

The child continually crunched and sucked on his *bonbons*. He also offered some to the other travelers with grace, ease and gallantry.

The train sped through the countryside. The window was half open: the soil was no longer arid as in summer. From afar, the hills seemed covered by a soft green color, as after the first spring showers.

The compartment was almost empty; with the doors also open, the draft of fresh air felt good.

Suddenly at the door a tall robust young man appeared, his two hands full. In fact, with his right hand he was holding a big suitcase tied with a string; with his left, he was holding a three- or four-year old child who, in turn, was holding onto his own brother, like a clinging appendage. There was no doubt that they were brothers, even twins, because one was the perfect image of the other.

In preparation for the trip, the twins had certainly been thoroughly groomed by their loving mother. With their hair slicked down and neatly parted, with their little freshly washed shirts, jackets, and pants of good strong material. Their bare robust legs were tanned above the cotton socks, and firmly set in cowhide shoes tied with thick shoestrings.

The new arrivals attracted the attention of all the other travelers, even of the little French child with whom they made an enormous contrast.

He was like one of those light candies with no substance that melt in your mouth; the others were like good homemade bread that nourishes but is hard to chew.

The tiny French child, with his consummate *savoir faire*, tried some approaches:

"Dis moi quelque chose, dis moi quelque chose."

Smiling all over, he insisted on offering his sweets to one or the other of the two little brothers, but the little country lads withdrew into a corner behind the window curtains, silent and out of reach.

All of a sudden, the 1:00 P.M. express train passed ours: "two choo-choos!"

They were screaming with all their might; they had jumped out from behind the curtain at the unusual sight. They were seeing two trains at once!

"They are rustics, poor things," said the parent with the broad speech of his Lombard dialect.

It was their first trip, he explained to us, and they lived in the countryside in an isolated house.

But immediately after the encounter of the two trains, the little country lads regained their silence, their complete indifference. They chewed their bread and cheese calmly, accepting them trustingly from the hands of their father.

I was happy to return and happy that my parents were far from the city. I was supposed to meet them at my cousin Uccio's estate, the old villa at Poggio, which was surrounded by a few peasants' houses and green fields.

Annalena and I had left the town behind us, the old houses huddled together, most of their shutters still closed in the quiet of the night. Only a few were open and the window panes reflected the beautiful, almost perfectly clear, September sky, a light water-color blue.

It had rained all night. Now only a few white clouds moved, like sails, in the clear sky. We could hear bells in the silence of the morning. Our car passed the church belfry, the embattled walls of the town, the double line of peeling plane trees, with their light yellow spots.

The road ran through the countryside between vineyards and olive trees. On both sides were freshly plowed fields. The upturned granular soil looked like the pulp of a fruit. It had turned a deep red. The earth clods had become water-logged, having greedily absorbed the night rain that now was evaporating. The early morning sun was drying up the soil, creating a patchwork of lighter and darker shades.

We encountered a wagon drawn by oxen, a horse-drawn cart, a few bicycles; cars, none.

Some peasant women and children were standing at the door or on the terrace near pots filled with geraniums. Shading their eyes with their hands, they were watching us go by. Some of them would greet our driver: "Oh, Michele, where are you going?" Michele would slow down briefly but leisurely. To us they would say: "Good day to you!" The "good day" of those Sienese peasants is unforgettable once heard uttered by those bright, lilting voices, in their Tuscan tongue, the most beautiful in the world.

At a road crossing we were welcomed by a little Madonna and Child decorated with carnations, smiling from behind a grille with a little vigil lamp aglow, looking like a pale firefly in the early morning light.

Where the road rose up on the hill, there stood a long row of cypresses. It was alive with clamoring sparrows taking off from the brown foliage in small restless flights, diving into the grass, upsetting its uniformity, playing hide and seek, grouping and regrouping, almost weaving tangles, forming flying chains of two, three, ten, whispering, chirping, trilling.

The shadow of death, lurking every evening behind the silhouette of those trees, at that moment seemed forced back by the spirit of life.

The sun spilled its gold on everything.

"We're almost there," Michele said to us at a curve. "From now on, the road goes directly up to Poggio, to the 'palace.'"

The car proceeded slowly up the steep hill, between two low stone walls. "All the land around here belongs to your cousin," he whispered slyly and greedily, like an innkeeper who lets you taste some of his good wine that he had put aside.

I looked at the beautiful vineyards, interspersed with olive trees, their dry, twisted old trunks silhouetted with graceful dignity against the sky. The foliage, etched against the sky, allowed the air to filter down between the leaves and berries – lightly, silvery, yet in a regular pattern. Those fields evoked an unchanging fourteenth-century landscape of Tuscany, similar to the Umbrian Franciscan landscape of the *"Fioretti."*[1] "Also Boccaccio's!", I suddenly thought as I was looking at the clusters of grapes peeking through their leaves, in bunches of round, ripe fruit, with the veil that softens their gold and brown colors.

Leaning from the car window, I breathed in the country air...the smell of soil, sun, grass; of hay, manure, and must; smells that already tasted of grapes and ripe figs. Birds pecked at the pinkish pulp that now presented itself unprotected, with bees buzzing around.

Smells of honey, mint, catnip; fragrance of blackberries and wild roses...

Cascading from a small well was a pomegranate tree with fruits already burst, like red smiling mouths.

When Michele opened the car door to help us out, I didn't have time to look around: I found myself squeezed tightly in my sister's arms.

"Isa," Lia said. "Do you know how long I have been waiting for you? I was worried! Did you ever get my letter?"

Mother, too, poor dear, had come out to meet us and without speaking hugged Annalena and me tight in her arms.

In the sweetness of that moment there was a prick, a sense of remorse in my heart. To think that I had wanted to remain in Switzerland for a year, perhaps forever. The war could have separated us, allowing us never to see one another again.

I couldn't stop looking at Mama! She was wearing a large dark apron and low tennis shoes. With her timid air, sweet, uncertain, her blue eyes like those of a child, she looked like a child again. She looked as if she had just stepped out of the fifth-grade photo of her grammar school group, the teacher in the center. I had great difficulty singling her out from all those serious young faces, already women at eleven years old, with stylish hairdos and long dresses with high neck-lines, puffed sleeves, ruffles... Suddenly I recognized her.

My sister Lia looked different too.

I looked at her eyes: new eyes. It seemed as if the light of a clear September morning were reflected in them.

"Wait and see; you'll see, Isa!" she said to me with those new eyes, as if she knew about secret hidden treasures that she would soon reveal to me. Meanwhile, she encouraged us, "Come, come on the swing!"

Against a background of grass and sky, she swung higher among the branches. The wind ruffled her fine, wispy hair. Among the leaves, her face was one moment in the shadow, the next moment in broad daylight. She challenged me and our cousin Annalena, coaxing us, laughing as never before.

Mother wanted me to tell her about Switzerland. My sister, on the other hand, was anxious to show me the house, "the palace."

While Annalena had hurried down to the kitchen to ask for a breakfast made of bread and freshly drawn milk, Lia called me:

"Come, Isa, come; Uccio is still in bed, don't make any noise..." She seemed happy to be alone with me while Annalena was in the kitchen getting her own breakfast and Uccio was still asleep.

Suddenly I noticed, with great joy, the same atmosphere of secrecy, a magical air that at times hovered about us, engulfing my sister and me.

"Don't look, Isa! You must not look yet."

She put her hand over my eyes, pulling me upstairs, laughing. We went up many steps, with my eyes still covered and she holding my hand.

"Where are you taking me?" I asked her.

But she went on climbing and laughing.

When I finally was allowed to open my eyes, I saw nothing at first, partly because I had kept my eyes shut and partly because the light in the immense attic just barely penetrated the round windows, shaped like the eyes of an ox.

Little by little, to my astonishment, the rays of light revealed the "*treasures*."

Just like a fairy tale: "*Before the light of the lantern appeared mountains of precious stones, mountains of gold coins.*" There on the trellises, lit by spots of sunlight, were mountains of grapes like clusters of rubies and topazes. Further on, mounds of corn ears, with innumerable golden kernels like gold nuggets in a purse, all covered by transparent leaves. On dark wood planks, split figs like shells of pink mother-of-pearl; on other planks, other varieties of figs were assembled geometrically, like red roses in a stained glass window, an almond set in their vermilion hearts.

In the blue enamel container was the tomato paste, a thick red-brown velvet. There were more wood planks with the split tomatoes revealing their jewels: a diamond of coarse salt, next to a little green basil leaf.

I woke up as from a dream. The sharp smell of tomato mixed with the fragrance of basil had reawakened my appetite. I had not eaten yet and I could not resist the temptation. I devoured half a tomato that tasted exquisite, even though it was overly salted.

Then I plucked some muscatel grapes from among those that were already a bit dried. The juice of these had coagulated into a rich, sweet pulp like a gem.

But there were still more "treasures."

This was only the beginning.

On tiptoes, my sister and I looked out of a little window.

We were in the heart of a small estate, a closed world, protected by an imaginary circle that seemed to embrace it on all sides.

The palace stood in the center. From the main door, the grassy meadow stretched like a carpet all around, creating a soft, green island of silence.

To the right and left were the peasants' houses, the stables, and the haystacks. Behind the house there was a garden, surrounded by crenelated walls; in front, the chapel with the burial ground was dominated by a very tall cypress.

We leaned from the little attic windows and looked down. Our view was obscured by the immense, umbrella-shaped foliage of the gigantic plane trees under which coolness and rest were always possible at midday.

Farther away we could see the cultivated fields, the vineyards, the olive trees, the houses, the paths as thin as ribbons...the woods like a dark spot. Still farther down, the spring water glistened among the pebbles.

The soft wavy outline of the hills on the horizon faded into cobalt blue.

Such a compact, self-sufficient panorama looked like a toy village.

High up in the little window, I felt as if the air had escaped, leaving me in a vacuum.

Surely the peasants were at work in the fields. I could see a few tiny men, standing by a wagon, or guiding an ox-drawn plow.

In the distance, cars, too, seemed as small as toys.

The front terrace was empty. Not a sign of life. For a few moments, everything remained suspended, as if held immobile and silent.

Suddenly something enlivened the scene. A twitching, bizarre, horned figure passed by against the green background. A goat had come out of its pen, and a young peasant girl with a red kerchief was running after it.

As if aware of our gaze, after recapturing her goat, the girl looked up at us.

"Good day to you!"

The spell was broken.

The leaves of the plane trees quivered in the wind, a flock of doves flew by, a white and black chicken crossed the meadow, a child began to scream...

Another peasant was coming up from the spring, carrying a water jug on her head, walking steadily, knowing by instinct how to balance it, with no apparent effort, as if executing a dance step.

She could have been symbolic.

The ascending stony path, the water, the jug, were all real. Real, too, was the toil she was undergoing. Yet that toil seemed lightened, transfigured by the measure and miracle of her gracefulness.

Symbolic of a living world that followed its own laws and purposes, at the price of hard work and pain, yet symbolic of a world that still seemed to exist in that September 1939 for the benefit of our contemplation, for our ecstatic joy.

"Where were you hiding?" asked Annalena. "I can't understand why you aren't starving. We haven't eaten since dinner at seven last night."

Suddenly I realized that I was terribly hungry. The half tomato had served as an appetizer; it had awakened an overpowering appetite. While I was cutting an enormous slice of dark peasant bread for myself, preparing to spread it with butter, I heard the warm laughing voice of our cousin Uccio.

"Where are the refugees?"

The "refugees," Annalena and I, jumped on his neck and hugged him.

"You're 'buttery' refugees. Did Michele Strogoff bring you up here? Why did he go away?"

"Who?" I asked, thinking of our driver.

"Michele Strogoff and I are good friends, you know, even though I am 'the young master' of the estate, whereas he is politically aware, as they say around here. In general, he has no kind feelings for owners, but I'm the exception."

"Why do you call him Michele Strogoff?"

"Don't you understand? His name is Michele and I added Strogoff, who was the courier of the Czar. *He* is my driver and *I* am the little Czar. Besides, "Michele Strogoff" has a Russian flavor, and he naturally is a Russian sympathizer. He also wears a fur cap like a Russian, even in the summer."

"You're right, Uccio. Now that I think about it, Michele Strogoff's face looks Russian, like a Tartar, with large cheek bones and slightly Mongolian, naïve eyes. 'Michele Strogoff' fits him well."

"Good, Zippo, you've got it."

He called me 'Zippo,' addressing me in the masculine, as he always did in one of his sudden bursts of sympathy for me.

"Zippo" was my nickname as a little girl.

"You know, Zippo, I'm happy that you are back. We'll have fun together. Your sister is no fun! She's cooped up in her room all day, alone, she and her 'Cattaneo.' You know what the people around here say about her? 'She looks like a cloistered nun!'"

He said "nun" tightly, with a slow singsong so typical of country people. Everyone laughed, including the "nun." Uccio was laughing too, one of his primitive guffaws.

As Annalena unpacked, a variety of objects appeared in her hands, one at a time: a pair of slippers, the photo album, a book called *An Adventure in Budapest*...

"Where do I put this?" she asked, interrupting the heated conversation between Mother and me, persisting until she received an answer.

Mother had pulled me into the bedroom. She made me talk and told me about the month we had been apart.

"Do you know," she said, "that we have no water, no gas, and no electricity in this house, and we're over seven miles away from town as well. Back home, your father used to ask me, 'What war? There is no war here in Italy!

What are you going to do way up there in that villa? Do you want to be another 'Pia dei Tolomei?'[2]

"Well, I've come for Uccio's sake," Mother continued. "What can a twenty-year-old boy do alone in this house? Someone had to be a bit concerned for him and Aunt Freda, his mother. You know her. She didn't want to come with him yet. It was high time for her to come and see her property. The manager had summoned her.

"You know poor Uncle; he hardly enjoyed his property. Yet he did everything he could so that the family could get together here on vacations. But his wife, never! She didn't want to stay here, even for a single month of the year. Perhaps she was not completely wrong – no water, no gas, no lights, and over seven miles from town as well..."

It was the second time I heard her say that, and certainly it would not be the last! From then on, "water, lights, gas, seven miles..." became a kind of compulsive, sad refrain our mothers and aunts used whenever they spoke of Poggio. Hardly would they strike the first note, "water," when we cousins would supply the chorus: "lights, gas, seven miles..." with a certain mournful and nostalgic tune created by Uccio.

Mother continued: "Uncle is dead, and nobody has come to stay here for quite a while. I, too, feel remorse at not making him happy by coming here. If the war broke out now, here in Italy... Well, maybe he thought about that, too.

"Do you remember toward the end, how he kept listening to the radio? He was always worried, sad... My poor brother." I saw Mother saddened by the memory.

"Now," she explained to me, "we're not alone here. The manager has rented the rooms on the first floor. He had written about it to Uccio, but you know him. Uccio always takes his time in answering business letters. The tenants are country people, good people. However, one never feels as comfortable as back at home. I'm going to leave with my sister soon. Aunt Clara will come here to see Annalena. You young people will stay here; Lia will do well with you..."

In her voice I heard hesitation, like a crack. "Why, Mother?" I asked. "Lia has been doing well. She has to hand in her doctorate thesis. This is her main concern since some new laws do not allow us to postpone our graduation. Later, she would not be eligible."

"Yes, yes, of course it's so. Your sister's a little nervous...sometimes I can't understand her." Mother blushed. "Nevertheless I can't..., I don't want to disturb her. I go quietly into her room where she writes in the midst of all those papers. Sometimes, you know, I have to take something out of the closet. She doesn't say anything to me, but she looks annoyed... I don't know, sometimes your sister makes me feel uncomfortable even though she's my daughter."

"You'll see, Mother, now that I'm here you'll be happier. You won't be worrying about me anymore."

"You're right about that," she said, "but, you see, I'm worried about your father now."

"How come mothers are always worrying about something?" I asked. "Father's okay. He has his work in the city. Our maid Teresa is home, and by now she knows how to do everything. You should enjoy the countryside a little more – it would be good for you. You get so tired at home!"

But mother shook her head. "No, no, I'm too worried. Here, I miss my house, my things. I don't know. Everything here is Uccio's, Aunt Freda's. The other day I broke a glass..."

"But a glass, what do you want, Mother? Uccio would only laugh at it."

"I know, I know, it's nothing to him, poor thing. But I still feel badly. See, I've broken up a set. I'll look in the city to find one like it, but it won't be easy, you know." And Mother sighed, truly upset by having broken a glass.

She felt out of place. The house was so big she hardly dared to straighten up things; making some space was like emptying the ocean with a spoon. There were mice in the kitchen, and they scared her.

"Uccio laughs his head off; he says the mice are his friends. You know, he is never serious.

"On top of that, he said he doesn't want any traps. Mice should be free to roam as they like. Can you believe it?"

After having vented her feelings, poor Mother was full of remorse. "But what am I talking about? We'd better put everything away. Let's unpack your suitcases."

"There's time, Mother, time for everything. Come, rest a little bit; I'll take care of it."

But she wouldn't rest, not until there was no lingerie left to fold, nothing to iron or to hang up in the closet. She had sheets ready to make my bed immediately, afraid I might be tired. I watched her while she bustled about, getting all confused by the hodgepodge of what had been removed from the suitcases. Wearing a large apron, she appeared somewhat clumsy with her short plump arms which seemed to grow tired while slipping a pillow into the pillowcase, held firmly against her chest by her chin. Once again, I was struck by her childlike manner, a little uncertain, as if she had never truly become an adult.

"Look," Lia said to me, "it is better for Mother to return to the city. I can't keep her company and she probably feels lonely and uneasy.

By the way, do you know that 'a wing of this villa' is being rented out? The building looks huge, but it's full of cellars, attics, stairs, cubbyholes. There is a big hall upstairs, on the second floor, but actually there are not many livable rooms.

Mother doesn't like to sleep alone, so we share a room. She insisted that I work on my doctorate thesis right there at the desk. She would be quiet, extremely quiet, even if she would have to come into the room. The problem was that she appeared every five minutes. You know how she is, always forgetting something, so she's always rummaging through the closet. Maybe she felt lonely, as I said before. The fact is, she insisted that I leave the door slightly ajar; she would come in so carefully, taking tiny steps, without a sound in her rubber-soled canvas shoes – those she is wearing now. She would enter furtively...

"Can you guess what came to my mind on those occasions? Sometimes here in the country, a chicken finds a door ajar and enters through the opening into the silent, empty kitchen. Noiselessly, it advances, tentatively, stopping now and then in the semi-darkness, with one foot suspended and its comb slightly tilted as if bewitched. It is almost halfway across the tile floor, when someone notices it, and 'shoo, shoo,' quickly chasing it away, maybe with a broom."

"Oh, Lia," I said, "please, don't tell me you were chasing Mother!"

"No, Isa! I felt so bad thinking of the chicken like that, and knowing that Mother realized she was bothering me.

Maybe it was those rubber-soled shoes and her timid, irresolute air! I think that it would almost have been better if she had thrown the door wide open and entered stamping her feet. I know, I know, she did it so as not to distract me. But, believe me, Isa, it was worse."

I understood very well and couldn't say she was wrong. On the other hand, I also understood how uneasy our mother felt, poor dear.

"How is it going now, Lia?"

"I don't study in that room anymore. I've found a refuge up in the solarium. It's just a little nook; there is only a small table of which, fortunately, I took possession. It's a bit too low for a desk, and I must hunch over, sitting on a bench. But I feel comfortable up there, and 'Cattaneo' consoles me. I shut myself in and stay there all day."

I smiled, thinking of the "cloistered nun." Then I asked, "and what about Uccio? Does he work? Does he paint?"

"I really don't know" Lia said. "Ask him. We don't see each other much, you know. He gets up late and rides his horse a lot. Undoubtedly, he, too, has his retreat. He claimed part of the basement for himself: it's his kingdom. I told him that he had descended into Hell, while I had ascended almost into Heaven, into paradise."

She laughed, rolling her luminous eyes.

"As for you, Lia, you look very well," I said. "You have a nice complexion. I never saw you look so well, even though it seems that you are living like a 'cloistered nun'!"

She continued to laugh with a slightly mysterious air.

"You can see how country life is good for me, even if I stay inside. You remember how one ray of light is enough to make one leaf green, as we studied 'chlorophyll in photosynthesis'! With me, you see, one whiff of country air is enough to make me rosy..."

For the moment I was satisfied with that semi-scientific explanation. However, I knew my sister too well. There had to be some other reason, some other secret!

Of the people in Poggio, the first I met was Nevo, a fifteen-year-old boy. He was part of the Mennozzi family, the sharecroppers who lived in the house to the right of the villa. To the left lived the Albieris, and almost 300 meters away, at the top of the hill, was the Stelli house. Nevo knocked timidly at the door.

"Come in," I said.

At that moment I was alone in the kitchen. Nevo stood on the threshold as if he was glued there. After the customary "Good day to you," he seemed to have nothing else to say. When I asked him what he wanted, he said, "good day" again, blushed, and turned and ran away.

I went out to call him back, but he had already gone into his house. An old peasant woman was coming down the outside stairs toward me.

"Are you Miss Isa?" she asked. "You're back? Your poor mother was so worried."

It was Beppa Mannozzi, Nevo's grandmother.

"He was supposed to talk with the young owner; he had a message for him. Didn't he tell you?"

"No," I answered. "He said 'good day' and ran away."

The old woman laughed, winking slightly, saying, "for taking care of animals, he is okay, but in other things he is not so tutored!"

I smiled too, but did not feel sorry for his not being "so tutored," for I remembered his beautiful, serene eyes, eyes that seemed to have looked only into the distance.

I asked Beppa to come in, but she refused. She remained standing and knitting, glancing up at me now and then. I felt the strength of her small eyes, like those of a tortoise, lighting up under heavy, wrinkled eyelids.

I looked at her, too.

Her face, probably round in other times, now had no definite shape, its skin tanned and wrinkled like the skin of an onion that had been placed under the ashes to roast.

She had to be very old. Yet she gave the impression that one could remove the first layer of skin, exactly as from an onion, to find a face much younger and livelier, with a new skin, as if from under a mask.

Even her stocky figure looked complex, due to her numerous layers of clothing, jacket upon jacket, skirt upon skirt, apron upon apron, shawls and kerchiefs – a figure blown up like a brood hen jealously guarding her offspring. I don't remember ever having seen her with her head uncovered. A big black kerchief was draped over her forehead, in her unique way, with innumerable knots and bows, mysteriously hiding her abundant, or scarce, or nonexistent hair.

From her apparent decrepitude emanated a powerful and secret charm.

"How do you like it here at Poggio?" Beppa asked with her strange voice: veiled, hoarse, yet deep, as if she spoke from behind a wall.

Then suddenly, out of the blue, like a sly cat who seems to be asleep, and, in a twinkling, leaps to catch a mouse, she added, "and what about the lady of the house?" Without waiting for my reply, she continued, "we haven't seen her recently. The young owner arrived alone. The first year, she came only once with your uncle – the poor owner, may he rest in peace. She went into the villa, but an hour later she had already left."

Her short wrinkled neck seemed to lengthen and immediately retract, disappearing with that tortoise-like motion, while the small set eyes in her desiccated face lit up with curiosity.

"How come?"

I realized that Beppa was fascinated by the unexplained mystery of the lady of the house and was therefore trying to wheedle an answer out of me.

"How come?"

But her question remained suspended in mid-air.

I had forgotten to ask Beppa what Nevo's 'message' was for my cousin; but before midday, his mother, Corinna, came and knocked at our kitchen door. Her eyes, of the same blue as her son, quite vapid, stared at me from beneath her dark kerchief.

Her square face reminded me of the faces of the Flemish peasants in some of Van Gogh's paintings: plain faces emphasized by starched bonnets, in contrasting light and shadow. Beneath the bib-apron and the monastic pleats of her skirt, her figure seemed flattened, almost stylized.

A pleasant sense of order, of cleanliness, and of composure exuded from her, while that slight rigidity that was part of her nature was lightened by her lovely Tuscan speech. Corinna, in fact, was a "good talker," as they say here, one who has a taste for and likes to carry on a graceful conversation, which is quite different from being a 'gossiper' – God save us! – which has, undoubtedly, a derogatory connotation.

Mother, always apprehensive, would say to her, "I am anxious for you. It is noon and you must have a lot to do, Corinna."

Corinna would not show the slightest haste. With enviable serenity, she replied once, "time is always regained."

I never saw her worried, notwithstanding the incredible amount of work she did. She was always at ease, relaxed, secure, as if time would multiply prodigiously for her.

Finally, Uccio was informed that the ox-cart with 'that stuff' that he had ordered, would arrive that evening.

When I asked him about it, I saw his eyes light up.

"But what is it?" My curiosity was aroused by the air of secrecy. Nevo had refused to say anything. Beppa had perhaps pretended to have forgotten, and now Corinna was vague and reticent.

"Will it arrive with the ox-cart?"

"Zippo, you'll see. You'll see tonight." Then, with sudden afterthought, he exclaimed: "Why not? I'll tell you now. I need to talk to somebody, and talking with you is the best I can hope for. You understand me. I must tell you all about it in my '*buen retiro.*' Come along, let's go this way!"

We had to cross the basement. It didn't seem real that Uccio was taking me through the very door that had attracted me so much, with its inscription in marble, '*MORITURO SATIS.*' It sounded like a severe, almost religious, admonition 'Enough for him who must die', like a call to moderation, not to accumulate too much. Those big letters, all capitals, of *MORITURO*, in black characters on white marble, seemed like a lapidary pronouncement that went well with thoughts of the grave.

Once through the door, we were in the fragrant coolness of the must, among enormous oak casks, each with a date written on its top, and a small bench that invites one to sit down under a spigot and draw some red or white wine. Then Horace, my favorite Latin poet, seemed to sing the *'Morituro Satis'* in a different key:

"Unseal the wine, seize the day, for tomorrow you will die...*morituro satis...* Do not accumulate too much because your heir will arrive and drink all the wine, even though it is locked with a hundred keys..."

Near a little cask of *Vin Santo*, I thought I heard another voice saying, "How is this one, Cisti? Is it good?"[3]

Undoubtedly, the merry spirits of Horace and Boccaccio hovered over that place. The shadows of death had been evoked on the threshold, yet the effect of *chiaroscuro* gave more warm light to life itself.

Behind the iron grate of the little windows, one could see a strip of sky and a branch hung with pale green leaves and quince apples.

"You're lucky, Uccio, to walk through this place often. The smallest whiff of such a fragrance would be enough to make one feel both inspired and a bit intoxicated."

He laughed contentedly. Then, behind a huge cask slightly away from the wall, he opened a small door.

It was a rather large room, with two exits: the small secret door from the cellar, and a door-window opening onto the garden.

A cold, greenish light shone from the closed shutters, the glass panels veiled by a curtain of dust, as if they had not been opened for a long time. The books were aligned along the shelves with an orderliness that amazed me.

On an easel, in a corner, was a white canvas, like an eye without its pupil.

"I cleared the room," said my cousin, realizing that I felt detached and disillusioned.

"But you do work here, don't you, Uccio?"

"Yes, of course, Isa," he answered somewhat evasively,

"It's *she* who inspires me – don't you recognize her on the wall over there?"

Then I noticed some charcoal sketches on the plaster wall...a lady's eyes and the striped iris of a tiger.

"No," I said smiling, "I don't recognize her from her eyes. I don't know who she is..."

"But, Isa, *she* is the same one all the time. I mean the tiger. You know I have always been in love with her!"

He was still the same boy, with the same grey iridescent eyes of the young tigers he loved so much. Whenever he laughed, his eyes disappeared under thick lashes, like two long, bright slits. When he opened his eyes wide, they looked much larger, and they became aquamarine.

He loved tigers. His love for them had begun when he started to read Salgari's and Kipling's books. He would draw tigers over and over in pastel, on thick Fabriano granular paper, and also with white chalk on black paper.

I can still visualize the various studies he made when he was a child: a head, two big eyes, one leg and, more often, the outline of the tiger's back – soft and loose. Above all it was the jungle tiger seen through the jungle grass.

He was mesmerized, enchanted by the shades of green, light and dark, that formed an iridescent background where the tiger's striped fur coat appeared and disappeared. "Feel here; feel the softness of her fur coat," he said once, as if really caressing a live tiger under her throat where the soft fur is lighter and brighter.

As a child, when he sketched he would actually forget about his playroom. He could imagine himself crouched within the grass that had grown high after a night of heavy rain, surrounded by the harmonious disorder of the jungle.

As an adolescent, he still loved tigers, perhaps even more than before, with that passion and love one might feel for a woman. Once he mentioned to me a passage from Cecchi's book *Trotting Races*. He asked, "Do you recall the white tigers?" He dreamed of those white tigers, picturing each one as the image of a graceful feline, a supple woman's body: a girl with long thick hair, bright yet cold eyes, like those of a wild beast. Childish memories of books and movies, no doubt; one could easily recognize Mowgli's or Tarzan's girl companion.

The "real" ones he met embodied his ideal girl, his beloved, only partially. They seemed to flash through brilliantly like the fleeting light of a firefly – a greenish bubble, a star shining in the silky darkness of the night, then dying out suddenly, to be transformed into a simple earthy black insect groping under a glass.

So it was with the girls he loved for one hour only. "Come down to earth, Uccio!" as Lalla, a young Roman shouted when she realized how far away he was, absorbed in his day-dreams, his eyes lost in a vacuum.

Where was he in those moments? Was he playing with the "white tigers," "in the sparkling snows under the sun," in the boundless desert, on the Himalayan glaciers?

The young Roman girl could not follow him there, she who had been transfigured by him because of her long shining hair, and the tiger-like line of her legs, barely veiled by the light clinging dress, which outlined her every movement.

"Uccio," I said, "I do recall your passion for tigers, but are you still really faithful to them? When you were little, you never tired of sketching them. You kept countless drawings of tigers on the blackboard in your room, in your school bag, all over. You were envious of the zoo keeper because he could see them any time. You said the old man must have been 'full of great joy.'"

Suddenly Uccio became sad.

"It's true," he said. "That child was better than I am now. He worked a lot...and perhaps he was happier. I wish I had never grown up. But how did you figure me out?"

"Look here, Uccio. Today you were happy – you brought me down here. But tell me why you were so happy and what is the material that will arrive this evening in the ox-cart."

Impatiently, as if he wanted to drive away a painful thought, he ran his fingers through his short hair and said, "Yes, Isa, you are right." Then, "clay will arrive this evening, different kinds of clay, too, because now I want to begin sculpting. In order to work seriously I need a different medium. I need "a third dimension;" you know, something more powerful than drawing. This whim of mine to mold, to create a form, to bring it into relief, probably came to me right here, among these peasants who are so real, so solid. Working more with my hands will give me greater satisfaction and warmth, as if I, too, were working as hard as they are. You see, a sculptor engages himself physically, he is directly in contact with the medium. Perhaps that is why he feels more fulfilled and happy. Tomorrow I'll begin for real!"

As he was talking, his words seemed to become livelier, his eyes lit up with joy. His voice became sure and warm.

The manager had given a counter order; thus the clay did not arrive that evening. Instead, Aunt Clara, Annalena's mother, arrived.

Aunt Clara looked vexed from the first moment she arrived in Poggio.

Michele Strogoff was not in town, and she had arrived in Benuccio's buggy. Her back was aching after that horrible trip. It was clear she would not leave the next day.

Aunt Clara had a good, logical mind, and an inclination for exact sciences such as mathematics, from which she borrowed expressions like "lack of coefficient," "the common denominator," and "to reduce to the lowest terms."

Aside from this "*forma mentis*," she possessed a sort of idolatry for being practical, or "pragmatic," as we would say nowadays.

Aunt Clara approved of only practical things; she wanted her home spic and span. Uccio used to say, "without a speck of dust." He imitated her very well, holding "speck" in his mouth, only to spit it out energetically as though savouring the effects of a scrupulous cleaning.

It was understandable that for such a personality, the "coefficients" were missing in Poggio, even more so since everything was just the opposite of the "practicality" that she cherished, and any kind of comfort was "in minimal terms." There were immense rooms, doors with rusty locks, very high windows that couldn't be opened without climbing. There were dark stairways, basements, broom closets, and store rooms everywhere, filled with old pieces of enormous, worm-eaten, inlaid furniture – real dust catchers – that once belonged to our maternal grandparents. There was also the typical Victorian drawing room with dark walnut furniture, and cupboards decorated with designs of fruit, fish, hares, and birds, all in relief. And then, there was not even water in the house! Water, can you believe it? Nor was there gas or electric light, and the house was six miles from the town!

For any need or service we had to turn to the country women, who never hurried, but were always as relaxed and calm as though it were five in the morning instead of midday, nearly time for the main meal.

Aunt Clara's lumbago persisted, and she was obliged to stay in Poggio longer than a week.

One wing of the villa had been rented to local people. According to the peculiar architecture of the time, there were many rooms in the house, but only one kitchen and one "retreat," as the lavatory was then called, a term that sounded both militaristic and cloistral.

To get to the "retreat," one had to climb an endless staircase and then venture down a long, dark passageway that led to a small square tower, seven by seven feet, a small window covered with an iron grill set high in its wall. Uccio called this place "the dungeon."

From the "dungeon," perched on the toilet seat and looking out through the iron bars, the temporarily closeted

person could admire a magnificent panorama: down below, the green fields stretched out as far as the horizon.
The window glass was broken, providentially letting in a
breath of fresh, albeit ice cold, air, refreshing the atmosphere of the room.

During our subsequent wanderings, I had occasion to
greatly appreciate the little windows of other country
"dungeons," which generally opened out to the most
panoramic view of the house. I'll always remember one in
particular. The view from its small, luminous rectangle
cheered up a "dungeon" crowded with mountains of old
shoes and discarded, unusable pots. Its window framed a
beautiful walnut tree with its leafy branches.

Aunt Clara, however, was far from appreciating such
beauty. She had developed a real hatred for the "dungeon,"
which she obstinately kept calling "the toilet," – such an
anachronistic word – certainly because of her nostalgic love
for the hygienic, sanitary plumbing that is the pride and joy
of the twentieth century. Unfortunately, at that time in
Poggio, such plumbing was only for the future, since Poggio was still back in the Middle Ages!

During that week there were real clashes in the common kitchen between the owners and the tenants, Mrs.
Grassi and her sister-in-law.

Before Aunt Clara's arrival, the owners' side at the
stove was represented by our mother, thus the ratio was one
to two, a clear superiority for the other side. Mother, so
sweet and timid by nature, would give in immediately as
soon as the other two would arrive with their ladles and
pots. Regularly, then, every morning our milk would boil
over.

But now, with Aunt Clara advancing onto the
battlefield, exact and punctual like a clock, always resolute

and determined to get breakfast ready for herself and An-nalena, the owners' side had been reinforced – and how!

The tenants, however, did not yield so easily, which caused endless squabbles, long faces, complaints, all of which amused Uccio very much, as well as us three cousins. Uccio had invented a new expression. He used to say that "old people," among whom he included those thirty years and older, were fit "*da noiosario*" – for homes for the boring!   In fact, if taken seriously, these were awfully boring people, but pleasant if laughed at behind their backs.

Uccio also amused himself greatly by using a sort of secret language, "a langaaga," an old game with a simple code: all vowels were to be changed into "a". He seemed to really enjoy it. Because of his peculiar comic talent both in choosing the words and in changing the tone of his voice, "tha langaaga" became "vara amasang" on his lips.

Aunt Clara kept silent. She seemed quite impervious to our cousin's jokes and to his hearty laughter. He, on the contrary, never gave up on her and would say "Aant alsa wall smala at last."

At Poggio I used to get up early; while the others were still in bed, I would go down to the ground floor.

In the kitchen, the water in the pitcher was almost ice cold, as if winter had already arrived. I enjoyed its coolness on my skin and on my eyes. In the darkness the oil lamp spread its quiet golden glow, while the live embers of the kitchen stove glowed brightly from under the pot filled with barley brew.

At that hour I had the house all to myself.

I enjoyed that big silent room with the fireplace. The fire was out, the flue didn't draw; but I slowly sipped the hot coffee, holding the cup with my hands so that I could enjoy its warmth.

The door of the room leading to the front was closed. Here the pale October dawn filtered through the high, slit-windows, like an illuminated panel which revealed the thickness of the walls.

The first rays of the sun struck the fireplace, and I, still in the darkness, was able to read the inscription engraved on the stone:

SICUT FUMUS DIES MEI (my days are like smoke).

My days, too, marched on uneventfully, dissipating like thin smoke. Yet I was not growing bored; my problems had stopped tormenting me.

Switzerland, sojourn permits, study or work programs, even "the laws," suddenly all seemed remote, very remote. My anxiety was calmed: the anxiety to determine the course of my life somehow, the urgency to look for something, to make a choice or a decision.

I felt refreshed, more open. My sight, my hearing, all my senses were sharper, more alert. At the same time I felt a sort of peacefulness. Without any effort on my part, my feelings seemed to fall into place and grow richer within me like a decanted wine that acquires taste, fragrance, and color simply by the passage of time, by aging.

I opened the door half-way; the sun shone inside the room through the crack, lighting up the brick floor, cutting across it diagonally like a line of fire. I followed its course beyond the threshold as far as the meadow – the grass waving its green splendor, bathed in a liquid light.

Farther away, around the chapel and the cypress, there was a shady spot. I used to love going out in the open to breathe in the silence, the smell of the soil and of the grass. I used to sit on one of the two stone benches at the side of the villa where the sun outlined a luminous warm triangle and dried up the night frost. The stone would stay warm till sunset.

A few peasant women used to come by and greet me. They rarely accepted an invitation to sit down with me; quietly knitting, they would stand for a half hour, while their men were already out in the fields.

Once I insisted that Beppa sit down.

"What are you talking about? See, we are used to being uncomfortable," and she smiled slyly with a glitter in her small moist eyes.

"Being uncomfortable" seemed to fit her very nicely, and even to her own advantage. Chatting, we went together as far as the low wall under the plane tree. Only there, on neutral territory, between the owners' villa and her farm house, she finally accepted my invitation to sit down with me.

We talked about the war.

"If anything," Beppa said, "only poor people go to war. The *signori* stay home. Who knows why?"

This time her turtle-like neck seemed to grow incredibly longer, sticking out as if to trap me with that difficult and terrible question. Without waiting for an answer, as usual, she then drew her neck back in between her shoulders.

The pigs, "those beasts, with all due respect," according to the peasants' code of politeness, came out of the sty. Rolling awkwardly like big, pinkish eggs, they ran onto the lawn; their feet and fleshy snouts disappeared as they plunged into the grass. Young swine herders, generally slim young boys and girls, yelled at the pigs with frightening big voices, even daring to touch them with a stick whenever they threatened to run onto the sown fields. One particular pig, enormous and quite out of proportion, was nicknamed "the female piglet." It was Stelli's little girl who used this nickname to soothe it while stroking its horrid snout.

Beauty and the Beast, just as in the fable.

At times I tried to attract these peasant children. At first they were bashful and reluctant. After a few days, however, the ice was broken. They crouched near me on the stone benches, letting me caress their heads, remaining silent, but friendly.

One of the children was Pino, the last born after three sisters, whom Uncle Poldo would always call "the bottom of the barrel."

Pino, too, belonged to the Stelli family. He was almost six years old, and was as lively as a black cricket.

"Don't you go to school?" I would ask.

He would swing his shaven head and laugh, showing his pointed white teeth.

"In one year. I'll go next year!" he would say, and his mischievous eyes, as black as pepper, would glitter.

"He was born in December," mumbled his father, as if to excuse him. "He is not old enough." He would then turn to his child and say, "Next year, you'll see! You can't get away with it!"

Whenever Pino heard "you can't get away with it," he would move back, somehow delighted, though, and laugh, as when one tests cold water before diving into the ocean.

"I really don't know whom he takes after. He likes to be a vagabond, he certainly does."

As a matter of fact, Pino was always running away, refusing to watch the sheep or the pigs, and no one could count on him. The other peasants' children were already accepting their obligations, their good share of responsibilities.

"The vagabond!"

Pino would take my hand and pull me impatiently. He felt secure holding my hand.

His father would stop recriminating, adding, perhaps for the sake of formality, "Be careful now; if you bother Miss Isa..."

But he never bothered me.

I used to hold his little hand in mine. His was dark and warm; he held me tight. I felt an electric shock, a thrill, as though by holding his hand his young blood flowed into me. I would become a child again, eager to see, impatient to run off, to run away.

We would tumble down the green slope behind the chapel, holding hands, almost flying, both of us laughing for no reason at all, simply for the joy of laughing. It was hard for me to keep up with him as we climbed up the hill. His brown legs showed taut muscles straining under a golden skin as he climbed. He no longer feared thorns or nettles.

He never tired.

He enjoyed seeing me marvel at him, better yet he enjoyed my ignorance, for it was he who was instructing me, telling me the names of trees and grasses. At times I would pretend not to know something in order to make him speak.

"Pino, what is this big tree? An oak?"

"Noooo! It's an ilex!"

"Oh, well. I never do guess right."

As we were standing on a grassy embankment, I said, "Let's see if I can at least recognize the greens to make a salad. This is '*radicchio*.'"

"Noooo! It's '*radicchiella*'!"

And without taking a breath, he would begin to sing as if it were a nursery rhyme, naming different kinds of vegetables for green salads.

We would go together to pick blackberries and and all kinds of mushrooms: *porcini*, *morecci*, *ovoli*, *cocchi*, *lardaioli*, and *ditole*.

In the woods I would become distracted by the smells of moss and ferns, but he would pull me along so as to involve me in his enthusiastic and persistent search, as if we were playing a game.

"Look at this beautiful one!" and I would show him a brown mushroom with its brick-colored top, "What's this?"

"AGH!! It's a poisonous one!"

Laughing, he would toss it away.

"A baby calf was born to me last night," said Pino. He said "born to me" as Tuscan peasants always say. Their sense of possession grows strong from the time of childhood. "My" cattle, "my" house, "my" property. It extends, for love, not only to things, but to people, to all the family members: "my Bruna," "my Piero."

We entered the stable. At first I could distinguish only shadows, since my eyes were still blinded by the sun.

Little by little I got used to the dim light.

The baby calf was lying on the straw. Flies landed on its damp face, on its nostrils, around its eyes. Angrily, I swatted them away, but to no avail. I patted the calf's head and scratched him behind his ears. A hard bump marked the place where the horns would soon appear. I looked into its eyes. They were almost light blue. The irises had a sweet grey background softening into blue, and the moist, shining pupils were black.

Those eyes had opened for the first time last night.

I stroked its coat, the color of hazel nuts, with lighter spots, silky and somewhat curly, like a field of grass being blown by a gust of wind.

The spotted mother cow lowed and turned to look at her baby.

"Will you raise the calf?" I asked Pino.

"For three months, but when it's big we'll sell it."

The little boy smiled unperturbed, innocently removed from either good or bad. The idea that the calf was to be sold didn't bother him. That was its fate. Its life in the warmth of the stable was to last only three months.

During those long days, I would start off uphill in the direction of the Stelli home, where the sun seemed to take longer to set, looking for Pino.

Against the sunlight, among the twisted olive trees, two oxen, still yoked to the plow, advanced slowly.

The delicate foliage cast a silvery grey design on their big, muscular, milk-white bodies.

Uncle Poldo's voice reached me from far away.

Softly, like a tender mother caressing her baby, he spoke to his big beasts: "Come on, Sweetie! Come on little one!" When I neared him, he greeted me, smiling.

"Good evening to you!"

His was a peaceful face, as round as his hat, with a smile that spread like the morning light on the fields. An old peasant's face, burnt by the sun and wrinkled like an aged apple, but with two clear eyes like those of a child, limpid and merry. And yet Uncle Poldo had known grief. His wife had died young, leaving him a widower with a little girl to raise.

"She was too proud, that woman," he told me. "She never said 'Poldo, you get up, I don't feel well.' Never, in ten years! One day she was washing the laundry at the spring. Our little girl, standing nearby, saw her suddenly fall down and hit her head on a stone. She lived three more days – no longer the same. Nothing could be done; no remedy could be found."

Uncle Poldo never remarried. He and Cocca, the motherless child, went to live with his brother, Pino's father.

"We are now one family. Many years have gone by. Cocca is married. You know her husband, Miss Isa – Vico degli Albieri."

As he said this, Uncle Poldo's clear eyes darkened, and he sighed, as if he were suffering from another hidden sorrow.

One of the two oxen turned its head slowly, rolling its eyes. "Come on, Sweetie! Come on, little one!" The grey crust of the soil was breaking easily under the harrow, and the brown, upturned turf smelled good. There was peace in the reddish evening air. Under Poldo's round hat you could see his smile.

"I wish you had met her, my bride! So wonderful, but too proud!"

In his voice there was no longer grief or regret, but only exaltation, as he must have sounded when a happy young husband almost thirty years before.

"We were peasant farm workers whose homes were next door to each other. I began to be interested in her when she was only a little girl. On my return from military service, I found that she had bloomed into a beautiful young woman."

I knew those eyes. Cocca's eyes were like her mother's, black, glistening. They stood out next to the pale blue eyes of the Albieri family.

How old could Cocca be now?

Colorless Vico, her husband, with his thin beard and raucous voice, appeared ageless.

Cocca wore long skirts, shapeless, colorless jackets, and a black apron just like a granny, with her hair pulled back under a kerchief. She was tiny, and her pale lips had a downward cast that gave her a melancholy air. Yet her eyes had a fiery brilliance.

Corinna told me Cocca's story.

"You see, when there is no mother, the others can't possibly take care of everything. You wouldn't have recognized her then. At fifteen she was so pretty. She had lots of curly hair, and her face was as pink as an apple. And those eyes!!

"Not anymore.

"Why did she go with a good-for-nothing? We warned her, but she wouldn't listen.

"Her father, the poor man, just about killed her with his whacks. But it did no good. The fellow had bewitched her. After his wife's death, Poldo had to suffer this other shame. Five years later, that good-for-nothing abandoned her. They made her marry Vico Albieri. But for her it was a gift from heaven!"

At twenty, Cocca said goodbye to love and started wearing the dark kerchief which hid her pretty curly hair. At times her black eyes could still sparkle.

The Albieris' house was a sad one. All the children, Menico's children and Vico's nieces and nephews, had a serious, tense look about them, as did Vico and Cocca, who had no children.

"And they never will," said Corinna, with a malicious grimace, although she sympathized with Cocca's misery.

Lena, Menico's wife, with the smooth, gentle line of her neck, her pale face, her sky-blue eyes, looked like a madonna. Silent most of the time, when she did speak with her dull voice, her gums showed, and you could see that she was already missing a few teeth, like an old woman.

The house itself seemed sad. The big kitchen, with little light, had a huge black fireplace. It seemed to me that even the fire wasn't as joyful as in the other peasants' houses, perhaps because an old paralyzed man was always sitting in front of it to warm his numb limbs.

"He's a friend of the fire," people told me.

The Albieris' house was filled with old people: the great-grandfather, the grandfather, the grandmother, Menico's and Vico's father and mother, and Vico himself. All had that same fatigued, absent-minded, shabby look. Another old man stood on the threshold in the warm sun.

"They are all the same, without vigor," Corinna commented.

However, with or "without vigor," the Albieris exercised a kind of enchanting power on me. In their home I felt as if the pain, like that of the paralyzed man, melted away by standing near the fireplace or in the sunlight. The pain seemed to lose some of its severity, its daily strength, dissolving itself into melancholy.

Cocca was pressing the nipple of the milk bottle into the little mouth of the last born. Through the crook of her arm, the milk seemed to come out of her own breast as if she were giving nourishment and life to the baby who wasn't hers, in a somewhat metaphysically regained maternity.

Her eyes were downcast, her eyelids over her black pupils veiled their fiery light. She seemed at peace.

Living in the country was good for me.

The birds would wake me at the first sign of light, setting in motion another day of daily errands and chores. Each day was the same, yet new, like a flower in bloom, the birth of a little chick or the blazing flames of a fire.

I enjoyed everything and everything pleased me. Things from my past reading jumped out at me in the countryside: Virgil's food "not bought," Horace's water spring "clearer than crystal," but above all Boccaccio.

Both the atmosphere and the people seemed to have come straight from Boccaccio's *Decameron*: events, speeches, characters. By focusing on the poetic images, I understood the real people around me.

It was an endless exchange between art and life, a fascinating game that offered me the joy of discovering a true confirmation of the vital links between the past and present, as if six centuries of history and civilization had not occurred.

Then I discovered Benuccio, Friar Cipolla's[4] soulmate. He must have played tricks on the people of his home town, for they would shake their heads as they were talking about him, saying, "Ugh! What a scoundrel!"

Benuccio, whose name also came from the fourteenth century, had a horse and buggy. He was always glad to drive us three girls around. Our cousin Uccio was too lazy, with a metaphysical laziness. He detested having to get up too early, as he was fascinated more by the nighttime hours than by the dawn. I, on the contrary, loved to get up early and to venture out: I had succeeded in winning over Annalena and even the "veiled nun."

I used to set the alarm clock for five, but long before that hour I would be wide awake, my eyes staring in the darkness. The musical alarm would rhythmically repeat the notes of *Fra Diavolo*[5]:

> that man
> with his fierce
> look...

Under the blankets I was already anticipating and enjoying the day ahead of us.

I would jump out of bed and pull Annalena and my sister out of theirs. They tried to rebel, but to no avail. We would splash our faces with the cold water from the jug, in order to chase away the last remnants of sleep.

Benuccio was always very punctual.

He would not knock at the door, nor would he call. However, I knew he was outside in the courtyard waiting for us. Noiselessly I would open the window, sure to see a glimpse of the long shadow of the horse and the squat shadow of his charioteer, against a backdrop of haystacks lit up by the orange moon. Benuccio could easily be spotted in the fading darkness of the night by the lighted end of his inevitable "toscano-cigar."

While "the palace" was still closed and everybody else was asleep, we would leave quietly, almost secretly, as if escaping with Benuccio, the lover, who was abducting us.

At first Benuccio would not talk, but would wrap our legs in a rough grey woolen blanket that still had the warmth of the stable.

The biting cold air froze our cheeks while the horse trotted merrily along.

Above us the stars went by, and the trees took on fantastic shapes. No one said a word, in a sort of conspiracy: all four silent, just like a sparkling wine compressed by the cork in the neck of a bottle.

When dawn lit up the sky and the early sun tinted the grape leaves the color of red wine, and the birds began to sing, the cork popped out, and words, laughter, and songs overflowed.

Benuccio chatted and joked without ever "tying himself inextricably in knots," as Boccaccio wrote.

He was a little man, with red hair and mischievous eyes, slightly crossed, with a small creased, grimy cap, of uncertain color, unpretentiously cocked over one eye. His hat had a life of its own, a bit like a wild mushroom.

Benuccio's age was as uncertain as the color of his hat. He was no youngster, but neither was he a mature man. He did not have an old, decrepit, or venerable air, but he had that liveliness that only age bestows, as happens with certain wines of no renown that lose their sourness with time, but acquire strength and fragrance.

Like Bertoldo, he appeared somehow neither clothed nor unclothed, because, besides his cap, his clothes, too, were made of an uncertain material. It was neither wool, cotton, nor linen, but it was something alive, as if it had grown on him like fleece or bird feathers. All was saturated with his particular odor, or rather, multiple odors: hay, fodder, sweat, tobacco, wine, food, dust, open air, and wind. His coat and trousers were neither blue nor grey nor brown, and his shirt was far from white. The patches were both light and dark, in all sorts of marvelous colors that harmonized with the stones of the old houses, with the white-washed and mildewed walls, with the damp brick paving of the village lanes.

The horse's blanket and the harness were like this, too. They had lost their substance. The leather of the bridle seemed no longer leather, having lost its toughness, its odor, and its color. It seemed soft, almost sweetly tender. The whipcord no longer even showed the roughness of the cord. It was not a dead object; rather it had taken on the likeness of a snake or a country serpent, something into which the strength of the charioteer's flowed. The whipcord hung on the side of the buggy, at the level of the horse's left ear, and Benuccio used it to communicate only now and then. The few times that he gently caressed the lobe of Otello's ear with it, the horse began to trot vivaciously as if it had gone crazy. More often, however, Benuccio spoke to the horse as a human being that understood everything.

Each time, as we stepped down from the carriage, one foot unbalanced on the carriage step, I was afraid that the horse would start to move. But Benuccio would assure me, "No such danger, miss; I have warned him." What a miracle! Poor Otello would not move, but would remain rigid on his four legs.

"And he is not to pee now! That would be something, the dirty pig!" But "the poor beast" would shortly pee on the green, at an allowed stop on a solitary country road.

While Otello peed, Benuccio told us about a disobedient female pony who was so whimsical that she was sold.

"Whenever she made up her mind not to pee, she wouldn't, shame on her. But once in the stable, psshhh...

A heavy gush would come, and she would make enough to fill a barrel! The poor man, dead tired in the evening, had to clean up everything and replace the straw immediately, because she was a lady, that one, and she had no intention of staying on wet straw! No sir!

"She would even refuse to drink, if that's what struck her fancy. There was good spring water along the road that led to Castello, and it was so clear that the green reflected in it as in a mirror. By noon my friend would be there, and he, too, would drink and lie down under the ilex. But not her, the naughty one. God only knew why she didn't like it. She wouldn't drink a single drop, no matter how exhausted she was. She would just stand there, rigid, twisting her snout. Dammit! Afterwards she would start pulling like crazy. She could already smell the stable. Back home, she wanted buckets and buckets of water. Dead tired as he was, the poor man had to take care of her. She never had enough.

"She drove me crazy, too. Well,...she was a female... Poor owner, though. Yet I felt sorry for her, too. She was cute, petite, and curly, that black one!"

Benuccio still missed that whimsical black beauty, and he took it out on poor Otello, a jade, who was white, contrary to his name. Otello, slightly short-winded, had no fancies in his head, and was patience itself – I wouldn't say personified, but horsified! Benuccio and the three of us could do anything to him.

With us, Benuccio was particularly permissive and let us do what we wanted and tried to please us in every way. For him, we were "the Misses" first of all. At the same time we were female, and young at that!

Benuccio was very merry in our midst, but he never went beyond the limits of his station. High on the buggy, he would speak with all the passers-by, saying, "Hey, you there! See who I am taking around! What will heaven be for me?"

Everyone would answer his jokes with that joviality typical of Tuscans, mixing good humor, malice, and rustic gallantry. Thus, on our way, it was an exchange of greetings, laughter, and clever jests. Too bad for those caught off guard, since there in Tuscany, everyone liked to jest; even the beasts seemed to have pepper under their tails.

At the end of the day, in the crisp evening air, while the village was starting to light up, and we were returning home by the light of the little lantern swinging by the jade's ear, Benuccio would become even merrier, having drunk extra glasses of wine to quench his thirst. He would then make even more pungent remarks.

"Benuccio, you certainly chose three tender ones!"

"I have three all right! But being wedged in so tight won't be so good!"

The three of us, too, made drunk by the fresh air, by the sun striking our cheeks all day long, would start singing old *stornelli: Il mazzolin di fiori...*, or lines from the Bell' Alpino:

> Where have you been
> My handsome Alpino [mountain soldier]?

Our voices sounded different, as if moistened by the keen air of the silent countryside:

> Your colors
> Your colors
> Will come back
> This evening
> We'll make love.

Words like "colors," "evening," and "love" would suddenly blaze up and mingle with Benuccio's spicy remarks.

We felt alive, young, and in love with love.

Poor Otello would pant up the hill back to Poggio, while Benuccio, plodding along on his short legs, led the horse by the bit and traces. He cajoled the horse with a low grumble like that of a pot boiling over, and whenever the ground was bumpy, he would say, "Hey there, come on! *Maremma peperone!*" and other unmentionable swear words.

The lantern hanging on the shaft kept swinging. It was almost nighttime, and all the crickets had started to sing.

The peasant girls would come out to meet us. "What have you brought?" they would ask laughingly. "Careful," and they would pull our treasures down from the buggy: blackberries, sorbs, and arbutus berries. Full branches of knee-holly, juniper, leaves, and brightly colored red berries, and lots of common broom.

I liked to cut their rigid, resistant stems with a small knife, while the yellow petals would fall like luminous raindrops.

The girls were laughing, showing their Tuscan common sense. "Oh, there's a broom thicket right near here! And they went *all* that way to get them!"

One evening the clay really did arrive.

Pino ran up to give us the good news.

"Here they are, here they are! With the ox-cart!"

It was necessary to open the gate on the back side of the garden, a gate that had not been opened for ages!

Corinna immediately brought over the large key, the oil cruet and a feather to oil the rusted lock; Pino ran off to get a lantern. We stood outside.

It was a windy evening, and the cold air of October's final days was already announcing winter. Grey clouds passed over our heads, veiling and unveiling a slender crescent moon just starting to become luminous in the dark sky. In the circle of light projected by the lantern, Corinna tore away a few twigs of leaves and bits of resistant vines, and oiled the iron fittings thoroughly.

As the three of us watched silently, we could hear the frogs croaking in the pond.

Three or four peasants stuck together in a tight group watched from afar, but they would not approach. We knew they were there only by their shadows.

"Oh, are you there, Rigo?" Corinna shouted. "Why don't you come and help?"

The key was hard to turn. Each of the peasants tried. "Dammit" here, "dammit" there, but no luck. The key only turned halfway.

Meantime the white oxen were arriving. They proceeded slowly, straining up the hill, shining in the darkness. They were led by Pino's father, Vanni, with his resolute *bersagliere* stride, and by Pietro de Mannozzi, who was as sturdy as an oak although he was over seventy.

When they stopped in the courtyard, we could see the heavy clay they were carrying. The poor beasts were sweating just like the two men.

"Good thing we came when it was cool!" said Pino's father.

At the center of the courtyard, as if on a stage, the two white immobile oxen stood out, still yoked to the cart filled to the brim with what seemed like a brown mountain. Uccio and the two peasants were making gestures in the foreground.

Our cousin's voice was loud, and it reached us above the other two lower and indistinct voices.

The Mannozzi, the Alberi, and the Stelli girls had made a circle, and they were whispering among themselves. From time to time we could hear their laughter coming from the darkness.

Mother and Aunt Clara, bundled up in their woolen shawls, sat on the stone benches. Beppa, standing by the porch of her home, focused her turtle-like eyes into the darkness.

Since the back gate could not be opened, they decided to go in through the main door, passing by the hall with the fireplace and the *MORITURO SATIS*.

Quickly, as bricklayers do with bricks and mortar, the peasants passed buckets of clay from hand to hand, unloading them downstairs in Uccio's room. In order not to make footprints on the floor, they went barefoot. They moved silently, in single file. The full and empty buckets went in and out of the rooms, but the clay never seemed to end.

Mountains of clay, clay in mountains.

My sister and I stood together speechless, watching guiltily.

The dry leaves from the plane tree whirled on the meadow, and a few of them flew inside, settling here and there.

Aunt Clara was staring, horrified, at the bustling that was going on – the open doors that let in freezing gusts, foreboding bad colds and lumbago, and especially all the mountains of filth that were soiling the house.

"Well! Now the young master is no longer without a job!" said Vanni, laughing and rubbing his hands, a bit for the cold, and also as if to say, "We are through, so now it's his turn!"

The wind had put out the trembling flames of the candles. The only light was a lantern on a corner of the fireplace.

In the half-light, I could not discern the expression on Uccio's face.

He closed himself inside his room with the clay. I caught myself watching the French door from afar. I felt a joyful thrill because behind those panes Uccio was working!

I neither knocked on his door, nor did I ask him anything, not even when we met about the house. A strange fear held me back, as if I was afraid to break the spell.

At times I would sneak a look at his face. His grey eyes avoided me, laughingly at times, hidden as they were under his lashes. At other times, his eyes looked back at me, fixing me in his gaze, his green pupils wide open, a little mockingly, as if to say, "Can't you read them? Come on! Try! Guess!"

One day I decided to try.

"Uccio," I said, "let's bet that I am going to guess. Let's play a game, like when we were children. You say 'very cold, cold, lukewarm,' and then 'warm, warmer' when I get near. You know what I mean!"

"Oh you devil, Zippo! Hot! Hot! I know that you have already guessed!"

Guessing was too easy. For the last few days we had seen Uccio coming back with a girl in the buggy.

"Go on, speak badly about me, my dear cousins! You know now that I have found a model. But, be assured, she is a decent girl, and well behaved. 'Anly tha haad!' What did you think?" he said, bursting into laughter. "It is only the head that interests me!"

For several days, we watched as Uccio arrived punctually at Poggio with his girl.

Hiding behind the window panes, up in the attic, we, his cousins, spied on them as they arrived.

But he knew very well that we were on the watch up there. While he helped the girl climb down from the buggy, he was laughing, and he looked up intentionally. We feared she would find out.

"You must introduce her to us, Uccio!"

But he didn't want to.

"No," he would say, "because you would ask the usual unbearable questions, such as 'Where are you from, miss? From this town? And your family?' See, Zippo, I must build her up within myself. I must forget who she is, even what her name is. She is *the muse* now!"

Was she beautiful? We couldn't tell since we only got fleeting glances of her.

After a week of sittings, the girl disappeared. Uccio seemed to me unusually quiet, and I dared not ask him any questions.

Once, when he was not around, I went into his room.

In a corner was a little head, barely outlined, with a damp cloth on it to keep the clay fresh. It looked like a small fetus straining in vain for a breath of life.

I stared at the enormous pile of clay heaped up in his room.

St. Martin's summer[6] arrived.

The air was warm, the leaves red, spotted with gold, lighted up against the sun in a fantastic array. That splendor, however, ended suddenly. It seemed as if the sun would never come back again.

Standing behind the window panes, I looked at the trees that were almost bare and at the unlit sky, and shivered. One grey day after another, the hours seemed to have a timeless stillness. There was no rain, but a damp mist penetrated my bones.

It happened on one of those gloomy days.

We were in the attic. My sister was reading the last chapter of her dissertation to me. Suddenly, through the closed windows, we heard noises and excited voices. We rushed to the window.

In the courtyard, as in an arena, Vanni and two other peasants were forcing a cow to go round in a circle in order to put on the yoke.

The beast was big and strong, and she was frothing at the mouth while the two men, overcome with anger, goaded and whipped her ferociously.

"Dammit! What is it? A lion?"

The cow would rather die than have the yoke put on her.

The men seemed more and more driven by their "red" rage, as if by a primitive passion.

"Dammit! She wanted to live like a lady!"

Their terrible swears burst like firecrackers, followed by other unmentionable phrases. From the window high up, we girls, unable to crush a pigeon's head or to cut off a rabbit's neck, were fascinated as we watched the bloody fight, unable to stop watching.

The cow's crime couldn't be appealed.

"She wanted to live like a lady."

Now, there she was, a scapegoat on which to avenge centuries of slavery.

"To live like a lord," however loathsome the privilege, was still a privilege to which one was born. The cow's fate was not "to live like a lady," but to work "like a beast," or else to be butchered. Therefore, her rebellion was absurd. It was a violation of peasant law.

They had gone as far as the chapel when, suddenly, the cow made a frightening swerve.

Head down, the beast was aiming like an infuriated bull. She had the upper hand. Suddenly she came toward the Albieris' house. Lena, who was in the doorway, screamed and rushed inside with her child in her arms. A shout choked our throats, too, when that enormous head and the large powerful square thorax seemed to come up to us. We felt as if the cow had fallen on us like a mountain of stones.

Now she was in agony, all bloody from the whipping, but she still would not be tamed.

The following day she was slaughtered.

The last leaves of the plane trees fell from the branches.

The bare trunks, with swollen tops, suddenly seemed to me like big peasant's hands, stocky and knotted, raised toward the menacing grey sky.

Our cousin Uccio had left without warning, giving no explanation.

During the last few days he had been restless. He would stay out for hours. Back from his rambles, he would offer me an oak branch, a wool flock, a smooth stone.

"All this is for you, Zippo. My gifts: a piece of wood, a flock, a torrent..."

When the weather was unstable and a storm threatened, we could see his tall figure, in his light raincoat the color of dried leaves. With his coat swelling in the wind like a sail, he could be seen striding along with long steps or climbing the path at a run. Always bareheaded, he would return, happy from his escapes, his short hair wet with rain, like the grass.

He used to say that those downpours were not to be taken seriously, that they were mere "drizzles," made purposefully to refresh one's ideas. Under the "drizzles," he would keep his face raised upward, as if he were drinking. At other times he was sullen and gloomy.

One evening he told me that he envied the animals. He said that they follow only one sure law, their instinct. They have their own seasons, like trees. As trees bloom and give fruit, so the animals have their mating season. They neither eat, nor sleep, nor work...

"Have you seen," he would ask, "a cat in love? He becomes all skin and bones, his eyes burning like amber. He sears everything in the wild fire of his one passion!"

Uccio had left.

Without his voice, the house seemed empty.

For the first time since I had been at Poggio, melancholy rose up again from deep inside me, threatening to overwhelm me like a tide. It was Annalena who saved me. Resolutely, she was preparing an entire suitcase of provisions to bring to the city. Like an ant, she had piled up the mushrooms dried in the fireplace in long fragrant strings, green and black olives, bunches of raisins, and figs stuffed with almonds.

Now she began something new, the making of quince apple jam. Since our respective mothers had left, Lia was in the attic with her Cattaneo, and Annalena demanded my help. At first, as usual, I was irritated by her obstinacy. The apples were heaped in a big basket, and a week was needed just to peel them all.

Armed with a small knife, I started to work unwillingly with my cousin. But while I was peeling and cutting, I found myself meditating over my natural inclination to idleness. Suddenly I thought of the slaughtered cow. I couldn't free myself from that strange feeling of fear, a nightmare... Within myself I could hear that voice shouting, "Dammit! She wanted to live like a lady!"

To live like a lord, *fare i signori!*

If living like a *signore* meant exploiting and oppressing others, this was not the case with me, but as far as not working... Well, I found an excuse, meditating upon the fact that idleness, for me, for us, was a temporary privilege that had been forced on us.

I began peeling the apples again more willingly and quickly.

The large earthen pot was already boiling over the clear flame in the big fireplace. The entire kitchen was filled with steam and the odor of roses, as if a rose bush had suddenly bloomed.

What a fascinating jam!

Not only its scent was wonderful, but also the sparkling color that apple pulp takes on, like the color of dawn!

On the kitchen table, the jars were all lined up. They had to be washed and dried thoroughly, otherwise the jam would go mouldy.

With a kitchen towel of hemp, the type that does not leave lint behind, Corinna rubbed the glass, which became more and more clear and sparkling.

With the ladle, Annalena, my sister and I scooped out the quince jam from the dark pot.

The lovely pieces of apple, saturated with rosy juice, one piled on the other, were filling the jar, showing off the ruby-colored pulp against the crystal. What a masterpiece! While everyone admired the jam, Corinna chatted about the "former owners" of Poggio.

The lady owner, too, liked preserves, but she wanted the quinces strained through a sieve, and woe to anyone if a piece of rind or a seed were left in the jam.

"What were the old owners like, Corinna?" I asked, as I was curious to hear about them.

"Oh them," she replied, "they were real '*signori*.'"

But perhaps fearing to offend us – the new owners, who seemed to have been excluded – she immediately added, "but you, too, we can see you are gentry as well! Even from the zucchini-squash."

"From the zucchini-squash?"

"Yes, you see, we always choose the biggest ones because they go further; whereas your mothers say that large ones have too much center. They want the young ones that are so tender that as soon as you put them in your mouths

you have already digested them. Just like the old owner.
She, too, would throw out the peas that had gone to seed,
saying that they were swollen like balloons. She wanted
the very young peas, so small and sweet that they seemed
to have no skins. When I would bring them to her freshly
picked, she would shell a few and put them right in her
mouth, just like that, like she couldn't resist them."

I learned then that even zucchini-squash and peas
could become a sort of litmus paper to identify the well-
born.

But Corinna was right, the former owners were not
only *signori*, but genuine ones by birth. They were mar-
quises.

"Once," Corinna told me, "the *padrona* waded through
the pond. She wanted to go to Pieve to see poor Primina,
the child who, reduced to skin and bones, passed away that
winter. The *padrona* went to visit her every day, to take
her temperature and to bring her some broth, a couple of
oranges and also the quince jelly that was so good for her
cough.

"At the time the little bridge didn't exist and people
forded the pond on the stones. That night it had rained a
great deal, and by the following morning the water was still
half a meter deep: half a meter of very cold water, because
it was December. But the *padrona* immediately took off
her shoes and stockings and stepped into it, raising her
dress up to her knees. She looked so pale and lady-like!

"She was a real good lady, but she suffered from the
extravagances of the Marquis. He was really a bit crazy:
he used to say he was like St. Francis, that he preferred our
simple food, that of poor people, to all the delicacies of the
city. 'You don't know what you're eating,' he would say.
Every time he arrived here, if it was bean season, he im-

mediately wanted a tureenful of beans cooked by me; you know, those white beans that when shelled look like almonds. With them he wanted half a red onion, a Florentine one, salt, pepper and a trickle of our olive oil.

"As soon as I put it all on the table, he would take a spoonful and fill his mouth. He would become very serious, and he would chew slowly, with his eyes closed tightly, and say in a tiny, faint voice, 'Surely this is food for the angels!'"

I laughed. I had always thought that angels fed only on nectar and ambrosia. No doubt those who preferred beans and Florentine onions were big robust angels from Tuscany: nectar and ambrosia would only have been good enough to quiet their hunger pains.

"Well," Corinna went on, "beans and onions were really to his liking, but, then, money slipped through his fingers, as the saying goes.

"He had to sell everything. He threw his money in the well: one could see he had not earned it by the sweat of his brow!"

I observed one other distinctive quality of a *vero signore*. The true *signore* is prodigal with money he has not earned.

Corinna was telling the absolute truth. I, in fact, found out that the Marquis had, literally, not metaphorically, thrown his money into a well. In the garden was a large cistern. The Marquis had set his heart on finding water there. But there was no water to be found in Poggio. Anyone else would have understood that up there, water 'couldn't reign.'

"Water always goes down," Corinna would say. "Oh, yes, the water was there indeed, but at the bottom of the hill, where the spring is. He, though, hardheaded as he was, gave orders to dig down meter after meter.

"Did you ever look into the well, Miss Isa?   Have you ever seen how deep it is? Well, dig...dig...nothing but a dry well.   Only mounds of stones and earth came out. As for water, there may have been barely three buckets.

The cistern was not his only concern!   The Marquis would have had buildings built all over the town. He had a large outside stairway built with stones; he would go up and down it right across the facade. It was a beauty! But when it was completed, he didn't like it at all and what did he do? He had the stairway pulled down. Oh, no? The traces of the stairs are still on the wall, haven't you seen them? To remove all the stones, two trucks had to go up and down the hill for a whole week.

But that wasn't all. All around the garden he ordered crenelated walls to be built – "*merlons*" he used to call them. Each *merlon* must have cost him a pretty penny!"

I began to understand. The villa was old and the Marquis restored it. Perhaps he was also the one who had had the fireplace built in the big ground floor room, the ceilings redone with small dark wooden beams, and the inscriptions in Latin, as well as in the vernacular.

Going uphill as you arrive at the green open meadow of Poggio, you come upon the 'palace,' a solid square mass, surmounted by the clock tower, austere but not threatening.

Like a jewel set in its facade, was an inscription carved in the stone that recorded the stay of an illustrious humanist, Aonio Paleario, who in that aura of hospitality had found comfort and rest.

I still remember the last words which I particularly liked. They went like this:

TO THE BOLD
ASPIRATIONS OF HIS MIND
DISTRACTED
THROUGH AN EXCESS OF LOVE

Who knows, perhaps the poor Marquis himself, with his extravagances, had been distracted "through an excess of love."

As for me, besides everything else, I could enjoy, without remorse, the "*merlons*," the well, and the inscriptions.

How true that the fool pays for the feast and the wise one enjoys it. But was the wise one really me in this case? I realized that I was sympathizing with the Marquis; however, I was very careful not to let Corinna know.

On the other hand, "building was not the only cause of his ruin: he also gambled and "he never lifted a finger for himself: he was a real *signore*, that one!"

It seemed as though there were different characteristics of a *signore*, and the peasants could appreciate and catch these nuances very well.

Now that the tenants had left, after the first rainfall, Corinna made cutting remarks about them as well.

"The local folk!" she said, with her lips curled in contempt. "They put on airs, so many airs because they want to play the role of *signori*."

That was a good one! Too bad Uccio had left, otherwise I would have immediately run to tell him.

Certain characteristics of this "gentry," on the other hand, had not escaped us cousins either. They were people with an eye for the material, like eating well, or for the daughter's dowry.

Eating was a function that seemed to absorb the energies and the activities of the entire family, continually and totally.

The father, a hunter, with his big face flushed and euphoric, would come back triumphantly with the game-bag filled with little birds.

"Pa...pa..., how many have you shot?", his daughter would ask him whenever he returned, repeating each time the exact same question, without ever changing a single word or even the inflection, managing to make even the Sienese way of speaking, usually so lively, awfully monotonous.

Her slow voice, the dismal past participle, "shot," and those poor tufts of ruffled bloody feathers filled my heart with sadness. It seemed as if between father and daughter there was a kind of a challenge; each time he returned, the number of thrushes and larks grew fearfully, as indeed the hustle and bustle of the housewives grew fearfully, too: mother, aunt, and niece, who seemed to have come to the country with only the one precise purpose of sweating in front of the spit, as it turned eternally on the flame in the fireplace dripping fat.

The three vestals would go into the kitchen at dawn and leave at night, after endless tidying up.

The mother, so skinny under her apron covered with grease spots, probably fed only on kitchen smoke. She seemed held down by other overbearing personalities: husband, sister-in-law and even her own daughter.

The girl was junoesque and rather disheveled, even though she powdered her nose each time she made an appearance.

Townsfolk, then, well-to-do people! However, in addition to what the "being" was, they also put great emphasis on appearances.

They never failed to stress the difference between their social status and that of the peasants. The daughter kept boasting about her dowry, and if she met the other girls of Poggio in town, she pretended not to see them.

As for the aunt, so fat that she was almost bursting inside her Bemberg silk dress, she stayed in the kitchen mainly to give orders to her frightened sister-in-law.

She kept talking about an imaginary liver disease – or, maybe, it wasn't so imaginary, because she ate too much – and would insert in her conversation – protracted and gloomy like a hospital corridor – a luminous phrase that apparently was once whispered to her by her family doctor: "You, a flower of a lady!"

November.

It rains, and rains, and rains...

Annalena has left. Now we are alone, the "cloistered nun" and me. She stays closed in her retreat even more than before.

In a few days she will have to send her thesis to her history professor. It is cold in the room with the fireplace; the large door is closed. Up high, thin streams of rain sketch fleeting silvery lines on the panes of the slit-windows, then wash them away.

It is nine o'clock in the morning, yet darkness still engulfs the room. From the glimmer of light that comes through, my eyes barely distinguish the letters of the motto carved on the fireplace: *SICUT FUMUS DIES MEI.*

Days, days, or perhaps years?

Youthful years that fly away.

The melancholy of November, the silence of the room... A sudden anguish assails me. I cannot stay closed in here any longer.

I open the door; a biting cold quickly penetrates the room. It is no longer raining, but the sky is still dark.

The grass in the meadow is discolored, already nipped by the frost. The trees are bare, but their bleakness is only an appearance, their expectation is secure: in Spring new blossoms and leaves will come. Meanwhile, they sink their roots into the soil.

But what about me? What can I expect?

Suddenly, standing still, almost enchanted, I feel a sudden presence behind the crack of the door.

It's a robin, incredibly near, flying away, but I can catch for a moment its peppercorn-like eyes, its beautiful orange color, like a ray of sunshine.

A bit crazy this November. In the sky the clouds chase each other, airily, filled with light, then a big black hat covers the hill again.

My sadness is gone. Better yet, I am enjoying the rain beating down in torrents. I feel like going up to the attic where my sister is.

I expected to find her, as usual, sitting at the table, bent over her papers; on the contrary, she was standing by the open window. There was no wind: the rain was coming down almost silently in long streams, designing a tent, isolating the room from the outside world.

But my sister was not looking out, she was standing sideways next to the oval window that served as a mirror. She was fixing up a lock of her hair and smiling.

She turned suddenly, stunned, as if just awakened from a dream.

"Isa," she said, "you frightened me. I didn't hear you come in. What time is it?"

"Almost ten," I replied. "Usually by this time the mailman has already arrived. From up here I would have seen him arrive from the road coming from the spring."

"Usually? But he only comes once in a blue moon. Furthermore, he never comes at the same hour as in the city: You know, he stops on his route haphazardly, to have a drink, to warm up by a fireplace..."

"It's true," she added with a sigh. "We haven't seen him for five days."

"What?" I said, even more amazed. "You have counted the days! Are you so worried? Actually your manuscript was sent out not even a week ago! You'll see, everything will be all right."

But she insisted, "I am expecting it this morning. I feel it's coming – I can't stay still... Isa, do you think *he* is pleased?"

I realized she was blushing; the *he* coming out of her lips so suddenly sounded somewhat strange.

I knew the history professor who was to judge her thesis.

Tall and slender, dressed in grey, always with a black tie, an inscrutable look behind the thick lenses of his glasses..

"So young and already so professor-like!" a student from the *Università Normale* of Pisa had said. He was highly regarded, and his classes were popular.

The students never failed to notice in his lectures, so formal and academic, his weakness for certain significant words that he pronounced with the open vowels of his Lombard accent – clarity, commitment, rigor.

Study was certainly his bread and butter, his only passion, as if it burned him with a cold flame. He lived with his very old mother and spent his every free hour in the library. Always courteous; however, the austerity of his life and his scholarly, absent-minded air certainly did not invite anyone to become familiar with him or, worse yet, to take liberties with him.

"Assuming that your doctoral dissertation pleased him greatly," I answered Lia, "I hope you don't expect him to throw his arms around your neck. If anything, he might write something like this:

> *Dear Miss: your subject is satisfactorily developed. A greater clarity...*"

Lia turned pale.

"Don't kid around, Isa," she said. "He is always a perfect gentleman. I am sure he not only sympathizes with us but he is distressed by our predicament."

"I am quite sure of it, Lia. We all know that he is Croce's[7] follower and as such he couldn't possibly approve of what's happening today. On the other hand, he is one of those who keep opinions to themselves, whether it's his character or for the sake of caution."

My sister blushed.

"Caution, certainly not," she said, "for character, perhaps. He is not one of those who talks just to talk, without ever lifting a finger. You know that he has written to me several times..."

I did know that, for I had seen a few post-cards and some very short notes that my sister kept religiously. They invariably ended with the word "*greetings*" followed or preceded by the same adjective "*cordial.*"

While talking, we were both standing by the open window; I noticed, however, that Lia glanced outside every few minutes, always on the look-out. When there was a sudden lightning flash followed by a loud crash of thunder and a heavy downpour, the window banged and I closed it quickly.

My sister returned to her seat at the desk. She ignored me completely, as if she had dismissed me and I were no longer there. She isolated herself again. She was not reading, though, for I could see she continued to be absorbed in her expectation of the letter.

I suddenly recalled a minor episode she had recounted to me: the professor always spoke *ex cathedra* (from a platform) both figuratively and literally. However, once during a seminar, he stepped down from the platform and walked along the aisles. The students had a good chance to look at his tall grey figure from close by and catch a glimpse of his eyes behind their sparkling glasses. They could listen to his *voice* that no longer came impersonally from above, but was nearby and seemed to address each individually, or rather, *one* young lady in particular, who was listening to him enchanted.

When *he* got near her desk, a chill ran up her spine and she withdrew, like a "sensitive plant."

It was the end of the academic year, a beautiful sunny June day. Seeing her withdraw shivering, with perplexed amusement he had asked, "Are you cold?"

My sister came back to reality, blushing.

The rain and the dampness we had absorbed made me shiver now. I, too, was cold.

I went downstairs to the kitchen to warm myself in front of the fire. Only five minutes later, behind the French door, the unmistakable silhouette of our postman appeared. He was staggering forward under the heavy downpour and the gusts of wind, beneath his green umbrella.

"Come in, come in," I said, opening the door wide, while he closed the dripping umbrella and shuffled his muddy boots. "What weather! Come, come near the fire."

I heard Lia come flying down the stairs, straight into the kitchen, anxiously waiting for the postman to open the mail bag.

But our postman was never in a hurry. Habitually he would take his time, telling the story of the day, talking about the weather, his stops on the way, and the people he had met. It seemed he had to act that way because of the long tiring route, or as if he knew he was carrying a nice gift, or a surprise that entitled him to get something in exchange.

He welcomed bread and prosciutto with a glass of wine, all the while keeping the bag closed, giving out mysterious vague hints, enjoying the delay of the anticipated mail. When finally he would get the letter out, he would hold it a while between his fingers, waving it under the addressee's nose, just as a housewife does when she amuses herself by teasing her cat with a piece of tripe.

He was a little man, a bit smaller than average. It was a miracle that his thin crooked legs could carry him around. He walked for such long distances in all sorts of weather and road conditions. Although he was always in the open air, his skin was yellowish and pale; his health, however, must have been of iron. He stuttered a bit which rather irritated those who were impatient and ready to snatch the letter out of his hands and read it. Snacks, sitting by the fire, telling stories, postponements, all these were part of his ritual.

In front of this little character, the peasants became obsequious; they even spoiled him. They gave him a welcome as warm as that reserved, perhaps not for the overseer, but for the peddler who both sold and bought from them, for the butcher, or for the most privileged among the privileged, the shoemaker.

Our kitchen had filled with people; the peasants can spot things from afar, especially the girls. They can detect someone arriving from a great distance better than radar, particularly if it is the mailman!

After going through his usual routine, he seemed willing to deliver the mail. He would slowly pull out one thing at a time: a postcard for the Mannozzis, printed matter for the Albieris, for me a newspaper. He withheld until the end the fiancé's letter for one of the Stelli girls, and an envelope for Lia almost as if he knew their importance.

Once they had all captured their prey, they ran away in order to enjoy it in private. Instinctively, I didn't follow my sister. I had noticed that she was startled when the letter was handed to her in front of everybody as if someone had violated her secret. Of course, I had recognized the handwriting.

Later, she came looking for me. Her cheeks were pink, her eyes shining with that glow I had come to know so well. She tried to appear casual and natural, but her voice had a slight tremor.

"Everything's great, Isa," she said.

This time the message was longer than two lines, it commented on her work. The professor suggested that Lia should take a short trip to Florence, where he was at the time. Verbally he could be more precise regarding certain details. The letter ended with "*cordially.*"

"Will you leave immediately?" I asked. To my surprise, she answered, "I don't know, I don't know. Perhaps I would rather not go, but have him write to me again. It's more beautiful.

Isa, "*cordially*" means "*from the heart,*" doesn't it?"

Lia's dissertation defense was scheduled for November 20. We left together for Pisa.

Just that year a special ceremony had been initiated that included the handing out of degrees and a medal of remembrance for all the newly graduated.

Perhaps because no special procedure had been set for the Jewish students, an invitation also was sent to Lia and to a friend of hers who was in the same predicament.

The two young ladies consulted each other. My sister, being rather timid and shy, would have been happy not to attend, but the more aggressive one asked her this agonizing question, "If we don't go, wouldn't it seem as if we were ashamed?"

The answer was obvious; they would take part in the ceremony, and the ball as well.

Both defended their dissertations early that morning. Earlier still, their classmates, young ladies wearing fascist uniforms, had been glancing with interest at my sister's white blouse and her friend's blue-grey overcoat. How many times does a girl dream of her graduation dress? Just as one dreams of a first communion dress or a bridal gown... The requirement to wear identical uniforms had provoked some resentment since the graduates were being deprived of the innocent pleasure of choosing special dresses.

The zealous janitor, a busybody, had pushed back the two young ladies in their civilian clothes, motioning the others forward. When he was about to begin roll call, the history professor looked at my sister, who, in her blue and white suit, had flown to the back of the black flock, like a wandering swallow and said, "No, the dissertation on Cattaneo will be the first to be defended. Then will follow, in order,..."

No one said a word, and the janitor had to swallow his zeal! That morning my sister was very happy. That was the most beautiful memory of her professor, one that she would cherish for the rest of her life.

But in the afternoon, a few minutes before the ceremony started, when she and her friend were about to cross the threshold of the auditorium, the same janitor being on duty, more zealous and arrogant than ever, escorted them into an adjoining room through a separate entrance.

There, they found the entire Board of eleven, in full academic regalia, with the Rector Magnificum in the center. He looked uncomfortable, as if his gown was too tight; and his cap was lopsided. As a matter of fact, until a moment before, and just because of the two youths, he had been faced with fierce doubts and an agonizing dilemma. What kind of an act should he put on, what image was he to project handing out degrees to Jewish youths, he, a "Magnificum," not to mention a Fascist? Evidence, no doubt, of merit – especially if the grade was high, or worse yet, followed by *cum laude* – but written on a sheepskin marred by an infamous stamp.

With each letter printed in black italics, one could not help seeing the three words *Of the Jewish race*!

What welcome could these Jewish youths, who had come to receive a degree and a medal (!), expect from some fellow students anxious to put into effect certain unequivocal plans. And what about the others, and they were not few, those who were against the regime, how would they, colleagues and students, react?

Chaos, disorder, countless complications; already the unhappy Magnificum was in a cold sweat. Then he saw a light at the end of the tunnel: call in the Jewish youths and ask them – for their own good – to sacrifice the ceremony.

And so he did.

But, when he saw before him not two boys but two girls, two young ladies, two women, the poor man, taken aback by his remaining sense of chivalry toward the eternal feminine, began to stutter, "If a scou...if a scoun...if a scoundrel." But he couldn't finish the dangerous phrase. Dangerous because of his indecorous stuttering, being a Magnificum, and for letting the word "scoundrel" escape his lips in reference to the "bold ones" who would dare hurl insults against the Jews!

There was a moment of indescribable embarrassment. On one side, the two girls, glassy-eyed, on the other, the stuttering chancellor. Then, the notoriously anti-fascist professor of Greek, wrapped in his magnificent beard, his blue eyes glittering mockingly, said, "What do you think is going to happen? The boys have a weakness for the gentler sex!" So saying, he gave a friendly pat on the back of his senior colleague, as if to free him from his stuttering.

In fact, during the ceremony nothing happened. In the evening, the two Jewish girls didn't attend the ball which should have also been their celebration.

Tears didn't dampen their cheeks, but there was still that bitter taste in their mouths to which the Jews cannot become accustomed whenever they sense that they must suffer because they are Jewish, or that they are being offended, pitied, or protected.

At the ball the others were singing:

> of songs of joy
> of songs of love...

We left Pisa the next day, as if the ground were burning beneath our feet. We found refuge at Poggio, in the country. Soon winter would arrive: Uccio and Annalena had left, and our parents were insisting that we go back home. But nothing drew us back to the city. Thus we apathetically let days slip by, finding excuses not to leave.

My sister would go up to the attic as before, surrounded by all her papers, as if still waiting for the mailman, spending long hours by the small window. Downstairs in the ground floor room, while lazily leafing through the pages of my book, I looked at the inscription on the fireplace,

SICUT FUMUS DIES MEI

We were both closed inside our separate cocoons. Our wings had been clipped; we had no way out. It rained and rained, and it rained more.

Those were grey days, full of melancholy. In our hermitage nothing new was happening, and no one ever came.

But one morning Corinna entered, announcing a visitor. He came forward, with his hat in one hand and a little basket in the other. He was an old man, thin and white. Not only his head was white, with its fine silvery hair, but even his skin was pale.

He looked lost, as if he had come from another world.

It reminded me of Geppetto's reunion with Pinocchio in the stomach of the whale: all white, very old, with his last candle still lit.

This old man also, though real and alive, looked to me unreal, as if resurrected by magic.

His color was unusual for a peasant, who is used to being outdoors, and his skin was smooth, almost transparent at the temples where I could see one blue vein beating.

He spoke without raising his voice. Handing me the basket, he told me he was poor, and that what he was offering me was not much, although he had "much to ask." He said this disconsolately, as if he had no hope of getting what he was about to ask for. I encouraged him to speak.

Finally I found out what it was all about. Two rooms had remained empty in the meager peasant dwelling, a sort of addition to the side of the master's house, and the old man asked to occupy them with his wife and son. He would not bother anyone. He only needed a small piece of land to support himself and his old woman; his son worked elsewhere. He couldn't stay any longer at his present dwelling. While saying all this, suddenly, his cheeks, which a moment earlier had looked so white and bloodless, flushed.

Perplexed by seeing an old man blushing, I didn't ask him any more questions and refused his gift of walnuts: I felt as if I would have been stealing them from the poor man. But he looked even sadder.

"Don't you like walnuts?" he said. "We are poor, you see, and we have nothing better."

I reassured him, praising the walnuts, telling him that they were beautiful, all nicely gathered in a blue cotton kerchief, big, light-colored, looking as if they had just been removed from the husks.

My words brought a timid smile to his lips, happy that I accepted and praised his gift. I told him that I would write to my cousin Uccio. He went away comforted.

I had promised to write to Uccio, and I wanted to do it immediately. I thought of the old man and of what was unusual about him, of his sudden blushing.

Corinna knocked at the door.

As soon as she came in I knew from her expression that she had returned to exchange pieces of news.

"As for the rooms," she told me, "they will not bother anyone," (the exact words the man had uttered, I thought). "There is a door adjoining the 'palace,' but it has been locked for a hundred years. Besides, with these thick walls, one could sing and dance all night. With that family, however, oh no, there is no such danger. See, they are not that type, they are so quiet that one could hear the buzzing of a fly. But they definitely weren't so before."

Before? When? Corinna liked to speak a little ambiguously.

The "old man" was not as old as I thought. He could have been forty-six or forty-seven, because "the incident" had occurred when she was a little girl in school.

Oh yes, she could remember it well. She was then in third grade, about seven or eight years old. Now she was thirty-six, because her son Nevo was sixteen, and she had married rather young. The old man could even be forty-eight, but definitely not more than that, because at that time he was a young man of twenty.

I wasn't in the habit of interrupting when peasants were talking; I enjoyed the gist of their conversations. It was like when one starts out on a footpath through the fields that does not go straight, but goes a meandering way. One goes on lazily without hurrying, stopping along the way, to look at a lizard here, to pick blackberries there, further along to drink from a small spring, even half losing one's way, always to be found in the end.

That day, however, I was impatient. What was "the incident," that, after adding and subtracting, (it was now 1939) must have happened in 1911 or '12, an incident with such magnitude as to have struck a third-grade child, remaining so vivid in her memory, after almost thirty years?

"You see, Miss Isa," Corinna went on, "in those days he was a handsome, hardy young man. He looked like a gentleman, but," she added with a sudden astonishing disclosure that sounded to me even more brutal coming after that long introduction, "having been kept 'inside' for thirty years, he is no longer the same, he has lost his vigor. But, you see, he is a good man, even though hit by misfortune. Would you like me to tell you his story?"

Unexpectedly, I saw again the old man's bloodless face and the sudden blushing which had perplexed me.

"No," I interrupted, "I don't want to know anything else. I believe he is a good man and I am going to write my cousin at once." I was tormented by a feeling of guilt, as if I had wanted to pry into the painful mystery of a human being's life, merely out of silly curiosity.

While waiting for Uccio's answer, I went to see the rooms. How long had they been empty? What a feeling of cold and squalor! They were musty and moldy.

The kitchen was small and dark, with broken window panes, damp walls, the brick floor in disarray, and the flue of the fireplace out of order.   When Corinna and I tried to light a fire, the whole room filled with smoke.

And that poor man was asking as a great favor to live in this hovel?

I wrote to cousin Uccio again: those ugly rooms needed at least a bit of repair.   Luckily Uccio, usually so lazy in writing letters, replied promptly.   He wasn't able to come and watch the work being done, so he asked if I would oversee it.

On the margin of his letter there was a cartoon sketching an enormous red brick, under which I stood, a tiny dwarf, hunched over like a caryatid, with the writing in italics:

> *The weight of the construction*
> *will be on Zippo's shoulders.*

But I carried that weight with ease, I would say almost with brilliance, and I was the first to be surprised, not knowing that I had such an unsuspected skill.   I was really quite successful, because I was given a hand – two hands, and what hands! – by an extraordinary assistant.   It was no less a person than the master brick-layer.

"The Florentine," as everybody called him, because he had suddenly appeared from Florence, how I don't know, was certainly skillful and, besides, like all his fellow citizens, he had an outrageous sense of humor.   Furthermore, like a water-diviner pointing to the pool of water with his magic stick, it was he who discovered and revealed "my genius."   It was that simple.

While he was on the ladder doing dangerous turns like an acrobat, holding the plumb line, the chalk, and the ruler, I, on the ground, with my nose up in the air, followed his

movements in amazement. I admired his tricks of the trade
and his mental and physical agility. I don't know which I
admired more. To look at him, he was not at all athletic,
with his round belly like a watermelon coming over his
belt, and yet he moved weightlessly on the ladder, almost
hovering, lightly swaying, not taking gravity into account.
Not only his physical talent attracted me, but also the mag-
netism of his Florentine speech, so unique for its humor, its
turns of phrase, and its intonation.

My Florentine, perched on the ladder, would ac-
company his witty remarks by tipping his newspaper cap
that he wore to one side, like a rooster inclining its comb
with fiery hot eyes.

I was also fascinated by the subject of our conversation. The subject was the fireplace, which was blocked,
and then "fireplaces" in general, rustic ones and heraldic
ones, their fortunes and misfortunes.

"Once," he told me, "a gentleman, a marquis, living in
Florence, in the villa on the *viale de' Colli*, had sent for my
father. My father was a master-bricklayer, the last of that
breed.

"'Come and see' the Marquis said to him, and he
opened the door wide into a large hall with a grey stone
fireplace of *pietra serena* at the end.

"It was a beauty and worked like a dream. But his
wife, the Marchesa, wanted to modernize the hall, saying
that the fireplace was a piece of junk. She wanted a
radiator instead. Can you imagine? As for the stone, she
couldn't stand it. She said it was not in style, and if the
fireplace had to remain there, she wanted it in red marble
with small columns.

"The poor Marchese didn't like the idea of removing
his fireplace, but he didn't want to displease her, so he or-

dered my father to remake it in marble. That, too, was a real beauty, all ruby red. The Marchesa seemed pleased and so was the Marquis, but the fireplace itself wasn't pleased. It was angry because they had changed its face, so it quit working. My father went crazy to make it work, but to no avail. In the end the Marchesa won: the Marchese had to install a radiator.

"Also up here in the country there was a fireplace that filled the kitchen with smoke. There was no way to fix it, due, perhaps, to a mountain nearby and swirling wind currents. This time it was I who went crazy to make it work, but nothing doing. Finally I picked up my tools and left, as I felt I was stealing money from those good people.

"The following day they came for me, saying, 'Come see how beautifully the fireplace works! What did you do to it? Did you bewitch it last night?'

"What had happened was that the wind had blown away the shield on top of the chimney. That queer fireplace simply didn't like to wear a hat!"

I would give the Florentine plenty of leeway to talk and he did the same for me. What a wonderful bond of understanding was established between us, flowing amiably from the floor to the top of the ladder, going up and down like a brick-layer's bucket.

From time to time we would interrupt the work and go outdoors, sometimes to oversee Nevo who was mixing the cement.

Peasants occasionally passing by would stop and stand around us. Conversation went on, questions and answers flew back and forth, and the two of us felt heartened by that vivacious atmosphere and by the fact that we, like performing actors, had some kind of an audience.

It was then that the Florentine gave me the title of "architect." "We must hear the 'architect's' opinion," he would say, validating my "expertise" in construction business, because I had received the university degree. The peasants didn't know whether he was joking or not, since he spoke with such an imperturbable expression.

For a while I went along with it, and the conversation continued with "Yes, architect! No, architect!"

When the discussion became more serious, I explained to them that, yes, I had received a Ph.D. degree, but in the School of *Letters* and not of *Architecture*. I had studied for many years, but now...

I could see amazement growing on Nevo's face. Before his light eyes, mountainous piles of letters flashed, letters he thought I had written.

"But now it is like saying that her nice diploma has become a bill out of circulation," the Florentine said, "and she can't spend it in any way."

He was right, I could not spend it in any way, and there I was explaining to my audience what racial law was all about.

We weren't even allowed to marry...

"Then, it's like saying," the Florentine added, "that you girls, with your youth..."

It was true. Our youth, as well, was a kind of money out of legal circulation.

A solemn silence fell as the peasants listened to me speak. The evening stillness descended over the fields. These people understood; they were on my side, on our side. There is only one truth, and simple souls know it best. We were all brothers; *other races* didn't exist.

In that silence my voice didn't seem like my own. Big words came from my lips, such as "justice" and "liberty," words that when taken seriously make one's heart beat faster.

I spoke of all those, Jews and others, who, like us, even more than us, were suffering and fighting in the shadow and in silence. About those who were dying...

I, then, felt that our youth was money to be spent, even if out of legal circulation, and it was as valuable as a gold coin, despite everything.

PART TWO

April of 1943 was a beautiful month.

The roses bloomed and also the common broom, the swallows flew in the clear sky. Nothing seemed so unbelievable, so out of place as the war. However, many people were leaving the cities, though at that time evacuation seemed like an adventure, a holiday in the country.

The last day of the month was also the day of our last date.

"Don't cry," he had said. And I didn't cry.

As long as I was with him, I lived in a state of ecstasy, as though a magic circle protected me. My blood flowed faster, with a sweet rhythm that made each emotion more intense. Even sorrow was being changed into a kind of happiness. I would always remember that sky, that air and warm sun on my bare arms.

In the first days of May the weather suddenly changed. It looked as if spring was over as a dark sky, lightning, thunder, and a heavy downpour of rain moved in. A cold November-like wind shook the trees, one that made the petals fall from the roses, and made us shiver.

But I was shivering not only with cold. I felt like a patient whose temperature drops sharply, and remains spent, trembling. I went from room to room feeling weak, and listless.

Go away? That would mean tearing out my heart. In my city, when he was with me, even danger seemed wonderful.

My father, seeing me in that state of inertia, decided for me. I was to go to Poggio, as soon as possible. Mother and Lia would stay in the city for a few more days to pack our things. I listened to them talk about dismantling furniture, packing trunks with possessions, books, blankets, rugs, silverware... I heard without listening, wrapped in a single thought: an extraordinary time, a time of love was dead for me, and would probably never return.

But once I was back in Poggio, the miracle repeated itself.

There, May was in full bloom. That air, that green, that silence...

Once again, as if by magic, I was transported from this world, into a kingdom of infinite tranquility and peace.

I was in love and I could live with those marvelous images of my love.

I was no longer alone, no longer sad. Remembrances and thoughts seemed to have lost their daily strength, almost all that remained was an echo, a fragrance.

I had the house all to myself.

In the morning I would open the old shutters. With the early sun hitting my heavy eyelids I would plunge into the clean and clear air that seemed almost the natural breath of Poggio, in the deep resonant silence of the country.

At night I would sit on the crenelated wall enclosing the garden and contemplate the "fair stars of the Bear"[8] as we did the night he and I together had read Leopardi's poetry.

The solitude was favorable to produced fantasies and illusions. I would envision him arriving suddenly, standing behind me on tip-toe, covering my eyes with his hands. I expected him. I was wearing the white dress that he liked so much. I would set the table for two with the light-blue plates and the yellow scented blossoms of broom shrubs.

Corinna would catch me in the midst of my dreams while I was arranging the flowers in a glass pitcher.

"You don't get bored all alone, do you, Miss Isa?"

No, I never got bored. The empty house lived along with me.

Climbing the stairs that led to the bedrooms, I felt as if he was holding my arm tightly in his, and I could almost hear his breathing and see the flame of my candle flickering from the breath of our voices.

At nighttime I was not alone in the "palace." Three peasant girls used to come after supper to spend the night with me. In the evening I would remain in the kitchen, standing behind the glass of the French door to wait for them. I enjoyed watching them come in the dark, passing under the vine-trellis. They carried an oil-lamp, one of those shaped like a boat. I could hear the laughter of their young voices, and in the glowing light I could see the vine tendrils that brushed their faces, looking like delicate, dark butterflies.

Because the girls came every evening, I began to know them better and gained their confidence a bit. It was not easy; usually they would shy away from any intimate questions. They were very jealous of their secrets but at the same time also very curious about us, never daring to ask any questions.

In those evenings, however, in the big silent house, with a candle wasting away slowly, with the semi-darkness making it easier to confide, they told me "who was chasing after them" and how important it was "to say 'no' at least three times to the boys, or else one is taken as..." Besides, girls had to be careful not to remain *pinze*.

"What do you mean by '*pinze*'?" I would ask, and they would burst out laughing.

"'*Pinze, pinze*'...how do you call them? You know, when a girl doesn't find a husband, by the age of twenty-five she is a '*pinza*.'"

Actually there were no '*pinze*' in the area because all the young peasant fellows made sure they found a wife, for to remain without one "was the greatest misfortune for a man."

When I saw them during the day "tending the beasts" in the fields, they would greet me with their "good morning to you" and continue knitting silently, casting a coy glance at me and laughing every now and then.

At other times, in the company of small boys, we would become little girls ourselves. We would chase each other until we were out of breath, or we would enter a footpath and hide, waiting to jump out suddenly to scare a newcomer, or we would go into the barley field, with the green spikes already tall, and dive into that sea of green. We would pick handfuls of barley seeds, attached to the long slender awns of the barley beard and throw them at each other through the air, while we ran. As they fell, some would stick to our hair or clothes.

"Three, four, five 'grooms,'" the girls would count. At each one they would shriek with joy and surprise. They threw seeds at me, too, but suddenly one of the girls, Ornella, become serious and said to me, "One is enough to love, isn't it, Miss Isa?" And I, who at that moment was thinking of one, one alone, felt my heart sink. Was he still in love with me?

Another game we played with barley was called "*go to paradise.*"

We would be sitting on a low wall. The game required silence and great concentration. It consisted of removing each green and tender seed with its long and slender awn from the barley spike, one at a time and very carefully. The goal was to pick off the seeds without breaking the jagged stem which was thinner and thinner toward its tip. To go as far as the top of the spike meant to "go to paradise."

Such an undertaking was hard. The stems were so slender that the green color faded out like transparent silk thread. They would invariably break halfway up the spike or, worse yet, right near its top. Then you had to start all over again, with another barley spike. With infinite patience you had to pull each seed out carefully, using just the right amount of force, yet with a delicate touch, as if your weightless hands were airborne.

And so those days flew by, days during which I was still in paradise, suspended by a slender, fragile thread, just like the stem of the barley spike.

Unexpectedly, Aunt Clara and Annalena arrived and so did their furniture. I immediately caught a glance of disapproval in Aunt Clara's eyes.

"Your parents told me that you had an earlier start to get the rooms ready, but everything is just as before, exactly as before."

"Exactly" as before... Even though the word was unpleasant, it told the truth. As much as I could, I had left "everything exactly as before."

How I wished it would have lasted that way forever! But it didn't last "as before" from then on, from that afternoon of May 13, 1943, it didn't last anymore as before, not another day, another hour, not even another moment.

We often don't realize when *something* comes to upset our life forever. Changes, even the very important ones, occur unnoticed at first. Then they seem to creep in treacherously, imperceptibly, the same way faces change due to the passage of time, from infancy to old age. Yet, they look the same, or we would be frightened to look in the mirror.

But the "face" of the house changed all at once that afternoon of May 13, never to be the same again.

The van with the furniture was outside on the lawn, so there was no time to waste. Corinna and Vanni arrived to help unload. The two panels of the big entrance door were spread wide open to let the invaders enter.

As I looked at the earthen footprints on the floor, I felt ashamed again, as when I watched the peasants carry Uccio's clay inside.

For the moment, the furniture in the fireplace room on the ground floor remained unchanged. In the hall, instead, just in front of the *MORITURO SATIS*, the horrible shining pieces of early twentieth-century furniture with their chrome ornaments were stacked up high. There was no way around them, we had to look at them every time we passed by. Other pieces of furniture, beds, chests of drawers, chairs, armchairs, sofas, were all dragged up the stairs to invade the rooms on the upper floor. Aunt Clara was giving orders like a sea captain from the bridge of his ship. Perhaps even stronger than her love for her possessions was her earnest desire to assign a logical, rational place for everything. Waving dust-cloths like blazing flags, she finally went up and down the stairs to establish the kingdom near and dear to her, the kingdom of everything clean, orderly, and functional. She gave no respite to herself or the others until late at night, only after she had conquered all the outposts.

Completely worn out, she went to bed without supper.

Annalena, somewhat unwillingly, had been working as field assistant, but now she proclaimed liberty in the kitchen, since she was starving after all that running around.

I was not hungry, but I took refuge in the kitchen, as well, to avoid, at least for that evening, the hideous sight of the household goods and chattels.

While tossing and turning in bed, I was feeling guilty about Aunt Clara. Actually the poor woman was right, and those horrible pieces of furniture shaped like parallelograms represented her entire home, the fruit of years of effort and sacrifice. It was only fair that she should care for them so tenderly.

However, envisioning those absurd pieces of furniture, with their veneered wood, falsely solid even though so geometrically shaped, all stowed in that somber cloister-like hall with its stone walls one meter thick, was very strange. To see them there, their shining, flashy metal ornaments disrupting the cool semi-darkness right there in front of the *"MORITURO SATIS"*, was simply unbearable.   Even the Latin inscription seemed to acquire a new mocking significance. *MORITURO SATIS...*, "it is enough for those who must die..."   And this is what is granted to human beings today as the fruit of their great efforts, some ugly furnishings that can break easily, in the midst of which their ephemeral lives are spent.

Time moved on quickly, then more than ever.   The eternal values such as Beauty and Art were luxuries, luxuries forbidden to those who had little time to live in this world, a world that became, day after day, uglier, smaller, and more unbearable.

I realized that my thoughts were becoming confused, no doubt I was delirious, and finally I fell asleep.

As for the barbarian invasions, May 13 marked only the first of many more to follow.

Once broken into, the old house was violated several times.   First the evacuees camped within its walls, then the Germans, the French, the Moroccans, then the English, the Canadians, the Blacks, the Indians...

After the war, when we went back to see Poggio again, we found dirty walls covered with obscene graffiti.   Even our recordings of the English language course had been broken into pieces, out of spite, by the Germans.

That May of 1943, however, the invasions were by the family. Aunt Freda and cousin Uccio arrived and with them another van.

Mama and Lia arrived as well, and our furniture was to follow a few days later.

Mother said that everything was done; the "famous" trunks were packed and closed.

"I suppose you feel better," I said to her, because I thought I perceived a certain relief in her voice. But seeing her so pale, her eyes shining, I understood why. I knew how much toil and pain the whole move had cost her. To move our belongings meant to pull each piece of furniture from its accustomed niche, from the place where we had always seen it, the beds we had slept in for more than twenty years, the table where we had always eaten together. It meant taking pictures down from the walls, leaving marks and empty spaces that brought feelings of melancholy. Let alone the doubts and uncertainties that surrounded our move, questions such as whether to pack everything or discard the unnecessary led to even deeper thoughts. What really *is* necessary and what is really unnecessary?

Diogenes lived in a bottle and threw away his cup to drink from his cupped hand... We, however, were slaves of our possessions, and piteously, grotesquely attached to "things."

"There is no end to emptying the armoire," Mother would say. "Tablecloths, sheets, woolen blankets for winter... We don't have a home anymore!" she would repeat. "Poor things! All piled and wrinkled inside the trunks! And to think that I worked so hard to iron them, and now I wonder how they will arrive."

There was, however, another worry consuming her, our father.

"That poor man, he has to stay behind in the city exposed to danger! I feel badly that I left him alone, but he wants me to stay here with you, my daughters. I wish I could be *here* and *there* at the same time. If only we could be all together!"

To be "all together." This was the biggest yearning of my mother, of all mothers, I believe, who felt their hearts torn at every separation, at each parting. They would love, like brood-hens, to cuddle us all under the warmth of their wings.

"Poor man and poor things..." Mama was right. Both human beings and things had one and the same destiny of misery, when snatched from their natural environment, perhaps separated forever.

The peasants had been busy finding the best place for Aunt Freda's and Cousin Uccio's furniture. It was only fair, since it belonged to them and they were the real owners of the house. Thus, almost all of the big room on the upper floor was crammed with furniture, but the fireplace room on the ground floor had been changed only a little, out of respect for the owners. Even in my cousin Uccio's eyes, which were usually cheerful, I caught the same uneasiness that I felt. But soon after, his satirical nature returned. That was his way, hiding his feelings by poking fun at the others, especially at me, maybe because I was the most like him.

"You, Zippo," he would say, "are not like soft soil. You are like dry terrain that splits open with the rain. You mustn't be so damned sensitive, you must get used to it.

"Look, I had mother's piano put right in the fireplace room," he told me, jokingly saying "p-i-a-no" in staccato.

"That varnished 'dinosaur' is a real eyesore in that room. Nothing could be worse!" Uccio was very devoted to his mother, and for her sake he had not wanted to relegate the "dinosaur" with the other household possessions.

"Perhaps she will never play it," he would say to me. "At home she played at nighttime because she didn't want to be bothered. Here in the country she does not feel acclimated; probably she'll be bored a lot, and boredom is terrible."

He feared boredom, tedium, for his mother more than for himself.

I was surprised to learn that Aunt Freda played the piano at night, as if a secret had been revealed to me. On the other hand, not one of us knew what she was really like, she was always aloof with people. I don't think she had a single true friend, and she never showed friendship to her relatives or to her sisters-in-law. I was truly curious about how living together would work out!

Uccio, her son, her only child, was everything to her. It seemed, in fact, that they got along very well. The peasants were amazed to see them going for long walks through the fields and the woods, talking all the way, chit-chatting as if they had everything to say to each other.

"*Like two lovers*," Corinna would say, marveling that a young man in his early twenties had so much to tell his mother, whereas she said of her own son, nineteen-year-old Nevo, that "you would never get a word out of his mouth even if you paid him!"

Order, punctuality, and precision were Aunt Clara's program. However, the poor lady had a hard time carrying them out. At any rate, she had placed a big ugly clock in the kitchen so that everyone would budget their time and keep mealtimes intact.

Home is not a hotel!

Furthermore, she had assigned each one of us different duties.   She would do the cooking, Mother would be responsible for wardrobe, and we girls were to take care of household chores, including provisions. She had not dared even mention Aunt Freda and Uccio, and from the very first day it was clear that Clara and Freda "*did not cooperate.*"

Aunt Freda didn't show any interest whatsoever in the house menage. She would close herself in her room or take walks through the woods with her son. Uccio, on the other hand, was like the elusive *Scarlet Pimpernel.* We had no way of knowing whether he was in his "*buen retiro*" because the shutters were always closed. At times he was out all day long riding horse-back; if asked to do an errand, he would surely forget it. At other times, he would appear in the kitchen at noon, yawning and still in his dressing gown, and with an innocent refreshed look on his face, he would ask for "breakfast."

If Aunt Clara's "program" meant just about nothing to Aunt Freda and Uccio, it didn't have much luck with us either. For instance, Aunt Clara had committed herself to the onerous task of cooking, but, who knows why, Lia was always determined to cook the corn-mush *polenta* herself, whenever it took her fancy.

Why? Simply because Lia had fun doing it. But these were no times for fun! Aunt Clara would fume with rage.

My sister had learned to make *polenta* from the peasants in their crude manner, with a ferocious fire under the kettle, and with Lia blowing until she was out of breath, scattering ashes all over the fireplace.

Aunt Clara would follow Lia's every movement with angry but powerless eyes because my sister, as sweet as an angel, would never give up when an idea was fixed in her mind.

Over the high flame, the *polenta* would bubble and spit inside the black kettle, much to everyone's delight, including Uccio who always arrived in the kitchen as if by chance.

Most exciting was our anticipation of the final moments when Lia, usually so calm, would become more and more animated. She would get quite close to the fireplace, the reflection of the flame reddening her face. Then she would take firm hold of the kettle, turn it upside down, and plop the big mass of steaming golden *polenta* onto the wooden cutting board.

All of us cousins would then rush toward it, holding our bowls, fighting to be the first to cut a slice with the string. We furiously attacked the mountain of grated cheese, grabbing it, and while pouring generous amounts on the *polenta* we scattered some around, even on the floor.

Aunt Clara grumbled that, besides everything else, in times of rationing, it was a disgrace to waste the "grace of God." Actually, however, the "grace of God" never went to waste since Sultano, Uccio's big cat, would clean it all up with his tongue.

In addition to *polenta*, so beautiful and so golden, other things displeased Aunt Clara, including our mother, her own sister.

My mother, so sweet, was reluctant to follow a militant discipline. She would remain for hours and hours with a darning egg in her hand to mend stockings without taking a single stitch, her eyes lost in space... She kept saying that she had a sad premonition. She didn't smile any longer with that lovely smile of hers that would light up her beautiful light blue eyes so like a child's.

The last days of May brought an unexpected early onset of hot weather.

During the midday hours, only dark shadows cast by the huts and haystacks interrupted the blinding light of the sun resting on the meadow; further down there were jagged shadows made by the leaves of the plane trees. But there was not a breath of air. The still silence, as if suspended, alternated with the increasingly deafening chorus of cicadas.

Everyone looked tired and even Corinna didn't look fresh or rested. She didn't linger in the kitchen to talk as usual, but this was also because *chores* were pressing.

News from our city was getting bleaker and bleaker. Father wrote that every night he was awakened by the howling of the air-raid siren.

We cousins almost avoided each other, feeling uneasy and ashamed, as if our doing nothing in the country weighed upon us to the point of becoming unbearable.

I was feeling low. Up to that moment I had not experienced the torment of nostalgia; recent memories had kept me company, and dreams and hopes had been singing in my heart. But not any more. I, too, was feeling spent, as if the sudden heat had debilitated not only my body but also my soul. The joyful images of my love story were fading like sparks buried among the ashes.

Waking up to reality, nostalgia of a lost love, anxiety, yearning and fear followed the dreams.

To avoid thinking and boredom, I read almost all day, but even my dearest poets seemed mute to me.

And what about Lia, Annalena, and Uccio?

Perhaps Annalena was most at ease. Free from school obligations and work, except for the few errands to alleviate Aunt Clara, she could give vent to her natural laziness by sleeping until late in the morning and taking a siesta in the meadow in the afternoon. She had not lost her good appetite, but since there was no great variety of food in the country, she grabbed whatever she could: slices of bread and bowls of milk for breakfast, big dishes of tomatoes and salad for snacks.

Uccio appeared distracted and remote. On the walls of his *buen retiro* there were still sketches drawn with charcoal; he never showed me a finished work.

When once I questioned him frankly, because I thought he was wasting too much time, he answered, "Isa, you torment yourself, you worry, you are impatient, you go after a goal and you would like to reach it immediately, at once. You don't know how to save your energy, and you burn yourself up in a blaze. However, in life, in love, and above all in art, one must know how to wait. See, I don't care if days go by with me doing nothing. It's only an apparent fear, for I *do create inside*."

As he spoke, he was unusually serious. I looked deep into his grey eyes, so full of light.

I felt consoled; I believed him. Uccio was an artist. He had chosen his way, that wonderful way to art, his secret, his strength, as well as his risk.

At times, seeing him idling his time away, I almost reproached myself, as if I were partly to blame for this. But what right had I to egg him on, I who didn't even know how to find my own way? Didn't the bans against practicing our professions constitute a dangerous alibi? Meanwhile, I, too, avoided all serious programs of study and work, consumed by the uncertainty of the future, by the nostalgia of an impossible love.

Better to be like Annalena. She didn't make problems for herself, but waited calmly. Her destiny would probably turn out better. As for my sister, she seemed to be completely unaware of the ephemera of our present life, nor did she seem to be worried about anyone or anything. She kept getting up early in the morning. She kept busy as before, and even when I saw her doing nothing, her face showed neither torment nor boredom. If anything, it showed a calm melancholy.

She would often take refuge in the attic, as when she was writing her thesis and would sit at her desk behind the small round windows. If I suggested we read or study together, she would answer, "No, Isa, I really don't feel like it now."

So all of us fended for ourselves, apart from each other. Mama looked the most tired. She had lost weight, she was pale and, like a troubled soul, wandered through the huge disorderly rooms crowded with furniture.

On May 28, a singular event occurred.

I was worried about mother's health, for in the past few days it had grown worse. She was very pale, she wouldn't eat anything, and in the morning she got up with deep, purplish circles under her eyes. Even her look had changed, and her light blue eyes seemed to have lost their glow.

I entered her room to bring her breakfast. Usually I would find her up already, seated near the window with a prayer book in her hands and a distant look in her eyes. But that very morning I became distressed as soon as I saw her. She was still in her nightgown and the whiteness of the linen emphasized her ghostly look. She didn't seem to be aware of my presence.

"Mama," I said, "are you all right? What's wrong?"

She looked at me with a fixed stare without answering and began to shiver, a convulsive tremor shaking her all over.

Then I grew frightened; I dared not leave her alone to call for help; I hugged her to warm her up, but she was cold, as if drained of blood.

Luckily Aunt Clara appeared, and soon after, my sister ran upstairs along with Corinna, who had been in the kitchen.

Even years later the peasants remembered the episode and would tell of it.

> The poor *signora* began to gasp. She seemed out of her mind, like a cow being stripped of her calf. She remained that way all day; she didn't want to move from where she lay and didn't want to get dressed. There she was, all white, whiter than her nightgown, without any food. We would wet her dry lips a little; her two daughters were crying. Suddenly, she screamed, as if they were slitting her throat, and she appeared to have fainted. But then she began sobbing and calling for her husband, saying he was in danger back in the city.
>
> The poor *signora* was right to act that way, because she had supernatural powers.

It became common knowledge that mother "*had super-natural powers*," and this was repeated by all the peasants.

It was true, for mother had that crisis on May 28, the same day that the first terrible bombing raid occurred in our city.

The next day the estate overseer came to Poggio. Father had phoned him in Colle so that he could tell us of the bombing before we read it in the newspaper. We were to stay calm; everything was safe. A brief letter followed, and father repeated that we should stay calm, that he would join us as soon as possible. He did not say anything about our poor city, nor had he even mentioned *that other one*, that other one who was tearing my heart.

Mother, although very weak, was completely normal again and she looked at me with her light blue eyes, tenderly, without speaking.

But I had no peace: I had to find out, at any cost I had to know, so I would leave right away. I told my sister, but she seemed not to approve.

"Bad news travels fast. He must be safe. His family had moved to Marina... Why should he have been in the city just that day? He will write, you'll see. You'll see, he will write soon." She would repeat those consoling words, in a kind of sweet sing-song voice, like a mother trying to calm the desperate cry of a baby by rocking it in her arms.

As for my cousin, she advised me not to go, absolutely not. Was I crazy? Who knew if the trains were even running! The city was almost destroyed! And if the first bombings were to be followed by others in the days to come? Everyone was running away from the city and I wanted to return there? If he were dead or wounded (she would utter those terrible words calmly), were he dead or wounded, we surely would have heard; if he didn't write, because he didn't want to, it would have been better to get him out of my mind. To be in agony over someone irresponsible was not worthwhile.

"Enough, enough," I told her, "I'll leave just the same."

I had strong misgivings about telling my mother. I feared I would give in to her begging and tears. But, to my surprise, she said nothing. She only sighed and blessed me in Hebrew, holding her trembling hand on my head for a long time.

I left at breakneck speed on the bicycle, plunging down the steep hill, to reach Colle where I could catch a train.

Only Uccio had approved of my going, nicknaming me "Zippo the Adventurous," and singing the tune of Mascagni's *Parisina*:

> I leave on a venture and
> I take with me only a horse [the bicycle]!

I could understand that, in his joking way as was his nature, he agreed with me and followed me with his heart.

Three days later I was back in Poggio. It seemed to me like a moment, or an eternity, as if I had never left, and everything had been a nightmare, a dream.

The peasants said that after that trip, I was no longer the same, but they never asked me questions. Rather, whenever I met them, men greeted me from a distance and women kept silent, carrying on with their work. Only Beppa, who used to come and knit near the small wall where I was seated, would sigh now and then, almost voiceless, "you poor things," as she pushed her knitting needle beneath her kerchief to scratch her ear.

My family also chose not to ask me anything. Whenever I entered a room and they were talking, they would stop short. Thus, I lived with all the others as if alone, in another dimension of time and space.

I don't know if I was actually suffering: I only knew that I had suffered and it had increased to the point of agony, just as when you dream of drowning, falling into space, or being followed, and your heart beats furiously. You wake up in a drenching sweat and yet find it difficult to remember what caused so much fear. As if I, too, was not completely awake. I kept repeating that moment of waking up, when sorrow lingers and surfaces to the threshold of consciousness. That relationship, pertaining to a very recent past, had shattered in the mirror of my memory, leaving disconnected images, phantoms that I vainly begged to leave me, to disappear into nothingness, but they kept coming back mercilessly. They talked to me with indistinguishable lost voices, asking me to listen to them, to reassemble them, as if I, too, would find peace only by finding again the main theme of a short story.

One face, more than any others, was always before me, the one that I would have liked to forget, more than anyone else. He was no longer my friend, a part of myself, whose image I evoked by the strength of my love to console my desperate longing.

He had looked at me with a fixed stare, his light eyes as cold as ice, without a smile on his pale lips. What did he want to tell me? Why didn't he talk? His look, just like a sharp blade, cut into my eyes which I felt opening wide gradually, and remaining wide open, becoming like his, an image reflected in the mirror.

I, too, was speechless, my voice choked in my throat.

Everything was still. There was not a breath of air, not even a leaf moved. A strip of livid sea without waves, far in the distance, looked like stone.

Little by little a grey fog lifted from the sea and that face, those eyes, dissolving, disappeared into the mist. Then the fog became thicker and thicker and through the fog a faceless voice reached me, *his voice*, saying, "You must not wait for me, do not wait for me ever again."

But I couldn't make out the meaning of those words, I repeated them over and over again, until suddenly they became as clear as a red-hot brand piercing my heart.

Now the fog disappeared. Suddenly the southwest wind came up. Shadows swiftly fell down around the pine trees which seemed to moan under the gusts of wind.

Is it still me waiting there? I no longer know for whom or for what. I shiver with cold. The blood drains from my veins, like an hour-glass that has emptied. I get lost among the tree trunks, along the paths, one after the other, all the same.

At the end of the pine grove, I hear the dark voice of the sea. The last bit of sun, vivid as a clear flame, disappears in the midst of the dark clouds chasing each other on the horizon; up high in the sky, a violet color deepens bleakly. A seagull flies with its wings spread, skimming the crest of the waves. It goes up and down again, without finding peace.

Other images overlapped and I tried to untangle them with great effort.

I recognize myself, alone, in a train compartment. The train stops in the middle of the countryside. The window frames an immobile landscape, fixed in the afternoon light.

Time, too, seems to have stopped.

I look at my watch, but its hands have stopped. How long have I been travelling? Wasn't I, this morning, on the train back to Colle?

I seem to hear voices again, voices of *paesani*, of peasants, who met and greeted each other, saying, "Look who is here! You of all people! What brings you here?"

They all greet one another as if they haven't seen each other for ages. I, instead, apart in a corner, watch olive trees and cypresses whizzing by.

All those people are calm. Why do I alone suddenly begin to tremble? Someone has uttered random phrases,

"Didn't you read the paper? *Down there* not even a seed has remained."

Up to that moment I had been thinking only of him. I was wrapped up in him; he was my only worry. Now those words uttered carelessly by a stranger had made an opening, a new wound, but just as intense. A feeling of anguish, of desperate longing for my poor city, now that I am nearing it again, for what I would find and for what I wouldn't find anymore.

The train stops abruptly again.

It is not going to start ever again. I wait in a kind of torpor, with my eyes closed. I don't know whether I am falling asleep or if I am dreaming. Behind my eyelids a throng of people gathers. Who are those ragged people waiting on the other track? When, where have I seen "*the evacuees*"? Had I not met some in Colle? What was so strange about them?

Now I recognize them. As I look they become one vast blur, for they seem to me all alike, one grey face, with livid circles under the eyes. This was the new face that war has painted with hunger, fear, and sleeplessness.

"*The evacuees*," an attribute that was already part of our common language usage, had acquired a more precise meaning. It was already like a brand in one's flesh, in one's soul. It referred, sadly, to refugees, exiles, and deportees.

Someone is shaking me roughly to awaken me. How long have I slept?. I quickly jump down from a high step. I am on a dead-end track. I have a glimpse of distant, phantom-like, dark silhouettes of the platform shelters, and the bluish lights.

The first stars already appear in the sky.

I am tired, my limbs are numb, but I walk and walk for a long stretch along the tracks to reach another train, the one that finally will take me home.

In the compartment by now swallowed in obscurity, an old man is snoring, his head leaning on the drapes; two other passengers talk aloud.

> The flames could be seen from more than twenty kilometers away; the crashing thuds could be heard as if near, so near that it seemed to be the end of the world. At the railway station people were crushed to death as they crowded in the underpasses; the corpses had not been removed yet...

I would never know whether that news was true, but even after so many years, anytime I happened to be inside there, in that closed area, within those cold stones in the underground, I thought I could smell the lugubrious odor of death.

But this is the street leading to my home, yet I think I am still walking in a tunnel without air or light. The street is deserted and completely dark, with all windows closed because of the black-out rule.

I can feel my heart pounding; my hand trembles as I ring the door bell.

No one opens, no one answers.

It looks like the house of the dead.

I ring again. I wait.

Why didn't I think of it before? There is no electricity.

Who knows if the garden bell is still there? I walk along the wall and, like a blind person, reach out to touch the iron gate. I search in the darkness, then I gently pull the bell chain.

In that silence, the rusted chain squeaks and moans: a broken sound like a sob answers. I stand still for a few moments, then I go back to the door.

Finally the door opens slightly. It's Aunt Tilde, thinner and older.

"You are here?" she says, asks, and her voice doesn't seem like hers anymore. I notice the strange look of the house. There was hardly any furniture, with no beds in the bedrooms, but instead mattresses on the floor.

Strangers are in my home, people I don't seem to know. They wander through the empty rooms with ghostly faces, by the smoky candle light and oil night-lamps.

I have asked for a jug of water, a bar of soap, a towel.

"Just try to find a decent towel!" my aunt says, trotting through the house on her poor tired legs. She explains that the few linens that were left have disappeared, or rather are disappearing every day, with those people in the house...

My home, those people, all seem unreal to me! These images move as if inside a steamed mirror, more and more out of focus. Suddenly, as if I had wiped the mirror clean, a scene appears clearly, in sharp focus. These people are all sitting around the long, narrow table. No tablecloth, but on it there is a pot with a few beans and a little bit of chopped onion.

I wait for father who is not back yet; I stay in a corner to watch them eat. Nobody speaks, nobody even mentions that terrible night. Bunched around the table, like newborn kittens almost blind, each one sucking from its mother's nipples. They eat avidly, in silence, seeing nothing but the food in their dishes.

Father, on the other hand, ate almost nothing that evening. He gave me a gruff welcome, gruffer than ever before.

"Why did you come?"

But he knows why, and doesn't ask me any more questions. He also knows that I'll not leave until I see *him*.

Yesterday morning I left with my father to go back to Poggio. I am on the train again and it is as if I had never gotten off.

Father asked me nothing, for it was enough for him to look at me. He holds one of my hands in his large hands like those of a kindly bear.

The sky is pale grey, it's so foggy that one can barely see the poplars; a light rain falls like tears on the window. The monotonous noise of the train is attuned to my weariness. I shall finally go to sleep.

But suddenly I hear a voice inside of me saying, *"Don't wait for me, you must not wait anymore."*

Now I understand the meaning of those words. Perhaps he is "*down there*," buried under the debris.

It is the voice of a dead person. The one who talked to me was not alive.

For the first time now, I almost hated the countryside. My heart had remained back "*down there*," buried in the debris.

Returning to Poggio I had thought that solitude could cure me by granting me space and rest from my sorrow. But it didn't happen that way. Whenever I went through the fields and the woods, I had the feeling of wandering like a phantom in search of my soul. The earth, the trees, and the sky had nothing to tell me.

Even with all the activity in the house, I was in my own world. I got up in the morning and continued my daily routine, but I was like a robot, acting mechanically, like a sleep-walker, unconscious of my actions. I would remain silent for hours, absorbed in my gloomy reverie. It seemed as if I was to leave again, to go looking for something, but for what? I no longer listened to other people's conversation. It was only when I heard them speaking about the dead, about destruction, or about danger, that I would prick up my ears. I seemed to be waking up, shaking myself and realizing that it would be good for me to be there, as if on top of a trench, risking my life every minute, feeling the breath of death.

Nay, only in this longing for death, I felt alive.

At times I dreamt, always unhappy dreams, but with exhilarating visions of happiness foreshadowing death. This was in order for me to live still another moment of life and to be able to consume myself simply because it was the last.

I detested time, which is long, empty, and useless. With Dante I begged for death, for I was its color.

> ...see how I yearn to be
> one of your own; I even look like you.
> Come, for my heart implores you.[9]

The days were getting longer, the sun hotter and the evenings more fragrant.

Now the peasants would stay out until late at night to do their chores. They would not go back home even for supper. The women brought baskets of food covered with napkins, and some wine in a flask. After eating in the meadow at dusk, they would stay a bit longer to rest while the younger people played hide and seek. In the twilight, one could hear the girls laughing softly at the more daring jokes.

Cousin Uccio loved that particular hour, and at times he, too, would go to the field, mingling with the peasants. The good humor and the merry excitement that got into them all after drinking a little wine, as well as the fact that girls were near them, infected him too.

"They are young and happy," Uccio would say, speaking of Nevo and the other young men. "To them, love is still a surprise, a joy to live, not a drama, sorrow, or sadness."

One time, while going out, he passed the room where I sat, my head bent over a book, but I wasn't reading. The room was dim, lit only by a candle in the far corner.

He asked me to join him for a walk:

"Zippo," he said, "You can't go on like this. If I had a magic wand, I would perform a spell, a metamorphosis. I would touch you and you would become a dormmouse, a squirrel. You know, one of those little animals that hibernate. Then you could stay there immobile, curled up in a corner as you are now. You would sleep until winter is over."

"Winter?" said I.

"Yes, this is winter for you. You feel nothing, not even the heat of the sun. You don't see the sky brightening nor the wheat ripening, nor the red poppies. Sleeping this way, months would go by until one day you would wake up, and see Spring had come. Unfortunately, though, I have not a wand!"

Suddenly from the table he grabbed a steel paper opener, shaped like a sword. For a moment he held its point in the candle flame, and before I could draw back, he touched my bare arm with the hot point, as in fencing.

I jumped, as I felt my flesh burning.

"*You are alive*, Zippo," he said. "You must fight!" At that very moment Lia entered the room. It would have been difficult to explain what had happened. I was sobbing, surely not from the pain caused by the little burn, as Uccio bent over me, patting my head.

This was a sign of my cousin's compassion, and I carried its mark on my arm for a few days.

Looking at the minute scar, I felt like sobbing again, reawakening the wave of emotion, the shock that was triggered in me on that occasion. I could still feel a tremor inside me, and something dissolve in my heart. Surely I was not recovered yet, but I tried to keep myself less alone and mingle with the others.

After the second air raid, Dad, too, came to stay in Poggio. Day after day his health worsened.

He arrived late at night, tired and exhausted.

His dusty jacket hung from his sagging shoulders. Wrinkles appeared deeper and oh, those eyes that had seen the destruction! Those eyes were evasive as if within him lingered a feeling of fear and shame, of one who has deserted his post.

"But how can one endure it?" he said. "Night after night, that damned air-raid-siren!"

We still remembered our Dad in the prime of life, tall, stately, and strong. Now he looked bent over and shrunken like an old man.

Crumbled homes, entire families destroyed, or worse yet, people left alone, without home or family. What can one do, alone in this world?

He told us about a friend of his, our family doctor.

"After the bombs destroyed his home, he didn't seem to be himself anymore. It left him shaking, his daughter holding him by the hand. He came to see me before going away. They sat on the step outside our door as if they were unable to make it up the stairs. They stayed there, stunned and staring, repeating over and over, 'My home! We no longer have a home!'"

Home!

Now our home as well, the household goods at least, was being transported to Poggio. Dad had arrived with the last truckload.

It was necessary to arrange the furniture that had already been stacked to make room for the next load.

We had tried to keep the belongings of each family together to give a little sense of home. But it was as if one had dissected the limbs from a living organism, removing the bowels, the bones: the cupboard, the table, the desk, Mother's piano.

It was not a grand piano, like the more aristocratic one Aunt Clara owned. It looked like a poor soul, with its worm-eaten brownish wood, like a punished child, since the keyboard faced the wall, due to lack of space. I noticed that every day, Mother crept laboriously into the corner, dusted it lovingly, and even raised the green felt strip that protected the old keys.

The piano could be symbolic of mother, so out of place, helpless, almost reduced to silence...

All of a sudden Mother was young again. In those days she played the piano often. Her eyes glittered, and she, though timid, seemed to express another self with the music, as if it were her only form of communication.

At times she played and sang, with her voice thin but clear, and in tune —

> I followed you, as if you were a vision of peace,
> along the avenues of heaven...

The notes of Tosti's song would transpose even us children far away.

Perhaps it was through that music, sung by my mother's voice, that it was revealed to me how powerful dreams, art, and the "Ideal" could be.

> Enraptured by the sound of your voice,
> I dreamed and dreamed.
> And I felt you in the light, in the air,
> in the fragrance of flowers,
> and my solitary room
> was filled with you, with your splendor.

Rooms crammed with furniture, eight people constantly bumping into one another, each with a different personality and problems, often with dark, tense faces.

The spirit of dreams that once permeated the villa seemed lost forever.

Even my sorrow seemed to be part of another world, a world already far away.

Our misfortune had dogged our steps as though it were chained to our ankles. We, too, had no home; we were evacuees, with our possessions all piled up. Worse yet, we were Jewish, lost, uncertain of our future.

Now we, the young ones, bore in silence the frustration of the elders. We had become more sympathetic with their discomfort, their pain. We no longer made fun of Aunt Clara's little idiosyncrasies; rather, her drawn face moved us to pity.

Although we were in the country, food was scarce.

The lengthening of our enforced vacation made the peasants more stingy of their "possessions," and rightly so.

They had realized that money could buy almost nothing now.

We seldom went to town, partly because so little was available in the stores, but also because we didn't even feel like going for a walk. We didn't even go to get bread with our ration card since we had been granted our allotment in flour. Thus, every day, in exchange for the flour, one of the peasant housewives weighed our ration of their bread for us.

The task of us girls was to go to the Mannozzis', the Albieris' and the Stellis' alternately, to get our daily bread. In rationing the loaf of bread with her knife, Beppa of the Mannozzis, fixing her small, turtle-like eyes upon us and tightening her thin lips, sighed, "Poor souls!"

It wasn't clear whether her sigh was on our behalf, because our share of bread was small or, perhaps, because she was sorry to part with the half loaf. The fact is that after judging by sight where more or less to sink the knife, she would make a slit on the crust, cutting a little behind in order to avoid either having to reduce the portion if too much or, worse yet, being obliged to give more than necessary. When the balancing weight on the scale tipped too far, she would counterbalance with "an addition." The addition was a great temptation for us: the bread so cut, especially fresh, smelled so good... That piece would disappear in a pinch.

If Beppa was the least generous in giving us our ration of bread, at least hers was the best bread, compact, with its browned crust. Furthermore, her careful slicing made it seem even more precious.

At the Albieris', we always received a larger portion.

Lena, in the dim light of her kitchen, taking her large pale loaves from the kneading trough, also sighed as she rationed out our portion. Her sigh, however, matched her mournful, tired air; hers was a sigh of sympathy for everything and everybody.

"Go, go, poor children!" she would say to us, and she refused to be thanked.

The evenings were long in July, and the days seemed never to end. The sun was still on the horizon while the moon was already rising.

It was harvest time.

In the cool hours, we, too, went with the peasants to bind the bales of hay. We worked in silence, taken by the evocative, enchanting hour.

As the hay piled up, it settled gently, as if weightless, and all sound became muffled. As if in the sequence of an old movie, one could see the peasants making the same gestures that had descended from centuries past. In that perfect quiet there seemed to be no room for anxiety, fear. At least it seemed that there could be healing for any pain.

I felt my soul revive and expand.

I accepted my wounds, reopening like a red flower.

One of those evenings we cousins had stayed up late.

Arm in arm, the four of us were walking down the footpath to the spring. The water, sparkling between the stones, could be caught at a glimpse. Uccio began to sing a tune that was popular at the time:

How lovely to take a stroll
By the full moon...

And we girls would answer with the refrain:

With you, just the two of us in the night
With you, singing a song...

We went on like this for I don't know how long, more
and more exhilarated by the moon, by the song, by our
being young and somewhat crazy.

Without a roof over our heads
Without a penny to eat
We'll sing through the night
To daybreak...

Arm in arm, we let ourselves go, almost flying now,
laughing and singing, down the steep foot-path.

Looking at the full moon mirrored in the spring, Uccio
decided, "Tonight we are going to do what the song says!
Who on earth would have the courage to go to bed with this
moon?"

"Do you mean we have to lie down on the stones?"
said Annalena. "If so, I bid you farewell and good-night!"

"Good night and rest well," Uccio replied. "I am sure
that Zippo and Lia will stay with me."

"Listen, this is no time for separation," I said. "What
do you say if we go and lie down on a hay stack. What bed
could be better! A regular bed is nothing in comparison!'

We climbed back up the path, still singing.

From a distance we saw the three hay stacks, one next
to the other, two large and low, while the third, with a very
tall ladder leaning against it, as high as a fortress, formed a

kind of citadel in the darkness. Climbing the tall ladder, we got ready for the assault. A flat surface two-thirds up the fortress offered us a wonderfully smooth space from which to contemplate the moon and the stars, so near that night that one could touch them.

As for the bed, with its fragrant odor of hay, it smelled better than sheets. Giving no thought to the insects, we would do great somersaults, laughing our heads off.

"As I look at this sea of stars," Uccio said, "there comes to mind a charming Chinese panel, *The sea in bloom*. It made me dream many times, and it comes back to me in the most unexpected moments...like tonight.

"What was *The sea in bloom* like?" I asked. "What strange flowers, what color nuances had the artist found?"

"No, Zippo," he answered, "the etching was black and white, but as you looked at it you could see colors as well."

While Uccio was talking, I continued to look at that swarm of stars high above. It was almost dawn.

A car was coming up the steep road of Poggio.

Who was it at that hour?

Michele! There he was in the courtyard. We called to him. He turned and didn't look at all surprised to see us up here. He was out of breath, panting, but surely he wasn't bringing us bad news, because his large face was smiling.

We rushed down the ladder.

"I ran here immediately!" He could hardly speak. "The radio just broadcast the news! *He* (Mussolini) went away. Understand? *He* went away! Fascism fell. We are free!"

That night was July 25.

The news, incredible by itself, sounded even more incredible with Michele arriving at that hour, with dawn approaching under the starry sky, while we were waiting for a miracle.

We ran inside the house and woke up our parents.

The peasants, always used to sleeping with one eye open, had already heard the noise of the car, and leaned out the windows to look down into the front yard. Soon after, they all came down.

Michele was welcomed and hugged. He was asked to repeat the news which didn't seem real.

The peasants looked at us in amazement. We couldn't convince them that we just happened to be there that night, simply by chance.

"They knew it, they knew it! That's why they didn't go to bed!"

Nobody went back to sleep. The sun had risen, a sun that looked clearer and brighter.

We were looking forward to going down to Colle and talking with the others, now that a new dawn, a new life had come, for us, too. Above all, for us.

In Colle all the streets were crowded, and there was an air of festivity. There was not even a shadow of fascists, for they had evaporated, all disappearing in a few short hours! People talked in groups, mentioning names here and there, the name of someone who had run away in time. Others were in hiding at home. Some had to stay hidden for awhile because they had already been beaten up.

Out of habit, the majority dared not speak openly. They whispered, paraphrasing everything, looking around them as if the walls had eyes and ears. They winked at one another to make clear their mutual understanding.

We were greeted with wide smiles.

At the ice cream store, the coffee-bar was full of people. We entered.

The barman was perched on a ladder removing a picture from the wall. Whistles, howls, deafening noised accompanied the removal.

"Finally you took *him* down!" someone said. "*He* was looking down from on high and took away from us even the desire to breathe. His surly look will be changed now; never mind the Roman salute!"

In Poggio, Uccio planned special celebrations for that July 26.

Out came the flour, out came the eggs, out came the sugar.

Cakes and sweet wine.

Dances, ditties, and storytelling. Uncle Poldo told the most beautiful story. It was about a countryman who had left his home town to go around the world, making his fortune in an unusual trade. He had two small cans of paint and a long feather which he used as a brush. He bellowed through the streets, "Women, here is your chance for 'golden buttocks'!"

"Come in, come in," said the old and the young women, particularly the richest ones, and even the maids had theirs done, "in silver."

After the euphoric happenings of July 25 that marked the fall of Fascism, when everything seemed resolved, we realized that problems still remained.

Now that we were no longer banned, excluded, and could speak openly and hope with all the others, we had to act also, to take the helm of our boat and begin a real life.

I went to look for Uccio. It seemed as if for him, a young man, even more than for myself, an immense horizon had opened and he had to decide, to act at once, at that very moment.

I even thought I would not find him in his room, for surely he had run away like a colt.

To my surprise, I found him seated calmly at his desk with *The Three Musketeers* in front of him.

He raised his eyes from the book.

"You know, Zippo," he said, "it's fantastic! I read it, thinking that I know it by heart, but I am enjoying it as if it were the first time. It is a different world, and I am engrossed in it. I wear the characters' clothing, and I feel good in them, as in my skin."

"But, Uccio," I said to him, "I, too, am in love with fables... We certainly have lived our purest and happiest moments in the company of poets. However, don't you think that now is no longer the time to escape reality? Our time can be beautiful, real life must still be lived, and we, too, must be a part of it."

"I detest 'real' life," he said. "Real life is mostly stupid and boring. You are the one who believes that at some corner we may meet Virtue, Beauty, Love! But nothing exists of all this or, better, it does exist, but in art, in paintings, books, and music. The rest is nothing. It is a petty world that I have neither desire nor haste to go back to.

"Yet, Uccio," I said to him, "there are young people who fight, who die, in order to prepare a better world. It is they who want to change the one in which we live."

"They fight and die for an ideal. But see, I don't believe an ideal can become reality.

"Ideals are beautiful and make one dream just because they are *Ideals*, but they belong to the '*World of Ideas*,' as Plato calls it.

"But the '*World of Ideas*' is very far away, remote, a world of stars, totally separated from ours."

Now he had shut his eyes into two vivid slits. He was smiling as if only this way, with his eyes almost closed, he could contemplate the distant light.

The "*World of Ideas*"! I never thought I would speak about it again after my conversation with Uccio. But a few days later I was to tutor in philosophy and the program included Plato.

Once again I was tutoring a student. She had failed the July examination and was to repeat the exam in September.

To find a pupil at the end of July, when the exams were only a little more than one month away, was not easy, and I accepted what heaven sent me.

Riding my bicycle for twelve kilometers each way, downhill and uphill, was like a game to me.

As I emerged from my shell, I was preparing myself to face "my battles." Nothing is conquered with nothing, but I never thought that father's objections would prove to be a problem.

Soon after July 25th, as an immediate domestic consequence of the political turnover, our father repeatedly told my sister and me to get going, enough of the life of leisure in the country. But now that I had found my first job, he couldn't get over the fact that the teacher should ride twelve plus twelve kilometers to go to the pupil.

"What a profit!" he said. "That rotten brat! She should come up here, it seems to me!"

It was useless to try to make him understand that there were other teachers in town, better known than I, who had been living by necessity in the background, and if I had proposed to the "rotten brat" that she should climb up to Poggio, it would have been like putting salt on the swallow's tail. My tutoring job would have flown away at once. And it would have disappeared even more quickly since the girl was lazy, both physically and intellectually. Her appearance was normal, a rather pretty blond in a pink polka-dot dress. However, even though she was sixteen, instead of being alert like her peers, she seemed sluggish. Her house, set at the end of a lane, was a gloomy but solid building, and rather big, probably with many rooms, but my pupil never invited me upstairs.

She received me in the hall on the ground floor, with an air that she hoped to rid herself of me as soon as possible. I felt like an intruder who has been granted an audience reluctantly.

The furnishings consisted of a small iron table – only it was missing a leg – like those used in a garden, and two chairs, also made of iron, incredibly uncomfortable.

On the walls were old prints (I remember Othello and Desdemona) and on the floor a dirty carpet. Due to lack of space, we sat very close to the "lame" table, which wobbled, threatening to overturn at the slightest touch, even when we turned the pages of a book.

A heavy musty odor lingered, mixed with a strong smell of frying onions that came from the kitchen. There were no windows and the only light came from the small transom over the door and from the door that was slightly ajar.

Now and then the opening enlarged and someone would come in from outside. Then my pupil's small light blue eyes, until that moment so distant and watery, would immediately turn, as if they were on a hinge, and settle on the newcomer, following the person's every movement until she or he disappeared up the stairs.   Generally it was some member of the household, her grandmother bringing back re-soled shoes, her mother with a shopping bag, or her little brother with his tricycle.   What could I do?   Everything seemed to attract her more than poor me!

We were reading *Criton*, and I, too, had moments when everything disappeared, the lame table, the smell of the onions, even my pupil.   I could hear in my voice another voice: that of Socrates in jail when, before his intent disciples, he argued with the Laws as though they were living creatures, real people.

The clearest, most beautiful translation, by Manara Valgimigli, which I loved so much, recreated that magic for me.   Words came to my lips, and I kept speaking of the "*World of Ideas*," of that world, so far away, absolute, starry...

It was at one of those moments that my pupil interrupted me: "You really like philosophy, Miss!?"

Her small light blue eyes were staring at me.

Candidly I answered "yes," that I "really" liked *Criton*. At this, I saw her eyes light maliciously, with something like scorn, or as if she felt sorry for me.

One evening, in the cool breeze, happy and secure, with eleven and a half kilometers of our trip home behind us, I was getting ready to tackle the hill.

Suddenly, a root, protruding from the ground, made my front wheel jump. The bicycle jerked. I couldn't hold the brakes tight, and I tumbled, almost breaking my neck. Fortunately, I fell sideways, into a grassy hole. I was with Annalena, who had helplessly watched my sudden flight.

I tried to get up with my cousin's help, but a severe pain in my left knee kept me standing immobile, with all my body weight on my good leg, unable to take a step.

When Annalena saw me becoming very pale, she lost her god-like calmness and even though she had to go uphill, she ran to get help.

After a few minutes, which seemed an eternity to me, back she came with Nevo, the first person she had met. With one arm around her neck and the other around his, putting all my weight on the good leg, I dragged myself all the way up, feeling more dead than alive.

I tried to minimize what had happened, trying to appear as comfortable as possible, but even on the flat lawn I limped terribly. With great effort, I reached the stone bench in the courtyard and sat there until word got around that I had injured my knee a little bit.

Sitting there pretending nothing had happened, I was able to talk with all my family, but soon my efforts became useless. I couldn't stay there all night, and when I attempted to stand, the pain grabbed me worse than before. With my father cross-examining me, I had to admit that I had not injured my knee *just a little* bit, but *badly*, and that I had to be put to bed at once, because I couldn't stand it any longer.

As I lay in bed, Corinna applied beaten egg whites to my knee.

After saying good night to everybody, finally alone, I stared into the darkness.

I needed more than beaten egg whites! Days went by and the pain in my knee didn't lessen. It was impossible to go down the stairs, thus I remained upstairs sitting sadly at the window.

There was no news at all from my lazy pupil, who was told about my mishap. My father changed his attribution from "*that rotten brat*" to "*that dirty stinker*," who, in his mind, was the cause of my broken leg, yet who didn't even have the decency to come and see me.

His sympathy for me was expressed by grumbling and complaining, sometimes rebuking mother and sister also, "persons who are confused just being here in this world" as he used to say. Certainly, "being in this world" has always been rather difficult for everyone, but for us Jews it was a little more so.

God willing and with the help of the doctor who came to put a cast on my leg, little by little the knee got better, but I still had to go cautiously.

My bicycle was put to rest in the cellar under the stone vault.

Annalena and Uccio kept bringing news from town. From a spirit of solidarity, and so as not to anger our father, my sister also gave up the trips to town. Besides, she didn't mind staying at Poggio, while I, now more than ever, resented being cut off from any active participation. I felt impatient, waiting for something that would never come.

My sister consoled me, saying, "Don't you understand that we are not the only ones waiting? Everyone is expecting something to happen. Perhaps the war will end soon. Now at least, we have hope. Afterward, other expectations and other sorrows will come," my sister said.

"Why?" I asked "Don't you hope for better times?"

"Better, who knows!" she answered with a sigh. "Who knows if it really will be better, or if we'll mourn over this..." She was standing next to me at the window. She had taken my hand and pressed it in hers. Her hand was cold and she was squeezing mine as if both to give and receive warmth.

Her voice was cracking, as if she feared danger, a threat.

"Everything happens to me!" I thought as I watched a big black fly. It was trapped and insisted on butting its head against the window-pane.

"Big black fly! You bring us the arrival either of news or visitors." Annalena quoted the proverb, laughing as she entered the room. But surely we were far from imagining that an important piece of news was so near! The following day was September 8. The armistice was announced and the news was received jubilantly, especially by all the mothers. "We can soon return to our homes!" they said with smiling eyes and big sighs of relief.

Dad was shaking his head. "The bulletin says that 'War Continues.' Germans are still Germans," he warned us.

Now that the moment of parting, of going our separate ways, was approaching, we cousins felt disoriented and somewhat uneasy.

One thought was fixed in my mind that dominated all others: once back home, I would see *him* again.

This thought was not accompanied by joy, but by anguish and torment. My heart was closed to all hopes. But still, I felt in danger, like a desperate gambler who sees his ruin when he's lost his last bet and has nothing else to gamble with, yet trembles at the idea of finding himself back at the green table.

The big black fly brought not only news, but people as well.

One evening the boyfriend of one of the Stelli sisters arrived; he was starving and without a uniform. On September 8 he had escaped, like many other soldiers, and after a dangerous trip he had made it home.

Rumors were spreading that others, stragglers and outlaws, were taking advantage of the chaos to steal, or to do worse, especially in isolated areas.

Aunt Clara declared that it wasn't at all safe to remain in Poggio with three young ladies, that to stay was simply irrational. She and Annalena would go to live in town while waiting for a chance to return to their home in the city.

Mother agreed with her, but she herself couldn't make any decision, subject as she was to "*patria potestas*" – that is, her husband's authority.

Aunt Freda procrastinated, thereby avoiding any decision, as was her way. For her to "decide" – her sister-in-law's favorite verb – was always "unbearable," "terrible." On the other hand, she had no daughters!

Our father "evaded the problem," as Aunt Clara put it. "Relax a bit," he once responded calmly, with his provocative smirk which had the effect of driving my aunt crazy. And not only her! "There are not only our girls! It seems to me there are also the seven or eight beautiful peasant girls."

Uccio laughed his head off at those fears.

"I'll defend the honor of my cousins 'with a dart,' said he, while breaking a pointed twig, resembling a minute arrow, from a reed.

Other times he hummed a tune from *Cavalleria*:

> ...deprived of my honor,
> Deprived I remain...

Aunt Clara couldn't endure staying longer. She set off "bag and baggage," together with Annalena.

After their departure, the house at Poggio was larger and emptier. I noticed that Uccio had even lost some of his cutting wit, his inexhaustible resourcefulness. He had became more serious, even somewhat morose.

"See," he said to me, "Aunt Clara represented 'the rational' and just to be contrary we liked to be irrational. As for Annalena..." and he raised his eyebrow a little as if pondering, "here it is," his eyes glittering, "Annalena was a sort of Sancho Panza and thus we felt like Don Quixote!

"Want to bet that from now on we'll be reduced to clock-watching?   Won't it be sad?   'Order, precision, punctuality!' And what fun it would be to do the opposite if no one got angry? But without Sancho, how could we succeed in playing Don Quixote's role?"

One evening at twilight I was with Lia in the fireplace room, sitting in the semi-darkness. Silent and lazy, we had not yet made up our minds to light the candle; we wanted to finish rolling up the last skein of wool.

The door facing the courtyard was open.

Suddenly my sister let go of the skein and I dropped the yarn, causing the ball to roll across the floor.

Three men, rather three shadows, appeared at the threshold. Two were very tall; the third was shorter and his arm was in a sling. We couldn't make out their faces because the light was behind them.

Before we could make a sign or say a word, they slipped inside, closing the door and gesturing us to be quiet.

They were English prisoners, escaped from a concentration camp, trying to rejoin their unit. They were asking for shelter for the night. They hoped that we would let them sleep in the stable. They made themselves understood with some English, some Italian, and a lot of hand gestures.

We were breathless with excitement. "Our side" had finally arrived! We wished we had a royal palace for them, not a stable.

We rushed about looking for Uccio.

To our surprise, Uccio didn't insist on their staying in the house, rather he went out with them to speak with the foreman, Vanni Stelli.

We waited with fluttering hearts. After half an hour, Uccio returned.

"It took me a long time to make Vanni understand the enormous difference!" he said. "To the peasants, the English are as much foreigners as the Germans! And besides, perhaps they know better what could happen. After all, they may be right!"

I looked my cousin directly in the face. He was upset, uneasy, and I was, too. Wasn't it awful what we were doing? We were asking others to take a risk; we should have kept the Englishmen here, taking the risk ourselves.

"Those young men, however," Uccio insisted, as if reading my thoughts, "wanted it this way simply not to compromise anyone else. They can always say they found the stable door ajar and went in by themselves during the night. Besides, it's easier for them to run away from there at the first sign of trouble."

He repeated his reasons. Common sense dictated them, but he was not convinced. I remember one of his sayings. "'Common sense, generally speaking, is a hateful merchant' and I detest people who think that way,'*i buonsensai*.'"

At that moment he must have detested himself; that's why he was so upset.

We were silent.

When father came in, I could tell that he already knew everything. Frowning, with his eyes darker, in a bad mood, like someone who has been treated unjustly. Or perhaps he himself felt guilty? Whatever it was, he needed to take out his worry and uneasiness on the others.

"This is not a joke!" he said. "Luckily they had the good sense to leave this house and sleep in the stable! Don't you know that we risk being shot? And on top of that we are Jews! You had better stay in this evening. No one is to know about this. Go to bed early! Let's hope that they have gone by morning, and that the incident is finished."

I understood. Probably he was right... But how sad, how disheartening is fear!

No one spoke at supper.

Father, gloomy, Aunt Freda, enigmatic, inscrutable; both ate looking down at their dishes. Mother knew nothing, but she was aware that something strange was going on. Her eyes had a perplexed look and sought ours as if asking what was wrong.

Soon they went up to their rooms, after reminding us to go to bed early. We cousins remained alone as conspirators. We looked at one another.

"It's understood," said Lia, her face flushed, "it's understood that we are going out to see them."

Lia, usually so reserved and timid, had become daring.

"It's understood" Uccio answered, as if responding to a password. The two of them began to go. I followed them, limping.

Before going out the door Lia said, "At least let's bring them a little something, something that is ours."

Uccio answered, "I gave orders to the peasants to take care of their supper. Corinna was already getting a basket together."

We envied the peasants who had enough food to offer. We felt embarrassed for our limited supplies. However, we gathered a few things: bandages, because one had a dislocated arm, Uccio's small flask of cognac, some raisins, and a jar of quince preserves.

Silently we walked along the path to the Stelli house. The night was cool, the moon a thin sickle; from afar, sprinkled across the sky, the stars shone. In the dark we could barely see the silhouettes of the haystacks on the threshing floor. We walked behind the house and under the vault that led to the stables. Uccio knocked three times on the fogged-up little window.

A streak of light appeared from the door as it opened slightly. By the weak light of a lantern we spotted the backs of the cattle, their faces in the manger. Three shadows sneaked out, the three Englishmen.

Without speaking we moved toward the haystacks in single file, and, as agreed earlier, we climbed on the lowest one, from which a big slice of hay had been cut. We sat in a circle like Turks on their carpets.

Between their Italian and our English, a serviceable language evolved. The three Englishmen were the first to burst out laughing, even though muted; they had recovered their sense of humor. Their laughter was contagious and we echoed them.

Star dust...*polvere di stelle*..." my sister said, winking at the sky.

"Yes, star dust...*polvare di stalle*," the light blond Englishman answered with a dreamy look.

At his *polvare di stalle*," it was our turn to burst out laughing. We tried to explain the double meaning, but the explanation became complicated. Suddenly Uccio began mooing like an ox in the stable. The Englishmen laughed like crazy; they understood.

We were three young ones with three young ones. Little by little we picked up courage and despite the linguistic Babel we understood each other quite well. We liked being together and talking, even if we bounced around from one subject to another, with no logical sequence.

"Gigole...Gigole..." said the Englishman in a romantic way. We understood: we needed someone with a beautiful voice to sing. He had said "Gigole" instead of "Gigli," the tenor.

They told us their stories. They were three friends who had escaped together. They spoke of their families, of their distant homes. One of the three lived in South Africa.

"Much food, much gold, much everything...fewer men, very good!" he concluded with a big happy smile.

All of a sudden, one of them fixed his eyes on us and said seriously, "in Italy many spies, many spies! Maybe you too spy?..."

No one "spied" on them and the incident ended happily, at least for us. The next morning the Englishmen had vanished, like a vapor, so much so that we might even have believed it had all been a dream.

PART THREE

Many years have gone by, yet every time November returns, with its magic blossoming of dead leaves, I am overcome by an intense emotion that takes me back in time to November 1943.

Branches sway, already bare; with the sun, the last leaf lights up. It flutters from an invisible breath of wind, and with a shiver breaks off. Another bit of purple and gold is added to the immense multicolored mosaic.

November, that fabulous painter! But its artistry is ephemeral. A few days later the dark wind, the torrential rains reduce the trees to skeletons, the earth to decomposing mud; the desolation of winter is proclaimed.

During those first winter days of November 1943, with my tearless eyes I stared at the whirling leaves as if in this change of seasons I just saw another transition: *ours*. We were young then! Our life was bursting, yearning to blossom. However, this was our blossoming: not bright flowers followed by fruits, but dead leaves lit up on the branch with a final splendor, just before the end.

I had not been to Colle for more than a month. Michele came to get me with his car, to have the doctor remove my cast. If I was sad, Michele didn't look happy either, and not just from the serious gruff expression on his big square face.

It's well known that Tuscans hide their facetious humor under gruff appearances; but what struck me was his silence, an unusual stubborn silence.

There was no sunshine, and the fields were covered with dew. Suddenly, after passing the chapel at the curve that led straight to the upper town, we were confronted by a sign set on a tripod in the middle of the countryside.

It was in German, all in black letters:

ACHTUNG!

I shivered, anguish clutched my throat.

It seemed outrageous, sacrilegious, that that word in a barbaric foreign language could have arrived even there to violate that solitude, that serene peace of the countryside, where up to that moment only the free voices of nature and of hard-working human beings had been heard.

ACHTUNG!

It seemed to me that the two sides of the "A" stretched endlessly up to the sky, like the legs of a giant spider, to prevent not only men but also the beautiful fields, trees, flowers, and birds of the air, from breathing, from existing.

"It's high time to tear out those things," Michele said, breaking the silence. "The town is full of them, all our walls smeared."

In those terrible days German ordinances multiplied infinitely. By now, these words laid siege to us, both written and oral. Their harsh guttural sounds were incomprehensible to most Italians, who grasped only their hateful authoritarian tone like that of a fearful obscure threat.

The horrible news arrived one evening while we were at the supper table.

Again, it was Michele who brought us the news: "All the Jews in Siena have been arrested."

He said "arrested," but that was not the word generally used. "To arrest," in fact, presupposes some legitimate rights in favor of those who are allegedly guilty of a crime. But people usually said, "They came to take the Jews," as they might speak about hunted beasts in a brutal man-hunt.

We looked at each other, dumbfounded.

We had to escape at once. Even one hour more could have meant extreme risk. Most probably we were the only Jewish family in the area, and were well-known in town. The authorities in Colle could receive a mandate of arrest at any moment. To remain in Poggio would have meant to be in the wolf's grasp.

Suddenly, mother began sobbing, but softly.

Aunt Freda said nothing, but her ashen face, immobile, was frightening.

The dark sky, without a star, appeared heavy with rain.

There was a knock at the door. We all felt our hearts in our throats. It was Pietro di Mannozzi and Vanni degli Stelli. The look on our faces and our silence must have frightened them. They looked at us and asked no questions.

Uccio was the first to move. He signaled to Pietro and Vanni. They went off in a corner and spoke excitedly while the rest of us together, almost in a huddle, watched.

They had come up with "a plan."

For that night we would take refuge in the Stellis' house, the farthest away. It was on an elevation, with extensive woods in the rear.

"Being on watch up there," Uccio said, "we could see the truck arrive on the main road. From there, anyone intending to come up would have to take the path and climb on foot. Finding the villa empty, they might stop searching, thinking that we had fled still farther away. If, however, they came up here... If worse came to worse, we would still have time to run into the woods behind the house."

We didn't know whether Uccio spoke in order to convince Vanni and Pietro, or to convince us, or himself.

We all looked at him with eyes fixed in amazement: as though Uccio were telling us of an incredible event, one of those unbelievable stories that we used to read in the magazine *Domenica del Corriere*.

In fact the "plan" seemed fantastically absurd, that the Germans and the S.S. finding the villa empty would not "think" of looking for us in the peasants' houses! Or, that if they did look and climbed the path, we would have time to escape, to disappear, to run away, to vanish camouflaged!

During the night, in the dark, in a torrential downpour, through thick tangled brush, with the horrible fright that freezes the blood, how could our mother, not so "adventurous," with her poor feet always sore in her city shoes, walk, let alone run?

She was listening, all confused, she said "yes" to everything, so long as she was not left alone. And yet, fantastic as it was, Uccio's plan was the only one we could follow.

We were living in strange times; nothing conformed any longer to the usual rules of civilized life. Unfortunately, the most irrational, absurd events became real, while the most logical, believable ones vanished in the world of non-reality, of Utopia.

The night passed without incident. Vanni, Uccio and Dad stayed up to be on watch. But, thank God, no truck appeared on the horizon.

Aunt Freda had a room to herself; mother and we two sisters had "Uncle" Poldo's bed. We found a little warmth, the three of us huddled together, and mother stopped trembling. Next to her daughters she felt comforted. She whispered the first words of the *Sh'ma* and her eyes closed gently like those of a child going to sleep.

Lia and I held hands, listening to mother's breathing. The words whispered by her a short while before were coming back to mind:

> *Sh'ma Israel*
> Hear, Israel, the Lord is our God,
> The Lord is one.

The next day, I vainly tried to recall that special moment of the night before.

Anguish and anxiety gripped me. I thought I could detect signs of uneasiness even in the peasant family with whom we were staying.

It was natural for them to feel so; it was also a legitimate fear.

The hours of that day seemed endless. With six of us in the kitchen forced to do nothing at all, silent, worried, in other people's way just because of our physical presence, the others, who could come and go as they pleased and attend to their daily chores!...

All this depressed and tormented me, with a mixture of envy, discouragement and humiliation.

We had been in that kitchen a hundred times, happy to be all together. Why was it that suddenly they looked like strangers to me, as if a wall of ice was between us?

We had asked them for an act of courage, of charity. Could we still consider ourselves "*padroni*"? Or rather, were we not in misery, poorer than the poor – human beings to whom even the right to life had been denied – looking for shelter and a piece of bread in God's name?

We had been given a roof; now the women bustled around the fireplace for us. Their kind attention seemed to me quite absurd – broth, roasted chicken, *canapes*...

Or was it a kind of final meal for the condemned? A meal that could very well be the last one?

I noticed that Uccio often spoke in a low voice with Vanni. Who knows if they were hatching another plan? Several times my cousin's eyes met mine, but he seemed to turn away immediately, as if he wanted to avoid contact with me.

Then a painful discovery tore my heart.

I doubted Uccio!

I doubted Uccio, with whom so far we had been bound by an absolute friendship, more than brotherly! Yet this shameful suspicion had insinuated itself within me: our cousin was planning only for himself and for his mother, plotting with Vanni, excluding we sisters and our parents.

After dinner Vanni disappeared, to return late in the evening; they spoke together again in low tones.

Then Uccio communicated his secret to all of us: another house, farther away and safer, would accommodate us all.

Everyone was relieved. However, for me it was not only a relief to know that another refuge had been found, it also took a weight off my heart.

It was almost night when we started to move: bundled up in blankets, hoisted on the two-wheeled cart, Aunt Freda, Mother and we sisters.

The rain had stopped but the sky was livid, and the wind twisted the branches, tearing away the last of the leaves.

Under the arcade the peasants, speechless, watched us go; the children, also quiet, stared at us wide-eyed.

In that bitter weather, it was impossible to ride the bicycle, so Dad and Uccio had started on foot.

Choosing side roads to avoid any unpleasant encounters, the horse covered with oil cloth, wrapped up to his eyes, Vanni led us to our new destiny.

We went into the thicket where the path became narrow; soaking wet branches bent with the weight of water deluged us, our blankets, our hands, and our faces. Beyond the thicket the countryside extended almost bare before us; only the silhouetted skeletons of poplars in long rows seemed to move toward us in welcome.

Scattered lights shone in the distance from a few isolated houses on the hill. At that hour everyone must have been indoors enjoying the warmth of their homes, gathered together for supper.

The air became colder and colder, the dampness soaking our blankets and penetrating our bones. Suddenly, at a curve, the horse reared, and, at the same time Mother gave a yell and Vanni swore, "*Dammit!!*"

An enormous tree trunk, felled by the night storm, blocked our way. The splintered wood, like nude flesh, pale and bloodless, lay there where it had crashed. It lay across a small canal of turbid water that faintly reflected the clouds and tree branches.

I was aroused by Vanni's voice.

"We must detour for at least half a kilometer, and many more kilometers to come before reaching Montecchio. The place is isolated and not so pleasant, but it's what you need now."

The two-wheeled cart proceeded, bumping over holes and stones.

With aching bones and limbs trembling from cold, we dropped onto the straw like bundles of rags.

We had been able to find beds for only Mother and Aunt Freda.

A lump gripped my throat; despite my exhaustion, my eyes refused to close. They remained open in the darkness for a long while, tracing visions of horrible phantoms.

The cruel, hateful tyranny of inhuman laws, the fear and the cowardice of man, separated us from civilized society. Wasn't our refuge, like a stable for beasts, also a sign of this cruelty? Or perhaps it was better this way! That was the most appropriate place: not with men, but only with beasts could we feel like brothers and sisters – yoked like them to our destiny of suffering – condemned victims to pain, torture, sacrifice.

Beasts! More compassionate than men certainly.

Now, desperate and freezing, we felt their quiet presence close to us, their warm breath.

A sort of animal-like, benumbed peace penetrated me little by little. Finally I lost consciousness and fell into a deep sleep.

The following morning I couldn't make out where I was. I felt my limbs rested, my eyes refreshed, my forehead relaxed.

Through the upper window the sky was becoming freshly colored.

Little by little, I remembered. I was lying on a pile of hay, still dressed, and next to me my sister slept. On one side of the plastered arched wall were Dad and Uccio.

On the other side of the arch that divided the space, the big whitish spots of the cattle, lined up side by side, became visible in the faint early light. As my eyes adapted to the sunlight, I could see their legs from below, their strong loins, their tails waving away the flies.

The straw we were lying on was light and clean; here and there a timid ray of sun lit it with a touch of gold. One breathed in, along with the warm good odor of manure, a feeling of goodness, of perfect peace.

Lia stirred and almost at the same time Papa and Uccio awoke.

It is really true that sometimes the worst is not as bad as one thinks or expects it to be!

Who could have thought that sleeping in a stable would have cured us, restored peace to us, even good humor? We had almost forgotten the reason for our exceptional lodging.

While the cows and the oxen quietly chewed their cuds, Uccio, instead of greeting us with a "good morning!" started to moo with a fearful crescendo and so perfectly that we all burst out laughing, surprised to have such an unusual awakening, so unexpectedly merry. It seemed that we were participating in a joke, in a game, or as movie actors in an old comedy.

Were we irresponsible, or was it, perhaps, a miracle of Providence?

The kitchen had no windows. Up high, behind the glass in the transom above the doors, bare branches seemed entwined with the first glimmer of a November dawn.

A dark kneading-trough, a few chairs with tattered straw seats, a dingy table, over which an old kerosene lamp hung from a beam diffused a yellow glow.

On the hearth of the enormous fireplace, where the last red embers were dying out, an old peasant was sitting on a bench up against the stone hearth. He was motionless like a figure in a bas-relief, his ragged hat on his forehead, his elbow resting on his knee, holding his chin with a big hand deformed by arthritis.

At our "good morning," he answered with a kind of grunt, without moving. Meanwhile his wife, also old and bent in two like a hook, was boiling milk in a pan set on the tripod in the fireplace.

The few embers were not enough to warm the room; my hands were cold. I began to feel discouraged again; perhaps it was so for everybody after that wave of merriment. Cold and silent, we sat around the ugly table, minus even a tablecloth, on which a big loaf of bread, a knife, and some rustic earthen bowls were placed.

Using a ladle the old woman filled the dark bowls with the steaming milk. She placed one bowl and a spoon before each of us. She cut the bread: big slices with a solid center encircled by a brown crust.

The old man had received his bowl as well and we could hear him chewing slowly inside the fireplace.

Bent over the steam of the warm, aromatic milk, staring at the circle shaped like a full moon inside the bowls, we were lost in an innocent dream...we felt refreshed. Our hands around the bowl were getting warm.

It was like going back in time.

In that act of receiving the same food together, as if in a community, it was like returning to the customs of our childhood, a calm obedience to a patriarchal authority, meeting each other again around the table, in the protective circle of the family. But for how long?

Bread and milk, two simple basic foods, would enter within us to become warm nutritious life. We ate silently, almost religiously, quiet, comforted.

The bread and milk that Providence offered us were our manna.

At present we young ones had more contact with the "old ones." The small kitchen didn't allow us privacy; perhaps our carefree attitude, which popped up now and then, did them some good as well. In a certain sense, they were even more carefree than we were. They relaxed, they even began to complain again, a good sign that this life seemed almost normal to them. We, instead, fluctuated between tragedy and rebirth with our tendency to evade reality in dreams. Again we were living held by reality, as if inside a parenthesis, expectant.

A few days before our flight from Poggio, by chance I got my hands on Mauriac's novel, *Tangle of Vipers.*

Uccio had immediately paraphrased that title to "Tangle of Jews." We were playing roles in the "tangle" and we saw ourselves as characters in an absurd incredible mess: a serial complete with effects and suspense.

Among these characters was a new one, another Jew whose existence we had ignored up until then; another "Jew" momentarily trapped in the threads of the tangle.

He was an important Milanese merchant, a guest at the farm on which the small village of Montecchio depended. He was a friend of the *padrone.*

We didn't know whether the *padrone* knew of our presence in Montecchio. Vanni had spoken with the overseer, who had given him to understand that he would close one eye, or even two, feigning not to know anything. Regarding the two old peasants, perhaps they had accepted us in the hope of a compensation – they were very poor – or for human pity, or perhaps for both reasons.

They were always silent, so much so that at times we forgot they were there, almost as if the old man was sculptured into the fireplace, and the old woman was a part of the kitchen furnishings, the table, the bench or the chairs.

In the evening, after supper, the *Milanese* would arrive.

He was certainly over fifty, somewhat fat and short; however, he wore knickers, a belted jacket in hound's tooth check, and a maroon scarf tossed around his neck like a real sportsman living in the country. On his head, he wore a slightly slanted beret with a visor, similar to what De Sica wore in the movie "*Gli Uomini che Mascalzoni*"!

Despite the adventure – not exactly sports-like – into which he, too, had stumbled, he didn't seem depressed at all. Rather, as a real Milanese he was active and always in good form; so much so that we felt somewhat comforted when we spotted his big face in the open doorway. His nose and cheeks, marked by a web of little pink blood vessels that were emphasized by the reddish-brown scarf; his eyes, small and lively, constantly darting about; one little hairy ear poking out from his beret, so reddened by the cold that it seemed alight.

He would immediately take a cigar and a deck of cards from his pockets, and he would insist that we play not with "beans" but with some change.

"One must make it interesting! The game..." he said, in a fat hearty voice, with a touch of malice.

During the pauses in card playing, he was our political and social Gazette, telling us the latest news in the paper, always spiced with his jokes and juicy stories about the *entourage*.

A certain young lady, the "private secretary" of the *padrone* had been evacuated to the farm.

"Yeah, yeah," he said, his small eyes half-closed and a little crossed, "ve-r-r-y intimate, ve-r-r-y intimate."

The hearty voice seemed to drown, even to sink into the sinful whirlpool of that intimacy. Uccio, set in good humor by the phrase, delighted in repeating it, "Yeah, yeah...ve-r-r-y intimate, ve-r-r-y intimate."

Not only that, but seeing that the Milanese was a glutton for stories of intrigue, Uccio indulged in inventing some for his own use and consumption.

Uccio made believe that he was in love with Lia.

He pretended to confide in him, telling him that "unfortunately they were cousins," and he would sigh, "first cousins, flesh-and-blood cousins, and it's known that children of cousins at times..."

"Oh, the poor little one!" the Milanese said, glancing at my sister. As if he could become a referee and guarantee their destinies, he shook his big rosy face like the Olympic Jupiter, saying, "Marry her with tranquility. Children turn out very well."

Thus Uccio had updated his repertoire by no longer mimicking Aunt Clara, but "Mister very Milanese", as he called him.

Certainly Uccio did his best to cheer us up during those days, but one time his remedy produced an opposite, unforeseen effect.

Uccio played the narrator's role in our "Tangle of Jews."

It was the last installment, the epilogue, which had two variations: one with a happy ending, "and they lived happily ever after," as in a fairy tale; the other having an unhappy ending, with inevitable comments on the "very sad case." In that "very sad," Uccio mimicked a mutual uncle of ours, a meticulous type, one of those who foresees everything and provides for everything.

According to Uccio, with our eventual and tragic end, our uncle would have wept and also disapproved, actually more disapproved than wept.

To give a better imitation of our uncle, Uccio would walk a little bent over, an old beret on his head. Like Madame Pace in Pirandello's *Six Characters in Search of an Author*," there was our uncle, saying, "But their end was all foreseen! It had even been printed in the paper!" After a pause of suspense, "What the devil! They will get over it."

We all laughed wholeheartedly. We could indeed see before our eyes our very "picky" uncle who would even "pick" on our tragic end! As a further comment, Uccio would imitate a young friend of his, somewhat fatuous, who spoke with a lisp, "so distressing, I say, so distressing." And in so saying, Uccio lisped in an exaggerated manner, with a crescendo of more lisped "esses": "Uncles, aunts; aunts, uncles, cousins, finished, finished. So distressing, so distressing."

We continued laughing with tears in our eyes, when suddenly we looked at Mother sitting by herself in a corner: she had passed from laughter to tears, sobbing so convulsively that she shook, frightening us.

After that, Uccio didn't dare poke fun anymore. Thus, "the narrator" stopped reading our story, and closed the book "on that page." But, we continued living our story.

With the passing of days, the atmosphere became more somber. We would remain silent for hours on end, looking at each other. We couldn't bear being restricted to the small kitchen any longer, so we tried to go out, but the depressing season and the desolate landscape disheartened us more than raising our spirits.

The house was isolated, perched on a peak. In order to avoid the wider but more travelled road that wound around in a gentle slope until it joined the main road, we had to take a steep path, muddy and full of stones, that ended at a swamp. Beyond the swamp there were woods.

Anxiety, expectation of the worst hung in the air, weighing heavily upon us. The sky was threatening and gloomy.

In the swamp frogs croaked insistently and monotonously; in the thicket beyond the swamp, dead leaves had turned a reddish-brown color.

Usually on those "strolls," our parents would go by themselves and we sisters by ourselves. Going up and down that depressing unchanging path – as in a nightmare – we all would meet face to face: we going down, they coming up, or vice versa, like the condemned souls through the circle of Dante's hell.

On one of those sad evenings there was another surprise. For the first time the Milanese did not come to see us. Our surprise turned into anxiety when even the next day he didn't knock on our door.

On the third evening he finally appeared. We knew immediately that something had happened.

He was terribly pale and dropped onto a chair, panting. It seemed as if he wanted to avoid telling us what had happened, but at our insistence he told us the bad news.

The *padrone*, he said, had returned from Milan and had asked his overseer to speak to him, because "he himself didn't have the nerve to tell me, 'his friend,' that he is afraid and does not want me in the house any longer."

The overseer, he continued, had begun the conversation with flowery language, saying that "the *padrone* was sorry," "he had nothing against the Jews," but due to "the most elementary caution" and "orders being orders," he'd better leave.

Since he was coming to Montecchio, the Milanese had been asked to convey the same message to us.

With the tone of those offering a small consolation prize, the Milanese told us that he, the *padrone*, was also informing us that, of course, he will continue "to ignore (our) presence, but only for two or three days more, at the most one week."

Our blood froze at hearing this ultimatum.

"Don't be downhearted!" the Milanese exclaimed, his eyes severely fixed on our very pale faces, while he himself had resumed his normal color. He seemed relieved of a great burden. "One must get busy...there is no time to lose."

He had already made his own plans. Luckily he had friends all over, and he would go to his priest friend in a nearby rectory. Thus he was retreating "under the shadow of a cassock, where one is always merry," he added, trying in vain to make us smile with his last *boutade*.

Two or three days, at the most a week.

It was urgent that a decision be made, a solution be found! But the anxiety became a nightmare that gripped our throats, paralyzing us.

"*Decision*," "*solution*": quickly, at once, immediately! But we remained immobile, with a sickening feeling at seeing time run away, like a wounded person who watches stunned at the blood running out of his veins.

Thus, the first day went by.

The next day there were unexpected visitors, Aunt Clara and Annalena. They were going away and had come to say good-bye.

Aunt Clara herself, who usually didn't show any great warmth, spoke sweetly to Mother, patting her head as if she were a child. For the first time I caught a resemblance between the two sisters; my aunt's definite, almost harsh features, had softened. I noticed that her chin trembled and a tear was in her eye.

Meanwhile, Annalena informed us they were going to Fiesole. They had been able to get a letter of recommendation from the Bishop; they hoped to be welcomed by the *Benedictine* Sisters located in a convent right there.

"I got this brilliant idea from a letter I received from a girlfriend of mine, living now in a convent."

"We are going to a beautiful place. On the Florentine hills the air is clean; can you imagine what appetites? And no rationing cards! My friend writes that the requirement is *"to abide by the rules."* Do you know what *"abide by the rules"* means? To have a false identity card made out! Furthermore, she informs me that whenever trouble is in the air, she and her mother dress up like nuns. As for me, I am ready to dress up even like a friar! Imagine! But what about you? Have you decided where to go? Don't think too much about it, Isa!"

But something inside me rebelled. To beg for recommendations, to obtain false documents, even to disguise oneself. It was all right for Annalena to take on everything merrily, with no guilt on her conscience, but...

What a lovely chapter to add to the "Tangle of Jews," adventurous, even quite suggestive of Manzoni's pages, the *farewell*, the *convent*...

As long as my cousin Annalena would not encounter another *monaca di Monza*!

For us Aunt Clara and Annalena's decision was like a stone flung into a swamp, the putrid waters stirring and boiling enough to bring to the surface the filthy bottom.

Immobility was followed by a confused excitement as we looked for a way out. But, during that desperate search, between Father and us two sisters, old rancors, reproaches, mutual accusations came up again, adding bitterness to our torment. We accused him of being blind when *"the laws"* hit us: as if we wanted to show him *now* that we had been right *then*. We almost enjoyed doing this, but in a sad way. In his turn, Father threw our accusations back at us, saying that we were "good-for-nothing," "our heads always in the clouds." Then he began listing his own accusations.

"What do you know how to do? You can only read useless books. Besides, you are either conceited or full of whims; you don't know how to adapt. Oh, yes, I am a real wretch with these three women!"

In his accusation, he also involved Mother! "Were I alone..."

Poor Mother, she would start to cry, she would tell him to calm down, and she would ask us not to upset him. She would repeat her same old advice, "The Lord will not forsake us, we'll find a way, all together!"

But as time went on, it was precisely this "all together" that revealed itself to be more and more impossible.

Aunt Clara and Annalena had made their choice. Uccio also would go away soon. All of a sudden, one evening, he told me about it.

"We are leaving for Rome to stay with some of Vanni's relatives. You know, in a big city it's much easier to be camouflaged, to vanish."

I looked into his eyes.

"I know what you are thinking, Isa," he said, "I should 'do something,' like being a part of the underground struggle joining the partisans on the mountain. Were I alone, perhaps I would do it. But I must take care of Mother first of all. She worries me. She doesn't love life enough. She would let herself go without resistance, do you understand? But perhaps this is only an alibi, and I, too, am one of those *'commonsense people.'*"

He smiled sadly, a sad smile I had never seen before.

Uccio had not asked us to leave with him. This time, however, I felt no rancor. Our ship was sinking, and each one of us could become a burden for the other.

We had neither the means nor the contacts to allow us to live in a big city.

Suddenly we felt free of the nightmare, no false documents, no slyness, no compromise. We were going to leave the way we were, without wiles and disarmed. Our clean conscience, in addition to our desperate need of help, sustained us.

He who is poor has the courage to ask. Perhaps someone would welcome us, perhaps "*that someone*" already existed. There was a binding love between us and this land, between us and the people; why wouldn't someone respond to our cry for help?

Faith was being reborn, faith in someone's deliberate act of human compassion.

I was in the kitchen with my leg stretched out on the fireplace hearth; my knee had been hurting again for some time.

Mother was coming and going in the next room, packing the little we had. We were to leave Montecchio the next day.

But where to? Up until then every attempt had been useless.

Papa and Lia had left on the bicycles with a last hope. The daughter of one of the peasants in Poggio had been married not long before and was living with her husband on a farm about twenty kilometers from Montecchio.

She was a nice, good girl. Perhaps she could help us.

My mood was as changeable as the sky that I glimpsed from the transom in the kitchen. At moments a ray of sunshine lit up my hope; at other moments, I saw all black, like those big dark clouds that chased each other behind the windowpane.

Annalena and Uccio had left, swallowed up! Would we ever meet again? And where was the *other one*? I hadn't received one word from him.

Now, my immediate family remained alone, painfully holding onto a last hope. Probably yet another separation, another farewell awaited us.

Yet while we were still together, these days had been spent in bitterness, in hurting each other.

Hours went by, the faint light from the transom gradually disappeared, and the kitchen was plunged into darkness. Mother and I sat near each other, saying nothing, waiting for Papa and Lia to return.

I don't know how long we remained that way.

A flash of lightning suddenly lit up the transom; a shiver went down my back. They had not yet returned. It would be night soon and what weather! And what about a bad encounter? I couldn't stand being in the dark any longer, so I lit the kerosene lamp. Mother was extremely pale, silent. I took one of her hands in mine.

Finally we heard sounds from behind the door.

Seeing them come in, our relief was so great that all we cared about right then was to free them from their soaked clothes and muddy shoes. We didn't ask them anything.

Mother had saved a little warm wine and papa drank it all in one gulp. It was only then that I noticed the expression on my sister's face. She had refused to drink the wine and was leaning against the wall, pale as though she were about to faint. The yellow glow of the lamp made her look almost spectral and I saw that she was trembling. I was struck by the hard look that she fixed on Papa while he was drinking.

Father answered Mother's anxious eyes with one word, "Nothing."

Nobody said anything else that evening.

What was to be done? We had had no choice. What a return home it had been!

Again we locked ourselves inside the house in Poggio, with all doors and windows bolted.

"We told everybody that all of you had left and that the 'palace' was abandoned," Vanni said. "Nobody is to know that you are back. In the cellar there are still some provisions, enough for a few days. But undoubtedly you must leave, and as soon as possible."

Leave? Where to?

My sister could hardly talk when she told me what she had suffered the previous day. Her voice broke in her throat as if from great suffering.

"You see, Isa, unfortunately you can't move because of your knee, but it would have been better if I had gone alone, without Father. He is not to blame, poor man, but on the way he had already reduced me to exasperation. He took it out on Uccio, saying he was selfish and 'had had the nerve to leave without a word.' He took it out on us daughters, and on Mother.

"I asked him to be quiet, but we had such a long way to go. Then he stopped short, menacingly, saying he would turn back then. "What are we going there for? They would have to be saints, and I don't believe in saints. Besides, I don't want them to take us in unwillingly. They would repent after three days and that would be much worse. Better still, I'll put my cards on the table and I'll say so. 'We are persecuted; to take us into your home is very dangerous. What you risk, at the least, is being shot. Now, if you can't do it with your hearts, you'd better tell us right now.'

"I, too, am averse to being diplomatic, Isa, but, for heaven's sakes, can you imagine the effect of such a speech? But he insisted with his paradoxical logic that is so nerve-wracking. 'What?! Would you want them to be nice to us on the first day because they are too embarrassed to say no, and then, perhaps the next day betray us, or at the least throw us out? Better to know the truth to begin with. Anyway, I would have stayed in Montecchio.'

"'But do you know that we are being sent away from Montecchio?' I asked him. 'How could we remain there?' And he, again, 'It makes no difference. It's the same all over!'

"Climbing up the hill, pushing his bicycle by hand and leaning on the handlebars, while wiping the sweat that dripped from his forehead, he looked at me grimly, as if I were to blame for that as well.

"I could see that his health had failed. He had bags under his eyes. He was thinner, shrunken, his dusty jacket hung from his bent shoulders. Yet I felt bitterness welling up, something like hate, or worse, scorn.

"Finally, almost at two in the afternoon we came in sight of the house.

"Nobody was on the threshing floor, but the door was ajar.

"I knocked timidly, pushing the door open; a peasant woman was bent over the hearth, stirring a cauldron. She turned toward us; it was Maria! To find her, of all people, seemed at that moment a sign of Providence. However, I saw that she was startled to see Father and me, and she was disturbed, poor thing.

"I did not dare to speak; our eyes met, hers turning away immediately.

"'We are poor, but you will honor us... It is past the hour of dinner.' Meanwhile, she pulled out the table cloth, the flask of wine, the bread, and started to set the table.

"My stomach was churning, I couldn't possibly swallow even a drop of water, but I sat at the table.

"However, father had perked up. I could see the wrinkles on his forehead slowly straightening out, as he swallowed the wine.

"He chewed bread and *salami* avidly, praising them to Maria, with an emphasis that seemed awkward. Showing no sign of haste, as if he had completely forgotten the reason for our visit, he poured some more wine, took another slice of *salami*, and some walnuts, which he crushed, one against the other in his fist. Doing that, as if pleased with his strength, he even smiled, winking at Maria, who stood there looking stupefied.

"I blushed, like an embarrassed mother. Papa was really acting like a child. Yet at that moment, my rage included a mixture of compassion and sorrow.

"I beckoned to Maria, and headed with her to the threshing-floor, leaving him at the table.

"How difficult it is to beg, Isa! I don't even know what I said to her; I only recall her face as she was listening; I saw it through my tears, as in a photo developed after the plate has moved.

"'Do not despair... Poor souls! What can I say? Have courage... If it depended on me... But I don't count for anything.'

"Maria's voice broke a little, 'Here the *capoccia*, my father-in-law, does everything. He is in the fields. If you want to, I could take you there, but as far as talking to him, you'd better do it yourself.'

"I followed Maria around the house and onto a long path, until we arrived at the edge of a bluff: below, the fields extended to the horizon, all divided into beautiful squares. One of them had brown clods of earth turned over by the plow. Right there, the silhouette of an old peasant on an ox-cart could be clearly seen.

"'There he is!' Maria said, pointing to the man. 'I'll run down and tell him you are here. You wait down below.'

"She disappeared down the bluff. After a few minutes, there she was again, lightly running on the clods, her lined skirt flashing in the sun and shadow.

"I saw her nearing the cart, gesturing while she spoke to the old man, who remained immobile. The she turned, pointing to me.

"Meanwhile, I had walked down into a vast hollow. In that vastness I seemed to get smaller and smaller, as if nothing remained of me; I could only feel my heart throbbing in my throat, like the toll of a mute bell lost within the silence of a vast space.

"The sky was divided into two sections. The lower part, almost totally dark and gloomy, seemed to weigh heavily upon the earth. A strip of yellow light, like sulphur, on the horizon was so vivid that it blinded my eyes. Almost frightened, I turned my eyes away, and looked at the man, still far away, small, black against the light, slowly approaching.

"The squared area of soil was all dark by now, so the peasant had moved forward with his cart. Now he was proceeding in my direction, making another furrow that would line up with the others, at equal distance. Once the furrow was completed, he stopped a moment where he was, as the crow flies, only a few meters from me, and I heard these words coming from on high, 'this is not the place...'

"I had hardly made out their meaning when I saw that the cart had already turned around. The man was moving off in the opposite direction, making another furrow with his plow.

"I didn't know if that was a sign for me to leave. Trembling, I didn't move. Maria motioned to me to wait. Then the man reappeared and his voice reached me again from a distance: 'This is not the place. There are too many ugly beasts...'

"Once again the man turned away, back and forth like a pendulum, and once again some words reached my ear from a shorter distance, 'but she is being tracked...' *Tracked, tracked.* Visions of horrible images flashed before my eyes: a wild boar hunted by dogs, its eyes appallingly alive, a bleeding, torn and dying beast.

"Minutes seemed eternal. The yellow strip had almost disappeared, blending into the grey. A few blackbirds had plunged down to peck at the freshly plowed furrows.

"Brought by the wind, once again the voice without a face arrived to me from the darkness, 'She is being tracked... But let it be clear: for one night and one night only.'

"I stood there, unable to move, rigid in the freezing wind, while the cart disappeared into the darkness. Then I felt Maria's warm hands holding me tight. I stirred at that *human* voice, speaking to me from so near, 'a stormy evening is ahead. Go home now, for God's sake!'

"She insisted on my taking a loaf of bread. I hugged her. All her instinctive kindness was in that gift, as if to tell me that she would have liked to open both her heart and her house to me.

"The first raindrops began to fall."

At this point my sister interrupted her narration as if the last part was the hardest to tell.

"It was dark and there was still a long stretch to climb. The road was very bad; I couldn't move my bicycle. I put on the bike light and I saw that one wheel had sunk into the mud. Dad had stopped. He looked at my powerless efforts, without offering me any help, almost mocking me. At that moment, I really turned against him and I felt like spewing out senseless words, while I began to sob desperately.

"What will we do now, Isa? What will we do?" My sister began to sob once more. "I can't do it, I have no courage to try again!"

I tried to calm her, holding her even tighter, saying: "We'll stay in Poggio for now. Nobody knows we came back."

But from the very first day the new existence of being both dead and alive scared us.

The house seemed different; it had an unfamiliar, almost sinister look. The silence, the closed windows, staying inside during the day with the candles lit, as if we were at a wake. Mother, pale and ghostly, wandering from room to room repeating: "With whom am I going to stay now? With whom am I going to stay now?"

Papa packed and unpacked a small suitcase.

My sister and I also gathered our things together.
We were getting ready – but, to go where?
The wardrobe was wide open – like a door – on its double panels inviting us to enter another world, now so distant from us.

Once we had been "young girls", I mean "young ladies," dressed in cretonne, organdy, voile.

How could these absurd dresses be ours?

They hung swaying on hangers with no bodies inside, empty, in a surreal atmosphere, already belonging to the past, to phantoms. But we, we... Who were we?
We were getting ready – but, to go where?
At the sudden awareness of what *where* could mean, a veil was cast asunder, there was no longer a screen, a

defense against my own uncontrolled imaginative delirium: I had reached the very bottom of terror.

I was a prisoner in a labyrinth where someone was brutally pushing me, compelling me to look into the circle of a lantern light revealing horrible larvae, terrifying appearances.

With no way out, pulled from our home, from our land, perhaps separated from our dear ones; no longer persons but shreds of live bleeding flesh, our souls die.

Were we still us, those we once were?

Ghosts mixed with other, anonymous, ghosts, directed toward an unknown fearful destination.

Perhaps one way out was left, if there was still time. To choose to leave forever, to go to a world where there is no need to take baggage.

Yet that idea, the idea of death, which at one time I had invoked desperately in my torment of love, now appeared to me with a different face, scary and horrible.

That face appeared and reappeared like one's likeness at the bottom of a well; suddenly I recognized it. It was not the austere, clear, and fearless face of Death, but that of suicide, ambiguous, sneering and cowardly.

I withdrew, terrified, as if from a mirror in which I had unexpectedly caught a look at my face, distorted by a troubled expression of insanity.

My eyes blurred, I thought I was fainting.

When I recovered I was sobbing unrestrainedly.

I experienced a heartfelt tenderness for my mother, sister, father, and also for myself. A pious compassion for that spark of life, for that trembling flame still burning inside me, made me feel sacrilegious by wanting to end it all on my own.

Perhaps each one of us *had thought of it* and had suffered the same crisis.

It was not courage to live, it was just courage not to want to die.

Soon it would be night.

We lay down fully dressed. I sank into a deep sleep, I lost consciousness. Suddenly something like a headlight penetrated the room through the shutters; a white light hurt my eyes and, at the same time, within my brain, I perceived a humming of wheels, a loud grinding noise, an increasing rumble.

I sat up with a start, in a cold sweat, my heart pounding fast. I wanted to scream "*The truck! The truck!*" but no sound came out.

My sister hugged me. "Isa, Isa. Aren't you feeling well? What's the matter?"

We stayed awake a long while, clinging to each other. Through the small opening of the shutters, the cold light of the moon filtered inside.

I don't know how many days we stayed inside in Poggio. They seemed endless, like a long delirium that one forgets as soon as one feels better or sees the hope of a full recovery.

One morning Pietro arrived with an unexpected offer. Near Poggio, almost hidden by a thicket there was a home belonging to some peasants, friends of the Mannozzis.

"They are good people and until we find something better..." Pietro said as if apologizing.

But that was marvelous! That piece of news meant that we could hope again, start living again.

"When it's dark," Pietro continued, "I'll come to get Miss Isa. With that bad knee it would be a risk for her to walk on the road to the spring. I'll carry her on my shoulders."

My sister and I felt alive again, while our parents looked disheartened at Pietro's proposal. They were pale, trembling, uncertain, in need of help like children.

This new change aggravated them. Painfully, Mother followed us from room to room.

Papa repeated that it was no use, the house was too near, and everybody would find out the next day. He indicated that it was necessary *to sever the revealing thread*, the obvious trail.

"You don't understand that to really save ourselves, we must run away secretly, hide our traces, sever the thread. If we don't do that, they will find a way to our hideout. One tells the other soon everyone knows where we are; they'll come and get us easily. We must sever our thread. You don't understand anything. I'll stay here and not move until we sever our thread."

Poor man, he was right in theory, but in practice it wasn't easy at all *"to sever our thread."* Meanwhile, should we refuse Pietro's offer?

However, we were confident that seeing us leave, Dad would follow us.

In fact, he continued to fumble with things, taking them in and out of his suitcase and an old trunk, worried about how and when he could take all this away.

"Just take the necessary," I said to him.

He looked indignant and refused my help, as if he wanted to keep me away from his things.

To my surprise, I discovered that in the trunk he had piled many useless objects that he had no intention of leaving behind.

Wrapped in a woolen scarf, there was even his old toy steam engine.

When we were little we used to fantasize about his famous toy train, because he kept it locked in a drawer and we were not allowed to touch it. He would show it to us only on special occasions.

It was brass, with a small steam engine, like a real train. An antique, now a document and a mirror of past times. A toy, carefully built, allowing no fancy of imagination; a little model produced with loving care and extremely faithful to the real thing.

A small but heavy locomotive, complete with its connecting rods, handles, and pistons. It would start with much puffing. Once, to show us that it really worked, Papa placed a small bunch of violets inside the smokestack. After a few puffs of steam, the violet stems looked like cooked spinach. Eyes wide-open, we looked astonished at that wonder.

After almost fifty years, our father still held a naïve enthusiasm for the "*impious monster*" that had fascinated men of the late nineteenth century.

After his demonstration, he would put the toy train back with great care, wiping away the drops of water, and with a woolen cloth, rub the brass until it shone again like gold.

He never failed to underline how much he cared for his objects and how thrifty he had been since his youth.

The toy train had been bought by dint of continuous savings that still wouldn't have been enough without his own father's contribution toward the enormous cost.

As a child, the last of six other children, all girls, Papa was idolized and spoiled by his already old father.

Apparently, "We'll do what the 'little one' wants" was our grandfather's refrain.

I made believe I had not noticed the toy train... Moreover, perhaps each one of us had a toy train to cherish.

While cleaning out a drawer of the hutch, my sister suddenly exclaimed, "Look, Isa, look where this card is from! Castello! Signorina Gentileschi sent it to us on July 25. Remember? She escaped from the city before the air raids began and surely she is still there. She is a fervent anti-fascist and she showed a certain fondness for the two of us. But she is so old! She must be over seventy. Listen, Castello is nearby; what do you say I go there tomorrow on the bike? Yes, I'll go there tomorrow!"

I was surprised at Lia's excitement over her own idea. Her voice was full of hope, as if she had forgotten all about her many previous attempts. I answered, "tomorrow, we'll see. Let's just think about today. At least for tonight we have a place to stay."

When darkness fell, we left one at a time. Pietro arrived punctually and carried me on his shoulders, like a bag of coal. With him, I could overcome any obstacle, while breathing the night air looking at the moon. Stones couldn't hurt me, going uphill couldn't tire me. "Walk...walk." On we went.

After so many days of little food, we were grateful to eat a real supper: roasted potatoes, baked rabbit and apples.

These well-meaning people were trying to give us some encouragement.

The *capoccia*'s mother wondered if our mother would deign to sleep with her on her bed; after all, she always slept near the edge. Poor old woman! So tiny and bent by arthritis, her head heavy on her bosom, yet she was willing to share her bed with someone worse off than herself at the moment.

Papa and the two of us went down to the stable. It was an enormous room with one high window and filthy walls. It was so crowded that our space on the straw was minimal.

What a difference from the graciously clean stable in Montecchio! Here, nothing separated us from the animals, except for a draining gutter on the floor – vile, yellow, and sour-smelling.

The air was warm and thick: the animals were so near that we could feel their breath on us.

Despite it all, we fell asleep.

I woke up in the middle of the night. My eyes were dry, my pulse rapid: I was burning with fever. Through my dry thirst, I was tormented by a cruel mirage: a cool glass of orange juice like the ones always so handy during family illnesses. The next day I was somewhat weak but better. The fever must have broken, even though I had taken no aspirin. Everyone else was full of aches and pains, covered with mosquito bites and itching all over.

My sister, along with Papa, decided to bicycle to Castello. She would have preferred to go alone, but he insisted.

Back from their trip, they looked so tired that I didn't dare ask anything; but Lia said, "Isa, I'll tell you everything later. What counts is that the Signorina agreed to take the two of us."

Even with no radio or telephone, that piece of news got around: everybody in Poggio knew it the following day.

In order to cover our tracks, our destination had been kept a secret. However, the fact that someone had the courage to welcome us, not for one or two days, but for an indefinite period of time, was in itself very important. It was as though enormous ice blocks had melted and water had begun to flow again.

Vanni, Pietro, Corinna, and "Zio" Poldo came back to see us. There was no sign of fear. Their countenances were open, no longer uncertain or hostile. They were full of initiative and plans.

We refused to leave for Castello before finding a place for our parents as well. It's true that difficulties must be faced one at a time so that, as Guicciardini writes, they unravel.

Three days later everything was arranged. Our parents would go to a farm near Siena to stay with some peasants, distant relatives of the Albieris. No one would know them there and no one would even notice them.

We had to take care of a few more problems, since we couldn't use any rationing cards. We planned to arrive at Castello and at Le Piane with enough provisions so that we would not impose on our benefactors.

Money didn't have much value then, and besides, we only had a limited amount. We would have to ask for provisions from the Mannozzis, the Albieris, and the Stellis.

At first, they showed distrust and avarice. We needed everything and we no longer were the "Signorine." We were tired and we felt lost, realizing that they regarded us differently.

Once we were hurt: Corinna referred to our parents as "those old people" and a tenant said about us, "those

women, what do they expect?"   It was as, if in a flash, we
were older.   In no time at all, how could such a metamorphosis have occurred?

To do them justice, their selfishness lasted only a short
while.   In fact, there was another surprising change.

Although we once had been looked upon as the
"privileged," the "signori," the peasants had loved us.   Now
the situation was reversed: the privileged were those who
still had families, owned land and homes, and could play
the role of benefactors.   Now, we were the ones to be protected and saved.

With a gentle sense of human pity, they compared us
with their own children, their brothers, or soldiers who had
not returned home, their whereabouts unknown and perhaps
wanderers like us, lost in the world in search of a roof and a
piece of bread.

Thus the old affection was rekindled under different
circumstances.   Mutual understanding was reestablished.
At one point they even began to compete among themselves, to sell us something, even to give us something, a
flask of oil, or a bag of potatoes.

They took delight in providing us with necessities, especially after Lia revealed an unexpected talent – bartering.
Perhaps our Jewish ancestry had something to do with it.
As a matter of fact, if money was worth so little, "to barter
things" was something else.

It began with the ski boots.   It is well known how important shoes are for peasants, so Lia got her boots out and
put them right under Beppa's nose.   The old woman looked
at them stealthily, blinking her small turtle-like eyes.

"Are they yours, Miss Lia?   They are good for your
gentle feet, but not for ours."

She nodded her head, still fascinated. She even smelled them while touching them.

"Beautiful, soft leather!" Actually, it was extremely hard and might even have been fake. Like a temptress mermaid, Lia increased their value: "You couldn't find leather like this anywhere, and look at the soles, two fingers thick! Besides, the boots aren't small. It's cold in the snow, and I had to wear two pairs of woolen socks with them."

In the meantime, Beppa's niece, Rosetta, had come in. She too was attracted to the boots like a fly to honey.

The old woman tried to resist, but no longer was she so firm.

"...Well, how much wheat would you want in exchange?"

With a straight face, my sister answered, "One hundred kilos."

"What are you saying? Let's make it sixty... Come on, just to please this young girl."

Beaming with joy, the young girl grabbed the boots, without even trying them on. If the leather was synthetic, the wheat too revealed itself somewhat weevily.

An eye for an eye, a tooth for a tooth. Beppa was too astute!

"Zio" Poldo, however, generously exchanged the sixty kilos of wheat with sixty kilos of soft white flour. Sixty kilos of flour for us meant sixty big loaves of bread, enough for quite a while.

Encouraged by her success, Lia continued to use her new talent. The peasants were drawn into it completely. It seemed as if we were back in the time of primitive man, when the "wicked silver" didn't yet exist, but man exchanged only in kind.

After the boots, two heavy winter coats, woolen sweaters, sheets, blankets and even a generous provision of medicines we had brought along, departed in a twinkling.

"That one, yes, I want that one!" the peasants would say, but actually they "preferred" everything, pocketing "each thing": gauze, cotton, a little bottle of iodine, epsom salts. In exchange we got olive oil, honey, walnuts, dry figs, and raisins.

Yet they were firm in their refusal of our offering of a bolt of black cloth. Who knows, perhaps they were dismayed by the association of black with death, mourning to fascism. At any rate, Corinna passed sentence: "Only right for a priest!"

We all planned to leave on the same day at about the same time; that way it would be less sad.

Once Michele was informed, he would first pick up our parents and drive them to Le Piane, then he would return and take us to Castello.

Papa divided his money, Mamma, her few jewels, which included a magic golden ring with a little secret: by turning it around, the three small diamonds set in it would vanish while three little words appeared: *I LOVE YOU*.

That ring was a token of love; it was our grandfather's gift to his fiancée. Looking at it, Mamma said, "Oh, my dear mother, your grandmother, always wore it. Now I want one of you to wear it. You, Lia. I feel it will protect both of you. Always take good care of each other. Love each other and trust in God. Keep this in mind when I am far away and someday when I won't be around anymore."

She put her hand lightly on our heads drawing them close together, in order to give us her blessing. Mamma looked calm, almost serene.

While waiting for Michele, my sister kept twisting the ring that Mother had put on her finger.

"We are by ourselves now, Isa," she said to me. "Perhaps it's for the best. It was painful to part from our parents, but now that they are alone, too, they will get along better. Mother is so sweet and docile that Papa won't have any reason to get angry. Well, with me, it was unavoidable. We even argued on our way to Castello, yet I didn't mean to argue, I swear it. But I was so upset. Do you know that just that day new restrictions against the Jews had been published? Those big black letters in the newspaper read like a death sentence!

"At the inn where we stopped to eat, I had the feeling everyone was looking at us and knew... Papa didn't want to believe what I was telling him: 'Don't you realize, Papa, that if you come along with me to Signorina Gentileschi and you whine and beg for shelter at her place for all four of us, we won't get anything, anything at all.'

"But he kept insisting. 'We needed brave people! Honest ones and good too! People that would be disgusted with such a world. The laws! How can they call them laws? Murders, that's what they are – real murders.'"

When the war was over, the signorina herself told me about that encounter several times. She loved to recall those unforgettable events and would say, "just think, at first I didn't recognize your sister at all. I remembered her the way I had seen her back in the city, the last time. She came to see me before I decided to evacuate and go to Castello. It was near the end of winter, during the first days of March. She looked smart in her grey suit, with her bright and beautiful eyes shining from under the brim of her hat. The day she arrived in Castello, I couldn't recognize her, even though only a few months had gone by! She was as white as a sheet, with a scarf on her head. She was sobbing, the poor thing."

"I don't even know what I told her," Lia continued, "I was crying. I only remember Signorina Gentileschi's answer: 'You and your sister may come if you don't find anything better.'

"Yet I was so lost that I couldn't even thank her. She wanted me to have a hot drink to perk me up, but I told her I had to leave immediately. She called her maid, Edonide, who had been with her for twenty years. Edonide was wearing a black dress with an apron trimmed with white lace, like those she used in the city. She took a small silver tray and a crystal goblet from the cupboard; then she poured a jigger of *Vin Santo* from a frosted glass bottle."

I, too, knew Signorina Gentileschi and I could understand that she wouldn't give up that little ritual, even in those two rooms at Castello.

My sister went on, "When I was leaving, I didn't know how to thank her. I would have liked to hug her, but I didn't dare. Instead, I bent to kiss her small ivory hand with its long tapered fingers, a hand as weightless as a dry leaf."

"Papa was waiting for me outside. The moment I saw him in the cold light of the street, I felt sorry for him, poor man, already aged and tired, dragging the two bicycles.

"Why couldn't we ever get along together? I felt the need to reassure him by saying, 'Let's hope for the best. At least she hasn't refused to take us in.'

"But I didn't have the courage to specify that it was just for you and me. Then I said to him, 'Later on we'll see what happens. Perhaps we'll find another refuge for you and Mom together, and Isa and me. Believe me, it would be much more difficult for the four of us together. As a 'family,' it is much easier to be identified.'

"This seemed like a good idea to him. Soon after, however, he began to frown and said grimly, 'tell me now, how will you and your sister make yourselves useful? Literature won't be of any use! And what about your mother, who is always in need of something? Poor things! You've never learned to cope.'

"And he started nagging all over again, making a case of nothing."

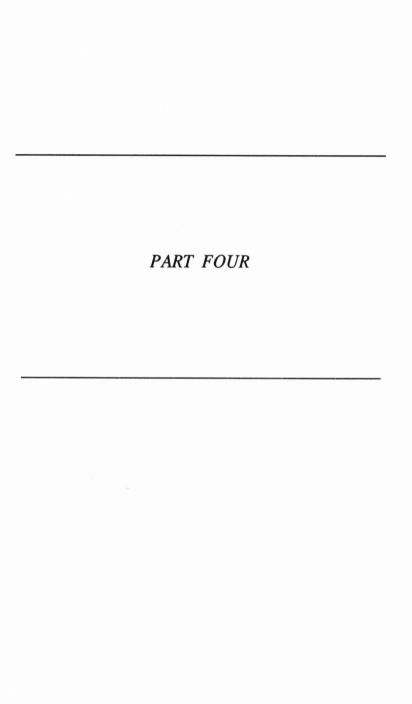

PART FOUR

It was almost night when my sister and I arrived at Castello. After entering the old town gate, Michele sped up the long, narrow main street.

We had been to Castello more than once, on sunny-day outings. We were always enchanted by the aristocratic aspect of the small old town with its walls, fortress, steeples and towers! The narrow medieval lanes squeezed between two walls, winding maze-like, suddenly coming out into the open. We were also fascinated by the airy glimpses of the countryside seen from new perspectives, through an arch, or from a height, when leaning over a low wall.

The square was in the heart of the town. Spacious yet intimate, well-defined in its boundary, as if shielded by the old palaces, of noble, simple lines. All the resources of art and nature seemed to converge there. Shapes and colors. One could detect a transformation of the color of stones and bricks into wonderful tones from yellow to ochre, from pink to blood-red. The rectangular windowpanes, reflecting the bright light, resembled mosaics.

On the window-sills and on the loggias, geraniums flamed in the sun. The large old cistern was right in the center. Every time I saw it, it was as if I were seeing it for the first time, as if a firm hand were tracing it in the air in its bare and perfect lines right before my eyes, according to the precepts of art.

That evening, however, when the car entered the square, crossing it diagonally, I couldn't help feeling anguish and fear. Doors and windows were tightly shut for the blackout. Only the moon, hanging motionless in the sky, turned everything to silver, creating the effect of chiaroscuro, as in a black-and-white film.

In the deserted square, the giant shadow of the cistern in that mute stillness seemed surreal and foreboding.

Signorina Gentileschi's house stood at a corner, with some of its windows facing the square. Luckily, however, the massive, wooden front door opened on a lane, completely dark at that time.

The car turned the corner with its headlights off. We went in through the door, which was ajar. Michele helped us unload our suitcases, bags, and bikes. He arranged everything in a corner of the dark hallway, behind a pillar. He slipped quickly into his car, his head leaning out the open window. Looking at us with slightly tearful, misty brown eyes, he addressed us in his usual gruff manner:

"Good-bye, signorine. Be brave, and if you need me, you know where I live."

He drove off quickly.

My sister went upstairs and came right back down with Edonide, our hostess' maid. They loaded themselves with things, then disappeared upstairs wordlessly, like thieves, under suitcases and bags. I stood guard over our bicycles.

My heart was pounding when suddenly I started. A door, hidden in the wall, opened a crack. For a moment I spied the glimmer of candlelight before it was immediately extinguished. I did not see anybody, nor could I know whether the door was still open, but I did feel a hostile presence in the darkness, the force of an evil eye spying on me.

The moment we entered the apartment, Signorina Gentileschi greeted us with a slight nod and an imperceptible smile on her thin lips, barely touching our hands, as if this were an everyday courtesy call. She invited us to "sit down" in the small guest parlor and, soon after, busied herself with giving orders to the maid: "Edonide, come here... Edonide, go there..."

"This is your room," she said, opening a door. "We go to bed early, and you too must be tired," she added in a slightly authoritative tone. "Good night."

We heard her go into the next room. After a little while, hurried footsteps, like those of someone who was still busy, echoed in the silence.

Our room was in semi-darkness, only a candle in a holder shimmered on the bedside table.

We quickly undressed and slipped between the cold sheets. After we blew out the candle, we lay awake in the darkness.

Finally, my sister dozed off; as for me, I couldn't stop thinking about that glimmering of light, those eyes whose disquieting and ominous power I had felt fixed on me.

I woke up so tired that I felt as if I had not slept at all. Yet, it was dawn: a pale dim light filtered through the shutters.

Lia was sleeping very quietly with her arm crooked under her head and her hair a bit ruffled on her forehead. She was breathing lightly and evenly, the way she did when she was a child. We two were still together: there we were, *the two of us*. I tucked her in a little. There was no hurry to awaken her. I tried not to make noise. I lay there looking about the room. Little by little, in that half-light I was able to distinguish the shapes and colors of the objects around me.

The room itself was large, but our bed, leaning against the wall, occupied only a small part of it. Across from the bed was a dark chest of drawers. In one corner of the room was an iron wash-stand with a blue and white china basin and jug, on which rested a linen towel with embroidered initials: "A.G." At the window, a pale-colored curtain hanging from wooden rings bore the same initials.

This small tidy space seemed fenced in by a good number of chairs. They were arranged in parallel rows, as if in a theatre, waiting to be used. The chairs had slip-covers. But where were the improbable, hypothetical occupants? Perhaps long dead?

I kept gazing at those chairs, which, even under their covers, revealed the slightly self-conscious charm of their style. For a long while I stared at those empty chairs as if under a spell. Suddenly the rows seemed to ripple and blend together before my very eyes. The small section that we occupied seemed to expand and grow larger with the chairs, withdrawing and arranging themselves in an orderly semicircle.

The stiff, dull slip-covers disappeared and suddenly the soft brilliance of the slightly faded golden velvet flashed upon me. On the velvet, like portraits in a medallion, some attentive faces appeared. Someone was at the piano. The strains of Boccherini's *Minuet* floated about the room.

Then it came to me: I remembered sitting on one of those chairs at Miss Gentileschi's home back in our city, for small musical gatherings. The atmosphere was the same as that described by Palazzeschi in *Stampe dell'Ottocento* ("*Prints of the Nineteenth Century*"). The guests were dear old friends and relatives...

After spending our first night at Signorina Antonina Gentileschi's, she was still almost a stranger to us when we met her in the corridor.

She had a minute face, like a Chinese idol, light-colored eyes, as if without pupils, narrow and elongated by fine wrinkles that stretched to the temples, where the skin turned to polished ivory under her light hair. Her thin body tended to disappear under her dark dress. Her voice was so feeble that it had little substance. Everything about her had a certain reserved secrecy, a mysterious inscrutability, though not lacking in charm. Her body gave off a mild lavender scent like that of the linen towel with the embroidered initials "A. G."

She was already fully and neatly dressed, her silver grey hair gathered into a small bun, her dark dress buttoned to the throat, where a small white collar was the only light touch. In a low yet firm voice she invited us to "hurry" and come down for breakfast.

Somewhat intimidated, we went to the kitchen. Edonide was at the sink, holding a blue enamel long-handled pan under a stream of water. She turned toward us and, without any greeting, said, "I must put it under the tap right away, otherwise the porridge stuck to the bottom will not come off."

While she was inspecting the sticky mass at the bottom of the pan with great severity, keeping it almost against her eye-glasses, she said, as the saying goes, "Either eat this soup, or jump out the window." *She* meant it, and she really was convinced that, without oil, butter, or cheese, the white porridge was nutritious. But it was certainly not palatable. The truth was that in those dog days of war, "to whet the appetite" would have been like pulling the tail of a biting dog. Ha! Ha! Ha! And she would laugh with a nasal old-maid laughter that made her face look ugly and of indefinable age.

Surprised by her familiarity, we didn't know how to answer, and we kept on toying with the matchbox and the coffee pot, without daring to touch the gas stove. We gazed at her, bewildered. Considering her destiny in general and her relationship to her mistress, Edonide was both a victim and a rebel, slave and tyrant. Brought up in a convent and as a "daughter of Mary," she combined certain bigotry with an anarchic inclination that quite often overflowed like boiled milk. After all, her inclination was justified by the fact that she came from a greatly subversive city where a picturesque dialect was spoken.

Usually these contrasting emotions were masked by the pallor of her face – her small short-sighted eyes almost disappearing behind the gleam of her thick glasses – but from time to time these and other emotions would suddenly emerge, and her face, rekindling, would regain color, as in a decal.

This happened in particularly unusual moments, as, for example, when she was overwhelmed by uncontrolled emotion.

Thus it happened on that December morning, our first morning at Signorina Gentileschi's.

"It's no use trying to light this stove," Edonide sneered, awkwardly sticking out her stomach under her soaked apron, as if to provoke us.

"The gas has not been working for months; but if you look under there," and she pointed to a stove full of ashes, "there is still some fire. I'll take care of it." And immediately she busied herself with a small shovel and a pair of bellows.

My sister filled a kettle with water and put it dangerously askew on three small, reddish embers. Edonide kept fanning, but after a few seconds, infuriated, knocked one of the smoking embers out of the stove. Trying to reach one hundred degrees centigrade for the water to boil was simply unrealistic, so we gave up.

"It doesn't really matter, Edonide," I said. "It's not worth making the fire again. It isn't even cold this morning." Actually, the kitchen was freezing. "Besides, we are tired of drinking barley coffee. Instead, we'll eat bread and dried figs."

Edonide approved at once with visible solace: "Figs are better than porridge!"

And she wasn't wrong.

Thanks to our exchanges with the peasants, we had quite a store of dried figs, which became very precious. Even though food was scarce, figs didn't cost much. Being considered frugal and unpretentious, they were almost looked down upon. As a matter of fact, figs don't attract your eye like other, more scented or colorful fruits, especially when dried, being all wrinkled and greyish. But how delicious they are!

We enjoyed chewing the red sweet pulp with the small crackling seeds that resembled sparks. They tasted delicious with bread but still better with walnuts. In contrast to life's false expectations, figs gave more than you would expect, so much so that once my sister, after eating them with real gusto and enjoyment, said, "Do you know these dried figs are really 'honest'." From that day on, figs were named "the honest ones."

At the end of a meal, when not quite satisfied, one of us would say to the other, "Give me an 'honest' or give me three or four 'honests'." With the addition of these figs, we were fully contented, just like Pinocchio after devouring the skins of the pears.

After drying the blue wooden spoon and the pan, which were used to cook the hated morning porridge, Edonide discreetly left the kitchen either to go shopping or, perhaps, to give us some time alone to eat our breakfast.

While eating, my sister and I looked around. The kitchen was big, somewhat like a farmhouse kitchen, a mixture of country and city: a huge stove with several coal-burners, and on one side useless gas burners. On the sink were pitchers, and also a spigot of drinkable water. The kneading-trough to make bread and a flour sifter; a rectangular table with a thick mottled marble slab; a glass cabinet with rows of different-sized cans, the small ones on the top shelf with painted labels as in a drugstore: pepper, nutmeg, cloves; on the lower shelf, bigger ones: rice, salt, pepper, sugar, coffee.

The light from the window picked up the gold reflections, both of the pitchers on the sink and the pans hanging on the wall. On the opposite wall hung a rack with ladles, knives of various shapes and sizes, and, in the center, a cutting board with a shining half-moon chopper.

With all that paraphernalia, one could cook for an army, but in a corner, a screened food-cupboard seemed practically empty.

Edonide came back after a few minutes and took the ration of bread and a big cabbage, with its outer leaves hanging down wilted, out of the basket. She moved into the corridor. The kitchen door was open; we could hear her reporting to her *padrona*, who, contrary to habit, raised her voice a little, saying, "I told you, you know nothing, nothing at all. And, nobody – do you understand? – nobody arrived here."

"But what could I answer? She kept asking whether guests arrived last night, that she saw a car stop right here and unload suitcases and bags, even two bicycles! So, how could I deny it? I made her believe that they were people only passing through."

"You did wrong!" retorted Signorina Gentileschi. "Once and for all, remember! Nobody arrived here!"

At this point, although sitting in the kitchen in flesh and blood, busy with the earthly function of swallowing food, we began to doubt our own physical presence, especially when we heard it denied in such peremptory tones.

Feeling very small, reduced in size, we tried to transform ourselves into floating acrobats, even to vanish in thin air. Then suddenly and forcefully the Cartesian *dubito ergo sum* arose within us. But Cartesio had no influence over *Signorina Antonina Gentileschi*, who repeated her thesis of our "non-existence" to us.

"You," she said, "you are not here. You must never go out for any reason, nor look out the window, nor make yourselves heard in the house."

Annihilated by her endless string of pressing negative imperatives, when we were alone, we said, "Alas! Surely we won't last long here!"

Several days went by without incident. We put on noiseless slippers made of felt. Continuous practice made us adept in the new art of non-existence.

"Hush! Hush!"

But we were craving to talk, so we learned how to whisper very softly. "Very quietly," standing by the stove in the kitchen, in an aura of tense silence, like in a circus a few moments before the dangerous somersault, there I was flipping an omelet. It was round, yellow, and so perfect that one might think it was a golden illusion, until you got it between your teeth and found it was real, edible, radiantly fragrant, and tasty.

At night, relegated to our room, wearing oversized nightgowns, we walked in circles like phantoms and every time we passed in front of the mirror we bowed. In the flickering flame of the candle, our ghostly figures surfaced slowly in the reflection.

Like thieves, we silently opened and closed drawers; quietly we disappeared into bed under a pile of blankets.

When it rained heavily (it was December), resounding thunder mixed with lightning burst in the air like a saraband, exciting us. We amused ourselves reciting aloud or dancing frantically, even daring to laugh aloud.

Once, as I was laughing, my sister interrupted me:

"Do you remember, Isa, do you remember how Uccio used to laugh? Where could he be now?"

His hearty laughter resonated, crackled inside us, alive again in the vivid flame of our memories. A blade pierced our hearts. Almost unbearable nostalgia overwhelmed us, and suddenly we realized how much we missed him. At the same time, as if touched by a live wire, we felt that no matter how far apart we were, something united us still, something that would last forever, in spite of everything, beyond space, time, and death.

"Perhaps," I said, "Perhaps at this moment he is thinking of us, too."

Thus we lived a *secret life*, a life of our own which, in a way, had its happy times.

At mealtimes we would gather in the small living room, with the *Signorina* sitting alone at a separate table.

She ate silently, almost motionlessly, with a certain mysterious air.   We felt somewhat like spectators in a theater, wondering whether the actors were really eating or not.

Judging from Edonide's basket, the portions couldn't be that large. At the end of the meals, however, *Signorina Gentileschi*, would always get the frosted glass bottle from the china closet and pour a small amount of red wine for us and for herself, adding to each glass a teaspoon of sugar: that was our dessert. Considering the hard times we were living in, it was quite something and we felt guilty for accepting it. However, she insisted, kindly, yet persistently, saying that "wine makes good blood," that my sister looked somewhat anaemic, and above all, we were "her guests."

Only later did we discover how much she had sacrificed for hospitality's sake.

The room with all the chairs was her sleeping quarters; she had moved into the living room, to the sofa. When we asked her please to take back her bedroom, she wouldn't hear of it.

She was actually sorry we had found out her secret, and would always wait for us to go to bed before setting up her place. She would get up at dawn and put everything in order, so that when we went into the sitting room, all was in its accustomed place, with all the knick-knacks meticulously dusted, the sofa impeccably puffed up. Nothing out of place, not a pair of slippers, a book, a glass, or any sign that would betray her.

Many years have gone by since Signorina Gentileschi left us on tip-toe, but these memories still trouble me and make me blush. I feel intensely warm gratitude for this wonderful, almost octogenarian, lady with a brave, fearless heart who risked her life by accepting us into her home. We as human beings are certainly attached not only to virtues but also to small oddities, and even to the defects of those we love.

Now Signorina Gentileschi sees and understands everything and hopefully she will forgive me.

We spent our waking hours together in that living room. We would read, crochet, make conversation, talk of music and books. We never talked politics; it was enough to exchange glances and sighs, especially when we listened to the muted voice of London on the radio, in the silence of the night.

Our hostess declared herself a free-thinker, but she would read the Vatican *Roman Observer* with respect.

Edonide always had her meals in the kitchen; only rarely would she be admitted to the living room. Signorina Gentileschi had no intention of lessening class distinctions.

In the city, when she went out with her maid, she wouldn't think of walking side by side with her or, worse yet, arm in arm. They would proceed one behind the other, at an understood distance. She would wear a small black felt hat, a "toque," simple but elegant, without any feathers, ribbons, or flowers. With her hat sitting squarely on her head, she would move briskly, militarily, as if she were a scout on her way to battle. Edonide, on the other hand, wore a cheerful flowered kerchief, tied carelessly under her chin, and walked behind, just the way "social status" dictated.

One day, the south-west wind was blowing. Despite its strong gusts, Signorina Gentileschi's black hat – with a long pin piercing it like a sword – remained firmly on her head. Suddenly, at a corner, a mischievous local boy, sarcastically acknowledging her hat, snickered "look at that old pot!"

Hit by a gust of wind and by the disrespectful comment, the small "toque" moved back a little, wobbling dangerously, then regained its position to proceed unperturbed and victorious.

Edonide kept that unforgettable episode in her memory and years after she would still crack up at the thought of it.

Though Edonide seldom remained in the living room, once, after having cleared the table, she lingered, clasping the tablecloth to her chest, hesitating before going to shake out the crumbs in the kitchen.

Signorina Gentileschi was talking about "property," about inherited wealth, which was useless during those hard times of war, while certain people who had started from nothing, perhaps involved in the black market, were swimming in prosperity. She respected those who were "born" wealthy, knowing how difficult it was to hold on to one's possessions.

Edonide kept listening, frowning, while still holding onto the tablecloth. She certainly was fascinated by wealthy, well-born people. She was aware that she belonged with that "class" and, in her turn, she scorned the maids who worked in more common homes. Yet unexpectedly, she reacted as never before.

"Social justice!" she said. "The day will come when exploiters or exploited won't exist anymore, and neither will masters or servants, rich or poor!"

And, as if inspired, she began to sing,

> ...In the international
> The future of humanity..."

It was one of "those moments"; her hair tossed from side to side; her eyes shone behind her thick eyeglasses. The tablecloth she was holding unfurled like a flag, gleaming in the sunlight.

Amazed, the *padrona* looked at her somewhat ironically, but didn't intervene. Only after "the maid" folded the tablecloth and marched out of the room, Signorina Gentileschi said, "Edonide is young! We must excuse her. She is only forty-seven years old!"

Quite aside from the arguable interpretation of Edonide's political stance simply as a youthful outburst, we couldn't hide a chuckle at that 'being young at forty-seven!' But with time we, too, learned that everything in this world is relative; now, unfortunately, we can't even appreciate its humor. For a person already in her eighties, it was perfectly natural that "only forty-seven" was young, almost a young girl... What was there to laugh at?

December was coming to an end. Signorina Gentileschi lived in seclusion; war demanded sacrifices from everyone.

However, the Christmas spirit was in the air; on the roof the snow glistened like sugar and the short days passed quickly into night. People stayed up later; thin smoke curled from the chimneys and the good smell of burning wood wafted in with the chilly evening breeze. Outside, the town was enveloped in a silent darkness, cushioning our house, as if to silence it. In the house – a pit, a small nucleus – four lives were lived together, but within this communal life, a thin thread of Jewish life, spun by our two lives, was unraveling.

A few acquaintances, a rare friend, came and exchanged best wishes and small gifts with the Signorina. As soon as the bell rang, the two of us would run and hide in our room. Through the wall, from the living room, which was next to ours, "the room with the chairs," we could hear steps, whispering, sudden coughs, giggles. Sometimes, peeking through a crack in our door, in the semi-dark corridor, we could see a cap, a scarf, a coat hanging on the hooks, or an umbrella dripping in a corner.

We never saw the visitors in person, but because of Signorina's dry comments and Edonide's copious reports, their names, surnames, status, habits would spin around in our heads as if in a prism, picking up different lights.

Thus, little by little, in our imagination, those vague shadows became bodies, figures, characters.

Besides Signorina Gentileschi and Edonide, who seemed more purposely made just for us, our theater was being enriched with more characters: the "sad" lady with the lilac-colored cloak, the "carefree" one with the plaid scarf, the "little one" with the red cap, the "uncertain" gentleman with his large black umbrella... Names and surnames would stick like labels on each character. Sometimes labels were attached incorrectly.

Amidst these characters, unfortunately, there was a cruel one. It was the same person whose malignant eye I had felt through the crack in the door the night we arrived. Transferred into a character, however, it became more familiar and less menacing. When we learned that the "cruel eye" wore a skirt, we named her "*Occhiaccia.*"

Actually, "*Occhiaccia*" was too often on the scene. She would appear inappropriately and intentionally at the most unthinkable hours, compelling us to escape to "the room of the chairs." Is there any play worthy of its name that has only good characters? And what about the fables? Isn't there always an ogre tied with a thread to the innocent child?

With all the visitors gone, we still remained in our room, curled up on a corner of the bed, still fantasizing.

Darkness began to penetrate the room, fading the colors. Our thoughts were carried far away, as we poked the embers in the brazier. Sparks glowed in the grey ashes, like tiny flames and we, too, would feel our young blood reviving, tingling, making us merry without reason. It was on one of those nights that my sister revealed to me her *secret*.

It was almost sunset. At a slight distance from the window, we were watching the luminous sky over the rooftops in front of us. Meanwhile the tower clock began to chime slowly.

"It's an enchanting moment," said my sister. "Don't you believe that *things* know this and they look for each other and they agree with one another?"

The room disappeared in darkness; outside the window the sky glowed with gold.

Lia lowered her voice, and I drank in all her words, perceiving a new, livelier, deeper intensity.

"Isa, I wish I could write...because I feel something inside me when I see the sky all aglow while the clock strikes... I remember that when we were little, Mother would come to say good-night, but as soon as she left, I would tuck my head under the sheets and tell myself my own stories. Well, after so many years, I have a new story. I'll tell you: its title is '*The Story of the Little Town With the Malignant Clocks*.'"

"See if I guess right," said I, "Is *this* the little town?"

"Maybe, maybe not. But surely it is a little town like those in fairy-tales."

After that night, Lia did not speak about her fables anymore, but I could still sense a light and happy aura about her, in the way that she moved, looked at me and smiled.

It was December 31, and we did not expect any visitors. We would spend New Year's Eve alone with Signorina Gentileschi, waiting for midnight. We had thought of asking Edonide to do some shopping for us to enliven the feast, after getting permission from our hostess.

Just then, the Signorina called my sister over. Nearing the window, from where part of the square could be seen, she said to her, "Look how many people! Even though there is war, they want to be a little merry tonight!" and then suddenly added, "You, also, go out with Edonide. It is cold, but the cold is healthy for young people. The dry winter air will do you good. Look how limpid the sky is! After a brisk walk, you'll see... "

Lia listened to her speechlessly. The fact was unheard of; *never* had the Signorina given us such permission. Had she also been affected by the euphoria? *Semel in anno* – "once a year" – and it was December 31! And the risk? In answer to the unsaid words, Signorina added, "Don't be afraid... With the commotion, who could recognize you?

The whole town is in the streets, but in the darkness, with the blackout, I myself could not recognize anyone. Go, go! But bundle yourself up, put a shawl on your head."

My sister did not have to be told twice. After almost a month of being cloistered, the proposal was too tempting to turn down. And how could she say "no" to the Signorina!

Wrapping her shawl around her, she ran out behind Edonide, being careful to keep a little distance, pretending that they were not together. The plan was this: Edonide would buy apples, oranges, walnuts, *Vin Santo*, Sienese fruit cake and cookies, and my sister would help her carry some of the packages.

Lia told me that everything went well. While Edonide went inside the stores, Lia wandered through the small streets that were alive with people. How great to be with people again! As if playing a game of hide-and-seek, she amused herself brushing against passers-by. She would have liked to have pulled the braid of some of the girls, saying laughingly, "Look, I am here, too!" She was attracted by the streams of light that emerged from the stores as if they were inviting her inside where it was warm and colorful, filled with flour sacks and fruit baskets and with the smell of pepper and tobacco. Instead she retracted into her shawl.

"Do you know," she told me, "the town, the buildings, the people stopped existing for me. As their outlines became dimmed and faded away, only the tiny sparkling stars remained over my head. Covered by my lacy shawl, I walked in the midst of grey shadows without being seen, feeling like a princess in a fairy-tale, wrapped in a magic veil that renders her invisible. Or I was transformed into a small fish...in murky water; then with a leap I immersed myself in a small limpid pool of water, silvery and isolated. There I swam freely and happily, in the light of the moon."

When she came back, her eyes were shining, her cheeks were flushed with a warm glow. Free from that reticence that had kept her from showing any sign of affection toward Signorina Gentileschi, she even dared grasp her hands warmly.

"Feel how warm I am now! I feel burning like a flame! Warm your hands in mine, Signorina!"

Signorina Gentileschi caressed her with a look, while her small clear eyes shone bright as if to say she understood and felt gratified. In those eyes there was also an almost conspiratorial glint, as if she, so old, had become young again, and was pleased to have taken a risk.

In that new, livelier atmosphere that had blossomed in our midst like a gift from Providence, other miracles took place.

Edonide was admitted into the small living room. After supper she took off her ever-present apron.

The *Vin Santo* had gone to our heads a little, making us pleasantly euphoric and tipsy. The four of us kept silent. The room still held the fragrance of oranges, cinnamon and marzipan. This was the beauty of it: being able to stay there so naturally, without saying a word, in the warm intimacy. Perhaps each one of us was following our own thread of thoughts, memories, dreams.

After a long pause, Signorina slowly got up and went to the piano. In all the time we were with her, we had never heard her play. She made sure to use the soft pedal.

Her hands flew over the keys:

Let's drink, let's drink
From the happy cups
That make youth flower!

These notes, dying away, weak, yet so intense and touching, were they a message? The words of the aria spoke of the joy of life, the nostalgia for youth, for lost dreams.

Signorina was very advanced in years; Edonide was on the threshold of old age; and what about us? The hourglass of our *good time* was rapidly draining. But in that enchanting hour, the four of us, united like the strings of an instrument vibrating to the same chord, experienced a kind of deep, heart-rending exultation.

Signorina closed the piano. The fleeting moment had gone forever.

Edonide, "to make us laugh a bit," began to talk of past times, of when she was a young girl, and was acting in the small theater of the convent on New Year's Eve.

"Mother Superior said I was very good! In the comical parts I made them all roar with laughter, and in the tragic parts cry like lambs about to be slaughtered. It upset me always to play the part of a male, but I was tall and I had a deep voice. But I, too, could please like the other show-off girls.

"I remember, once I wore a red necklace. I was in the sacristy where there was a chair-mender. He came close to me. I saw that he was trying to charm me, but I was naïve. He played around with my necklace for a long while, letting it bounce back on my chest. I laughed it off... Meanwhile, the sexton came in and ordered him to stop and me to go straight home. Well, the chair-mender was certainly attracted to me!"

We laughed and Edonide laughed also. Even Signorina Gentileschi laughed with gusto, so much so that Edonide picked up the courage to say, "You should have seen our Signorina when she was young! A young man waited for her for years and years, I, too, knew Mr..."

At this point her *padrona* motioned for her to stop, in such a commanding way that Edonide was speechless. Turning toward us, her cheeks a little flushed and her eyes like two slits of bright light, the Signorina said, "...in novels, aren't secret passions more interesting?"

Her sentence was left hanging in the air.

An unforgettable New Year's Eve. At midnight we turned on the radio. Fiorello La Guardia was talking to us from across the ocean: "Italians! Liberation is near!"

In the silence of the night at that summons, at those good wishes, our hearts trembled and lifted with hope. "Italians!" We felt bound together with all those who, like us, were in great expectation.

The night of December 31, the last of 1943, was also our last happy night at Castello.

Two or three days later, we discovered that the *Occhiaccia* had spied on us and had strung everything together. She knew all. It was imperative for us to escape immediately from Castello, but to where?

Strangely enough, this time I felt determined, ready. At once I worked out a plan and told my sister and Signorina about it. Even though at the moment we had no idea where to find refuge, it was important for us to notify Michele that same day, so that he could come and pick us up early the following morning, so that we could leave under cover of darkness.

Not even this first part of our plan was easy, but we did find a way. Michele would arrive at 5:00 A.M.

Night brings council. In "the room of the chairs," Lia and I exhaustively discussed the pros and cons of any possible decision. The best route was this: More than a month had passed since our flight, and the search for us had lessened, or taken other directions. We knew that the peasants of Poggio were satisfying the curiosity of the nosy: "The poor things! They've gone far away!"

We would ask Michele to take us to the last house where we had stayed before coming to Castello.

In fact, those good people told us as we left, "It's not safe for you here with us, being so close to Poggio, and our house is poor, but if need be you can always return."

We had eliminated the idea of joining our parents. Luckily, news of them was good, but our arrival might complicate things. They were weak and in more need of help than we. It was better that we not disturb their temporary and perhaps precarious shelter.

We felt more serene. Only a few hours remained before Michele's arrival, but after a short prayer, we fell asleep.

At four o'clock, as if we had an alarm in our heads, we awoke. We dressed hurriedly, collecting our belongings.

Edonide got up for our sake; in the kitchen she made barley coffee.

The Signorina also wanted to say good-bye. She approached us with such a pale face that we feared she was ill. Her voice was reedier but her speech as clear as ever, and her hands did not tremble as she laid them on our heads in a gesture that reminded us of our mother far away.

Finally, everything was downstairs on the ground floor under the stone arch: the suitcases, the bags, the two bicycles. We ran upstairs to hug the Signorina for the last time. She embraced us tightly against her heart.

It was one minute to five o'clock. Hidden behind a pillar we waited breathlessly. The dark silhouette of a silent cat crossed the big entrance hall; halfway, it turned its eyes upon us, flooding us with green light.

Michele was nowhere in sight. We were drowning in the anguish of waiting.

It was cold in the long, tunnel-like hall and darkness spilled over us like nausea. Chilled and shivering, we looked up through the arch and saw a sliver of sky turn from black to vivid grey.

How much time had passed? Dawn would soon be upon us. In the distance we could hear the barking of dogs and the raucous crowing of a cock.

Suddenly, a shuffling and mumbling; the beams of two flashlights crossed.

Our hearts stopped. Two shadows, two men. Flattened against the pillar, hiding, we saw them go toward the end of the hall; one lifted a manhole cover and inserted a tube. An unmistakable smell enveloped us. We breathed again! It was the sewer men this time, not the S.S.! They were laughing and joking in their local speech. At a certain point, something malfunctioned and after a few curses, they shut the lid and went out into the air, turning the corner.

Under the porch, the sky had become pearlescent when finally Michele arrived. We asked no questions. Just seeing him gave us relief, warmth, hope.

After the baggage had been loaded, we sped away.

Once the old gate of the tower was behind us, Michele asked where we were going. At our answer, he braked sharply in the midst of the countryside.

"Impossible!" he said. He looked so serious and perturbed that we didn't know what to make of it.

"Why, why Michele? What has happened?"

"Don't ask me, Signorina, because I can't tell you. I gave my word to say nothing to anybody."

Seeing our distress, he gave in.

"After all," he said, "it concerns your cousin!"

"Uccio?"

Yes, it was Uccio. Where he had been in the city, he had met some dirty bastards who spied on him! In short, he had to return with his mother after a few days to the house that we had planned to return to. That was the best that they could do.

"How can I take you there, too?" said Michele. "They are good people, but there's not enough room, as you know; you were there. You'd be crowded in together..."

This was the only good reason Michele gave for not taking us, but it was a good one. Of course there were many more; one above all. Granted, we could all "crowd in together," but how could we ask those risking their lives for two to risk them for four? Michele was right. That route was closed.

Meanwhile, dawn broke and such distress was etched on our faces that Michele said, "don't despair, signorine, we'll find a way. I have an idea. As you know, because of the air-raids, everyone left Colle, and my house is empty like all the rest. My family is in the country. I come and go because of my job, but most of the time I sleep in my house in town. The siren sounds almost every night, but I'm not afraid – what is to be will be. But I certainly don't want to put you at risk."

Good, kind Michele! He wasn't afraid for himself, but for us, and that was why he was so timid in offering us his house!

Air-raids? Even bombs seemed like confetti compared to the horror of the other risk.

"Michele," I said, "we'd be happy to go to your house if you'll take us!"

We felt relieved, almost merry, but immediately an obstacle presented itself. How dare we, in broad daylight, go into the town where everybody knew us?

"There's hardly anyone in Colle," Michele said.

But *that* was the trouble. Because the town was practically empty, the car and its passengers could not pass unobserved. It was imperative to arrive under cover of darkness, get out of the car in darkness and sneak into the house.

Against the sky, on the thin bare branches of the poplars, innumerable brown sparrows were dotted about like leaves. They flitted from branch to branch in the morning light.

You lucky birds! You can always find a tree, a root, for refuge!

At that moment, a shot was heard far off, and the sparrows flew away together, like leaves blown by the wind.

Then my sister, looking at the hill, saw a thicket of holm-oak and juniper and said, "Michele, leave us up there in those woods. It's too late now to go into town."

We were really living our "fairy-tale." For a moment I thought I had already heard the story told this way: "...then they hid in the woods and dropped lots of little stones to find their way back..."

Michele woke us from our fantasies.

"What about the evening? How can I leave you in the woods in the dark?" He was right. The sun would set...

"Leave it to me," Michele said, "I'll find a place." Without another word, he started the car.

Leaving the main road, he took a steep path. We kept quiet; we abandoned ourselves, putting all our trust in him, knowing it wasn't for us to think or make decisions.

After about 300 meters, we approached a haystack, a hut, and a small row of cypresses. Michele passed them, driving farther, braking in an opening bordered by three of four somewhat dilapidated houses grouped together.

Meanwhile, some barefoot children approached the car; an old woman watched us from a threshold.

Turning to us, Michele said in a low voice, "I know this isn't so great, it's a poor section, but a friend of mine lives here, someone I really trust."

As he got out of the car, I couldn't help saying, "Michele, even to your friend, please don't say our real names."

Michele smiled without answering "yes" or "no.

He disappeared through a doorway. Almost immediately he came out, accompanied by a robust man wearing a corduroy hunting jacket who stood motionless, making no move to greet us, while Michele opened the car door.

"Well," Michele said loudly, "I leave you in my friend's hands today. I'll come and pick you up early tomorrow morning."

We went inside.

Not knowing what Michele had told the family, we remained silent, being content to stay in the kitchen looking at the fire. In the evening, after supper, we wanted to creep into bed, to avoid endangering ourselves with conversation. But our hosts thought differently, asking some cautious questions. We answered them so vaguely and inconclusively that we were surprised that the good people didn't lose their patience and become suspicious.

On the contrary, making us talk amused them. They never interrupted us, so we gathered courage and made up an elaborate string of lies. They accepted everything we said as gospel.

Years later, after the war, Michele told us that "they knew everything." Certainly they had fun behind our backs, but without malice, out of that love of joking that all Tuscans share. Actually, their welcome had been warm; supper was very good, with salami, walnuts, and wine; the bed was comfortable and we abandoned ourselves to sleep, unaware that they knew of our innocent stories. But what was most important, Michele's friend was completely trustworthy.

It was still dark when Michele arrived the following morning. Rested and full of our first success, we chatted happily, looking forward to the rest of the adventure, while Michele was pensive and taciturn. We had the pleasant feeling that everything would go smoothly, like our car in that morning hour in the countryside. We didn't meet a soul before we got to the high section of Colle. However, crossing the deserted town, on the familiar street, I felt a knot in my stomach and a faintness of pulse that brought me back to reality.

"Michele," I said in a flash of inspiration, "I think we shouldn't stop the car in front of your house. Don't you usually drive into your garage?"

I recalled that the garage was in a small lane a short distance from his house.

"Yes," said Michele immediately understanding what I meant. "We'll back into the garage with no lights on. We'll unload everything there. Then, keeping watch that no one passes by, we'll walk very quietly, one at a time, into the entrance."

He was so wrapped up in his plan that he included himself with us sneaking like thieves into his own house. In fact, we two really were like thieves, stealing the poor man's peace and quiet. But there was no choice. Being so involved living that extraordinary adventure, we had no room for remorse!

Half an hour later we were sitting at the table. Michele, like a nurse, nourished us not with milk but with three or four jiggers of *Vin Santo* that he made us gulp, one after the other, with lots of cookies, to give us warmth and strength.

Not satisfied with taking care of our physical needs only, he was concerned for our spirit and turned on the radio that was on top of the china cabinet.

> In the grey skies I see Paris
> Through the smoke of a thousand chimneys

In the euphoria of having made it home safely, all three of us listened happily, imagining ourselves as *bohémiens* watching the grey sky through the window. But suddenly, as if coming to his senses, Michele jumped up and closed the shutters. To cheer us up, he said, "Up here, apart from a black cat, who can spy on us?"

After this light-hearted comment, he became serious, adding, "Listen, signorine, I am sorry, but you must try to keep everything shut and make no noise. You understand, of course. Usually there is no one in the house because I am out all day. I don't know, but people, especially the bad ones, see everything."

Attentive to all our needs, and to make us feel at home, he opened the cupboard where he kept the bread and other provisions; he showed us how to use the gas and light; gave us towels and soap. Meanwhile, Mimi kept singing:

> A rose blooms,
> One leaf after the other I inhale.

Michele was already at the door, but he came back saying, as he turned off the radio, "I'm sorry, but we must turn this off, too."

A moment later, he brightened, handing us the *Iliad, Orlando Furioso*, along with *Schiava o Regina, Tra Due Anime*, and *Il corsaro Nero*.

"These are my daughter's books, they'll help time pass more quickly. It's better for you not to read the newspapers now. See you tonight."

Unlucky are those who are alone with no one to wait for. In saying goodbye to Michele, we felt protected, connected by the thread of waiting.

There was his cap, wet with rain, left hanging on the hook, the smell of his cigar...

No, how could we feel alone? Michele would return at night.

Three of four days of this new life went by, and strange as it was, we were becoming accustomed to it.

Michele thought of everything.

One day he came back happy as a young boy because he'd thought of bringing us a can of tomato sauce, ready to pour on spaghetti.

But at times he appeared pensive and taciturn. One evening, the furrows on his brow seemed deeper, like scars. He was reluctant to look at us. Finally, with much effort, in his low voice, as if talking to himself instead of to us, he said, "This can't go on. This is no life."

"Why Michele? We are doing fine here."

"Poor little things," he answered, and those words, instead of the usual 'Signorine' were like a caress.

"Poor little things, you've had to give up everything, but even if you and I were content, there's always someone who would play a cruel trick on us."

A few years later, when his hair was grey but his eyes still young, he told us that a cruel trick had been played on him, but not what he had expected.

"They went and told my wife that while she was away, I brought women to my house – imagine, *women*."

That evening, he continued, saying, "we can't trust anyone. However, I'm waiting for an answer tonight. And if it's 'yes,' you can be sure that you will be well taken care of."

The answer arrived earlier than Michele or we had expected. The following morning a whistle from the street called him downstairs. Two minutes later, he ran upstairs, but not alone.

"I," said the new arrival, "I'm the one who will take you to Molino. I'm Michele and Pietro Mannozzi's friend. In my house you'll want for nothing."

My dear, dear Beppe!

How true was that promise!

In his house, not only did we "want for nothing," but we found a greater good: a love that even now, in sad moments, lives in our memory and still lights our path.

PART FIVE

"It's not that I don't want to stay," Michele said to the *capoccia* – the head of the house – who was insisting that he remain for supper. "My family is waiting for me." Yet still he stood there in his coat and fur hat, warming himself by the fireplace.

"With you here, Beppe has two new daughters," he added. "So, you can all be informal, since you are part of the family now."

As soon as he saw us sitting around the table with all the others, and after the *capoccia* invited me with a warm "scoop yourself some hot soup, Luisa," Michele's face literally glowed; rubbing his hands together, he finally walked away happily.

With Michele gone, it seemed as if no one had anything to say. Perhaps that sudden informal kind of invitation caused us all some embarrassment.

We kept eating in silence.

It was nice to be in the warmth of the kitchen, close together around the table. Somehow that silence was a happy one, feeling the coziness from the fireplace, the ceiling light swaying gently over the table, the dishes, the glasses, everything on it.

Upon entering the room when we arrived, I had noticed with surprise the carved stone door shining in the dark. I heard a kind of humming sound. The wheel in the basement was making the motor run.

Noticing that we were watching the light-bulb spellbound, the housewife said, "see? Here at Molino we have lots of water to waste and so we make our own electricity."

In the rustic atmosphere of the mill, surrounded by the same ancient fittings that had not changed for centuries, the racket of the turning wheel, and the small carbon lamp seemed almost pathetic, yet it restored a sense of miracles and brought us great happiness, as when one discovers something new. Perhaps the state of grace in our spirits was ready to be triggered at any vague sign, to interpret it as a foreboding of happiness, a wish for good luck.

We continued to eat in silence. Every once in a while, two shining black eyes, like swallows in flight, would lift, catch ours, then immediately lower. We talked that way for a long time, exchanging glances that gradually became less timid, freer, and livelier, seeming to imply, "yes, we'll be all right, all together."

Needles of light were penetrating the green shade, though it was still lowered. In her nightgown, and *barefoot*, my sister ran to raise it. She remained in front of the window for a moment, leaning far out, "Isa, come! Come! Come!" Her voice echoed clearly through the room, almost like a birdsong greeting the morning.

I could feel sleepiness, like a smooth ointment, soothing my half-closed eyelids; but there was impatience, surprise, and happiness in that calling. "Come! Come, Isa! Come and look."

For the first time, standing close to each other, we breathed the air around the Molino. There was a light, pure breeze, a fragrant caress of flowers and snow. The open window framed a miniature dream-like paradise.

In the shadow, in front of and below the mill, stood the dark moss-covered grotto, separated from it by three tall poplars. The water glistened in the sun, flowing around clear blue pebbles. The water was alive, even where it widened, mirror-like, colored with light and green shadows, its surface cut by narrow circles left by dragonflies and other water-skimming insects. It was broken by eddies made by wagtail fish as they darted between rocks and plunged in their beaks as if to drink. A small bridge connected the two sides, on one of which was a path that disappeared into the tall grass.

Suddenly, like a ray of color, a kingfisher darted across the sky. I was startled when I recognized the little blue-green fairy-tale bird.

"Water to waste."

"The mill canal is always full, you don't have to worry about the water. The small spigot is at the entrance and you can drink as much as you want. It is good water that comes down from the rocks ice cold, so refreshing and so clear that you can see through it to the very bottom of the bucket." Elvira said this politely, while providing us with a pitcher of water, big hemp towels, and a brazier. On the hot stove a coffeepot was brewing, giving off an aroma of roasted barley and anise.

In response to our appreciation for the morning goodies, she suddenly turned around, and said, with a touch of joy and pride in her voice, "in your home, in the city, you would have other comforts, but here, too, we have our little amenities."

Seeing how happy we were with the things she had brought us, she gave a big smile that illuminated her flushed face, saying "however, air like we have here at the mill is nowhere to be found in the city. It's cold. In the last few days it has snowed, but the sun makes you feel heavenly."

The house, near the cliffs, was almost completely immersed in the shade, while on the opposite side, in the morning coolness, the threshing-floor was open to the sun. Not far away, yellow haystacks outlined the blue sky.

We walked up there and sat down in the hay that was strewn on the ground, with our shoulders against the stacks, where part of the hay had been cut. Wearing a white kerchief on my head and with my sleeves rolled up to my elbows, I felt a freshness on my forehead, and a light warm caress on my bare arms.

A tall ladder leaned nearby. My eyes followed its rungs to the top and beyond to the blue sky, criss-crossed by doves. In that restful state of perfect stillness, I felt an extraordinary sense of levity, almost like one in flight. Spellbound, I looked at the hay all golden in the sun.

Only one year had passed. It was January again. We were in Poggio for three days; the setting sun became tinged with color, vermilion, like blood inside the eyelids. Beside me, on the hay, someone was tightly squeezing my hand in his.

I could still feel the warmth of his hand. I thought of that moment, I thought of him, yet I asked my sister, "Lia, will we find everyone at the end of the war?"

"Everyone?" she questioned. "We must hope so. We will find them in our hearts, at least," she added, sighing.

But I was afraid. A crown of beloved faces came before me. How could I dare, even secretly, ask for a particular one or show a preference?

My heart fluttered and stopped for a moment; it was like leaning out into an abyss, into emptiness... No, I don't want to, I cannot look. We are here, in the sun, under this blue sky, in the serene air, but in the meantime...in this same moment...

But even if all our beloved ones are safe, isn't it horrible that hundreds of others, thousands of innocent people like ours, for whom life is equally precious, should perish? And even if only one perished, how horrible it is.

"Isa," my sister said sweetly, "listen to me. This morning, when I leaned out the window, I felt reborn. Once again, I felt inside me a small seed of hope. We, too, are in danger, we are at risk even here. But we have to cultivate this small seed. It's like a blade of grass that must grow. If we rip it out, nothing has value, not even our safety. What does survival matter, if we don't survive with hope?

"Hundreds, thousands will die, and maybe we will be one of those, but, again, what does it matter? Some will remain, some who have more strength, more courage, more faith than others, perhaps some to whom a mission has been assigned. Who knows which one?"

"But no, Lia," I said, still prisoner of desperation. "Often it is chance that decides, chance with all its brutal blindness. At times the very best succumb."

"But that is not the case," she said. "Do you remember the Psalm?"

> Oh you righteous who dwell in the shelter
> of the Most High,
> I say of the Lord in whom I confide.
> He will deliver you from the snare of the fowler,
> And from the destructive pestilence.
> ...Under His wings shall you take refuge.
>
> You shall not be afraid of the terror by night,
> Nor of the arrow that flies by day;
> Nor of death that wanders around in darkness.
> ...A thousand may fall at your side,
> And ten thousand at your right hand;
> But it shall not come near you.
>
> Because you have said: oh, Lord, you are my refuge,
> He will give His angels charge over you,
> They shall bear you upon their hands,
> Lest you strike your foot against a stone.
> You shall tread upon the lion and the asp,

You shall trample on the young lion and serpent.
Because, the Lord says, he has set his love upon Me
I will deliver him.

"You see, Isa, this may be the meaning of the Psalm:
the righteous are those who believe most strongly; they
have faith, no matter what. For them, death is not the end;
one is not lost through this faith, they will be saved.

"But faith is not an act of will! It's a gift, a grace."

"Oh, yes, only let's pray that it may be granted to us.
Do you remember Mama, how serene she was at times?"

Once again I saw those beloved blue eyes, so full of
light, and I bent my head without trying to question myself
any longer.

In the days that followed, my sister appeared serene. But for me, happy moments alternated with moments in which I'd become anxious and fearful. These two states of mind opposed each other vividly, like black and white, shade and light.

The house, wrapped in verdure, was so solitary that it seemed as though we were a thousand miles away from the world.

Our hosts, confident that no one knew us, permitted us to go out, and reveled in our new liberty. There was no room for boredom; it was a continuous succession of discovery and encounters.

Beppe went back and forth between the house and the stalls. His son Tonino, a young man of fifteen, would comb his horse, then come in with a bundle of twigs and grass for the rabbits.

The daughters, who slept in our room in the bed beside ours, were in the fields all during the day. We could hear them calling to each other from a distance.

"Rosa-anna! Marti-ina! Lu-ci-ia!"

There were three of them: twelve, fourteen, and sixteen years old.

Often we would explore the surroundings of the Molino. We would cross the bridge over the water; the path beyond it led to a fork. One went up steeply, the other descended and disappeared in the grass.

I used to choose the small uphill path, even if it was narrow and stony; at every step the thorn bushes and other shrubs made the path difficult for us.

Sometimes Lia rebelled. "But, Isa, where are you taking me?" she would say while showing me a scratched knee or a bleeding finger pricked by a thorn, but I was anxious to climb higher and higher. I didn't look at what was around me, I just enjoyed breathing the pure air, feeling the accelerated beating of my heart. It was the joy of feeling still alive, free, like the birds flying in circles over our heads. I wanted to savour this sensation to the fullest, with an avidity almost as painful as that of a hungry person fearing that someone might suddenly snatch away his plate. Perhaps my sister did not understand me. At times she would smile and say, "I am a little tired, Isa! It seems to me that for today we have trotted far enough." It was not enough for me, but, to please her, I would turn back.

The house was quiet in those afternoon hours. On the newly-washed floor, the wet bricks dried slowly, the copper jugs shone in the twilight.

Everyone was out in the fields.

In our room Lia sat at the small table reading a book. From the slowness with which she turned the pages, I could tell that often her thoughts wandered far away. She was at peace with herself. At times I caught a smile on her slightly-opened lips, as if she spoke with someone secretly. She remained there for hours, until night came. Darkness filled our room, but she was not aware of it.

Without making any noise, I would go out alone. I could not stand staying in any longer; an overpowering anxiety urged me to go out.

I breathed in the fresh, strong odor of the grass. The house faded into the darkness; only a thread of smoke from the chimney rose into the dull blue sky.

The silence of the night was barely interrupted by voices calling from the distance.

"Hey, Rosanna!"

"Where are you, Martina?"

On the way to the grove, the birds alighted on the bare branches of the poplars and from there they flew to a cypress. Their chirping grew more and more intense, their wings flashed through the leaves, then stopped fluttering. Their song became more and more subdued, a feeble whisper, then was silenced.

Only the monotonous song of the horned owl could be heard from the distance.

One evening I continued wandering among the shadows, overhead the clouds ran, veiling and unveiling the slender crescent moon.

"Whoo...whoo...whoo..."

I felt anguish and fear, as if the horned owl was inviting me to brave the solitary countryside. An anxiety, almost a need to touch the unknown, pushed me forward, making me lose track of time.

Suddenly I heard a voice calling me from the distance:

"Isa! Isa! Where are you? Where are you?"

Meanwhile, Beppe met me with a lantern.

I was in my sister's arms. She embraced me, dragged me on, reproached me. "Isa...Isa!"

Upset as I was, I followed them, stumbling in the dark. At the entrance to the house, I didn't even realize that a stone was protruding from the wall. I hit my head, blood flowing over my temple. In the light of the kitchen, Beppe examined the small cut. "It's nothing," he said. Meanwhile, Elvira wet a napkin in cold water and put it on my forehead. The grandmother, the three girls, and their brother watched me silently.

I was embarrassed, I couldn't control my sobs until Beppe smiled at me, sat at the table and called to me. "Come on. Come and scoop it up, Luisa!" The steaming soup was dished out.

My sister and I, however, could not eat anything. During supper no one hinted at what had happened. With their delicate intuition, the peasants had understood.

After many years, they still remembered the episode:

"Remember the time when Luisa hit her head on the stone?"

That night we went to sleep early.

The three girls, side by side in their big bed near ours, fell asleep right away. A little later I heard my sister's light breathing.

Rain flowed softly down the window panes, washing them.

The room was almost completely dark. On the little table between the two beds, something glowed – it was from the small mother-of-pearl shells that framed some holy pictures. Little by little my eyes adjusted to the half light and rested on those small pictures that seemed to keep watch, like guardians of the house: the Madonna and Child, Saint Anthony, the Good Shepherd.

Perhaps in that pure faith lay the secret.

From one thought to another, in that drowsy state, I seemed to feel lighter, as if my doubts and anxieties had dissolved like snow, without exertion on my part, not so much by force of reason, but by a kind of intuition that seemed to touch the heart of things.

Suddenly, I felt an immense gratitude for all that had been given to us: a house, food, a bed. Marvelous, natural, simple things, which were neither natural nor simple to obtain in time of war. And love among those people was also marvelous. It grew more intense among the few left. It increased and multiplied, as it did between my sister and me, two shipwrecked souls alone on an island.

The rain continued to fall lightly on the window.

In the morning, while it was still dark, the three girls woke up one after another, in the order of their ages. As soon as the generator in the cellar began to turn, making the little light go on, Rosanna, the eldest, jumped out of bed and soon after she called her sister, the second oldest, in a low, rumbling, sleepy voice, a voice that faded with the morning light.

"Hey, Martina! Get up! You've got to get up."

Martina went on sleeping peacefully and soundly until her sister firmly shook her. Only after two or three attempts did she open her sleepy eyes fully, still adrift in an ocean of sleep. Once awake and up, Martina called the third sister threateningly:

"Hey, Lucia! Get up! You've got to get up."

And so it was every morning.

My sister and I pretended not to notice, and continued to sleep.

In the *casina*, – a small addition to the house that overlooked the threshing floor – were some refugees, a young mother with her four small children. Her husband, a bricklayer, came at night to sleep and left early in the morning.

The *casina* was a sort of shed, divided by a partition. The space inside was so restricted that mother and children always stayed outside.

Two of the young brothers and the young sister had light-colored hair and resembled each other. Only the youngest child, just a year old, had hair as dark as a black swallow. All the children, however, opened their mouths in hungry anticipation like swallows.

At noontime big pieces of bread dipped in red wine and a little sugar on top were laid out; the little swallows gobbled down the food. The youngest swallow, the dark one, lay asleep, all wrapped up in a military blanket, his eyes closed, his little rosy mouth slightly open. On his head his new "feathers," his first hair, very black, as delicate and smooth as strands of silk.

His mother wiped his forehead, slightly damp with sweat. His soft tiny arm jutted out of the blanket revealing dark skin. On this perfect skin there was one mosquito bite, standing out like a flower. I felt like caressing his little bare arm.

Not far away, his sister barely managed to stand up on her chubby legs. She tried to get to the dog, Vespa, in little leaps. The dog stood still, wagging her tail and waiting. The child was irresistibly drawn to the dog, yet she gave a screech every time she touched it, then dropped her piece of bread, which Vespa immediately snatched.

At this point my sister and I were also hungry, so we went into the house.

Under the stone vaulting, next to the door upon which the word "Molino" was written in green, was a small room from which warm air and a delicious fragrance arose. It was the room where the baking was done. Elvira, the housewife, who oversaw the baking, was almost hidden under the arch of the door. Hearing us approach, she emerged, somewhat awkwardly, as if she had been caught red-handed. She was eating a piece of *ciaccino*, a kind of Tuscan oiled seasoned bread. Right away, she took a paddle and removed another *ciaccino* from the hot oven and gave it to us, round, whole, crunchy, and golden. When Beppe passed by, he exclaimed, "no way! That's all she eats until supper time. That's just the way she is, and she works hard from morning to night."

"Gee, I don't count my work as anything," she answered gaily.

"Well, it just means that I found myself a wife who doesn't ask for much!" added Beppe smiling.

Elvira turned to us and asked, "would you young ladies like a couple of eggs? I'll go look in the henhouse." She addressed us formally; the familiar form of conversation still embarrassed her.

During the day, everyone ate anywhere – in the house or in the fields – but in the evening, everyone dined together in the kitchen. The place that we chose to eat that noon was at a little table by an open window that looked out on the grotto, the three poplars, and the footbridge.

Elvira handed us a black pan with a long handle and the eggs. "They're nice and fresh from this morning. You can fix them yourself," she said. She poked the embers, which sprouted sparks.

My sister set the table. She placed a couple of flowered plates, silverware, and glasses on the white tablecloth. In the middle of the table she put the *acquetta*, a weak, acidulous wine that peasants drink and that increases one's appetite. Meanwhile, I poured a drop of oil in the pan and broke open the eggs, two yellow and white sunflowers staring up at me. I sprinkled them with salt and pepper, and we dipped the good bread in the yolks while they were still hot.

Entering the darkened kitchen, we would spot Grandma Evelina always bustling about. Tiny and slim, she must have weighed next to nothing. A kerchief was tilted over her ear. Her face was like a withered apple and flushed from the glare of the fireplace. She moved soundlessly and agilely; her shadow, like an elf, seemed to flutter here and there in the fire.

"I'm a little old woman," she would say, nodding her head with a certain coquettishness, "and I'm left at home."

At times, however, she left the kitchen to take the goat out to graze. The two of them could be seen parading on the cliffs as if projected on a movie screen by a magic lantern. Two unmistakable figures: one white, jumpy, and horned, followed by the black one, slightly towering over the other, with her neck and stick stretched out, her skirt billowing in the wind.

She never got upset over keeping up with that bizarre animal which jumped from bank to bank, leaning over the very edge of the cliff.

"How come? Well, the goat likes it."

And the goat liked precisely those dry, thorny branches that would seem to pierce one's stomach. Spiteful and stubborn, worse than a mule, what a goat! Yet one could see that secretly the old woman sided with this crotchety temperament. It was her evasion, her element of folly, her "whim," to be exact.

"As long as my legs can carry me, getting out of the house is more than I could ask for."

Most of the time she was merry, but "once," she told us, sighing, "I would have remained shut in the house for all my life to take care of my poor baby who later died. One night I awakened and he was unable to move his little arms and legs; his little head was bent. I wanted so much to take him to the city to a good doctor, but the old uncle, the *capoccia*, yelled in my face, 'do you have the money to go to the doctor?' What could I do? I had very little money, very little! My neighbors told me, 'put some rue in his hand and a string of garlic around his neck,'

"But in less than a month he was dead. He was my first baby! Were he here now, I would take him in my arms, leave this house and find enough money to save him! But at the time I was young and shy.

"Then I gave birth to my Beppe. Still, I have never forgotten my first little baby."

Now that we were living together with the peasants, in the same house, we saw their ways close up, not only their joys, but also their toil, anxieties, and pain.

They still seemed fortunate to us, precisely because theirs was a real life.

Even the pain was never a torment, like a blight that dried up all the plants. If there remained a sigh, even a shadow from any pain, like Grandma Evelina's memory of her lost baby, it didn't shadow their faces forever.

They had work, religion, family, the entire country around. They were bound to that earth by tough, age-old roots.

The day was made to work, the night to sleep soundly and restfully. They awoke with the dawn. The daily routine of the chores followed that of the sun, the moon, and the seasons. Their habits were like immutable laws that accompanied them and sustained them.

On Mondays they washed clothes, Tuesdays they made bread, Fridays they went to the town market, Sundays to church. It seemed that such a life would have continued like this, from generation to generation, until the end of the world.

Even if the children were far off, serving in the army, one day they would return home.

The girls were certain of the future that awaited them. "When I marry..." they said, never doubting the eventuality of a different destiny.

Rosanna, the eldest daughter, waited for her fiancé, who was missing in action in Russia.

At times, she sang nostalgic songs of love, pouring out her feelings; at other times she withdrew in bitter silence and responded spitefully to her sisters, who always wanted to laugh and joke.

"She wasn't like this before," her mother Elvira said, comforting her with a sorrowful look.

Rosanna had tucked away in her trunk a dark piece of cloth that she had bought from a street vendor as a present for Piero. She showed it to us, caressing it delicately and poignantly.

"Beautiful material is heavy..." she sighed.

But once she said to us, "his mother wanted me to stay with her as if I was already married. But if he never returns?. I'm still young..."

The wound from which she still suffered would have healed.

There were only a few that didn't have a family or remained alone.

I knew two, two old men who had never married.

One was Elia, who worked in the vineyards, on the small sunny hill in front of our window. He was a tiny man, who almost disappeared beneath his straw hat, stained with verdigris that he used to spray on the grapevines. He wore it also during the winter with a dark blue smock that went down below his knees.

Elia is exactly like a woman," we were told. "You should see how clean he keeps his house. He knows how to do everything, he washes and mends his clothes and he makes his soup."

'He makes soup' was for the Tuscan peasants a sign of civility.

Some people from the south had moved in to a farm nearby.

"These people live like gypsies. In the evening they eat raw celery stalks with oil and bread with olives 'without even making a little soup.'"

Of Elia, people said, "he was always this way, even when he was young."

But it was difficult to imagine how he might have been, the young Elia, with his mosquito voice and almost completely bald head. With his work apron on, he had an almost spinsterish air about him, of an indefinable age. He was well-bred and well-spoken for the countryman that he was.

One time he said to me proudly that in the Sienese region "the true mother tongue" is spoken.

As a boy, he was, for some time, in a seminary, training to be a priest. Then, he, too, was needed in the fields. His seemingly weak arms performed the task well.

He kept his land like a garden. He didn't smoke, nor did he drink, even his own wine; he ate like a bird and had not a single vice. All his relatives had died and he, like an ancient sage, lived alone in a sort of limbo, "*his semblance was neither sad nor joyful.*"[10]

When he became so old that he could not farm his land any longer, he retired as a sort of honored guest at the nunnery, where he continued to care for trees and flowers, until death should come.

Undoubtedly Elia remained a bachelor by vocation, not through any choice of his own.

The other old man who remained alone was Beppe's uncle. He used to come to Molino once in a while. His name was Rigo, but he was called "Chickadee." When he was young, Grandmother Evelina told us that he amused himself by shooting at thrushes, quail, and hares. That was his passion. He was of marriageable age, but to get married meant to support a family.

The *capoccia* was a resolute man, who said to him, "either a wife or the shotgun, make up your mind!"

"Get me a hunting license," the young man answered, and thus he remained with his shotgun, but without a woman.

He now regretted having remained alone, even if the shotgun was always his "loyal companion," and it "cost less than a woman."

He knew how to imitate bird calls. By striking two coins together, "tee ti ti," he would call the robins. Even without a barometer, he knew everything about winds and weather changes.

He was old, but had not become lazy. He was slight but strong. He always wore a green corduroy hunting jacket, and he liked to stand in the kitchen doorway scrutinizing the sky, as if he were about to leave.

I remember him in the doorway, tall and straight, on a grey day. The rain was falling softly over the countryside. "It's coming down *comfortingly*, he said, half closing his eyes and raising his face as if to drink the rain, while the wrinkles on his face seemed to fade away.

The grey sky cleared, becoming turquoise; the raindrops on the bare branches glistened like silver and the earth gave forth a fresh scent. From the fluffy clouds, in tiny, silvery threads, the rain did come down quietly, silently, *comfortingly*, as he had expressed it so poetically.

Within this simple world, there seemed to be relief, comfort, consolation for every sorrow, for every pain. The sick were cared for in spotless rooms. If one of them was hospitalized in town, everyone else went to visit him.

"There were so many friends circling my bed that they formed a wreath," said an old man when he returned home from the hospital. It was not a hostile city hospital, where one is just another patient. When people fell ill here, they rarely went far away.

Once I heard of a poor little girl "who was taken to Genoa, never to return." In such cases, for them, it was as if the sea, or an abyss would swallow the sick forever. People avoided speaking of the little girl, except on rare occasions, whispering *povera Bianchina*, as if fearing to reawaken the evil spirits always hiding in ambush.

Even the incurable illness that could strike one down without remedy was here a little less horrible, a little less odious than in the city.

For the most part, the sick still lived with the family, not among the chronically ill in a hospice. Thus the loving atmosphere that develops in the bosom of the family warmed their weakened bodies. They sat by the fire in winter, or by the doorway in the sun. During the summer, in the heat of the day, they would sit under the shade of a tree.

Many years after the war, I went to visit Uncle Poldo, who was immobilized by paralysis. The poor old man was almost unrecognizable. Upon seeing me, a wan smile ventured forth from his thin face, revealing toothless gums. In order to hold my hand, he stretched out the only arm that he could still move. Meanwhile a young girl entered the room with a baby in her arms. It was Pino's child, as beautiful and florid as a round bud. The old man, reanimated, said "look at him, Signorina Isa! This is 'little Pino'."

The young mother laid the baby down near Uncle Poldo on the blanket. I looked and saw the baby's arm sprouting like a tender bud from the old man's arm, with its swollen, twisted veins like old roots.

Even Death had a familiar face. The dead slept in the little village cemetery outside the village up the hill.

On Sundays and other holidays, the families went to visit them.

"We are going to the *Cipressini* [cypress grove]" they would say. Meeting each other along the way, people paused to exchange news of the latest sad or happy events. On that hill one breathed an intimate air. The tombstones stood next to each other, with portraits of the dead when they were young.

People pulled out weeds and watered the little green meadow. Even on this cemetery soil, small carnations bloomed in the spring, and wild flowers in the autumn, the same flowers that bloomed in the garden near home.

But how many, how many others?

All those white crosses stretched out to infinity, crosses and crosses... How many did I see after the war, often without names to distinguish them!

And what about all those killed in concentration camps, even their ashes lost?...

At that time, my sister and I, too, were, or at least we felt that we were, fortunate. We were in an exceptional frame of mind, a little feeble, romantic, uprooted. The presence of danger probably sharpened our senses and allowed us to see things more clearly.

Once I remember descending the steep path that disappeared within the moist grass beyond the little bridge. I was alone. The sky was veiled with wispy clouds. As I walked, the path became more and more narrow. It was bordered by reeds that bent over a small brook. In order to keep from falling, I had to keep close to one side.

At one turn, the reeds thickened and the path completely disappeared. As in the beginning of musical impromptu, suddenly I felt a new mood. Farther out, the reeds began to thin, and beyond them I could see water sparkling in a luminescent green. On the other bank of the brook, to which I was unable to cross, fine soft grass and water lilies of a splendid yellow were growing.

Almost hidden in the grass were four stone walls with a small doorway. It had a slanting roof with old rusty tiles covered with patches of moss. For a long while I remained in my niche, holding my breath as I looked.

My whole being was becoming one with nature, as light as the shining dragonflies that flew hovering above the house. Through a light veil of mist, the old stones and the roof sloping into the grass were like a mirage.

Under the green roof, I though I might meet... What? Perhaps Happiness and Poetry.

I had been drawn so far forward toward the edge of the brook that I did not realize that I was sinking into the wet soil. When I got back home, my shoes were all muddy.

Halfway back, I had met an old man, also splattered with mud, carrying a bundle of rushes on his shoulders. "What a dump, my child," said he, "what a dump!"

"But for heaven's sake, where have you been?" my sister asked. "You look feverish, maybe you are running a fever. You are very hot."

That night, at dinner, I told about my adventure and my meeting with the old man.

"Worse than a dump! That grass, the canal, the little house," Beppe exclaimed. "It can't be true... Can you believe it? You were at the *ripresa* [dam]."

That's where the dam was at one time.

Beppe was amused at hearing my story, while mimicking the old man's comment, "What a dump, my child."

"I would love to stay at the dam forever!" I said.

Beppe looked at me, and even though he didn't understand me completely, he understood some of my intimate feelings.

"This means that you really like it, Luisa?" he asked with tenderness.

Our hosts were small proprietors, they did not have to answer to anyone. Therefore we did not fear that an overseer or a landlord would come to know of us, as had happened at Montecchio. One morning, however, after almost a month, something seemed different. My sister and I felt an atmosphere of uneasiness.

Someone had seen us taking our walks and talked about us. They were not bad people, but the danger was great. For our own good and for the good of the people who had welcomed us into their home, we had to be "more cautious," Beppe finally said. Telling us lifted a weight from his heart. But, he did not tell us how worried he was. He simply followed his conscience, the impulse of his heart, without measuring the depth of the possible consequences and the risk for his family.

"It seemed it would last only fifteen days!" Elvira sighed years later. But the war went on, and no one knew until when.

"We'll see," said Grandmother Evelina, while Rosanna burst into tears. Maybe her Piero, too, had been taken in by someone.

Many years later, we told about all this, and how Beppe felt relieved that his mother, the oldest in the household, and his daughter, the youngest, had agreed that we should remain with them.

"It had to be so," Elvira added. "We had become one loving family."

For awhile, as a precaution, we remained "closed up" in our little room.

Beppe, a peasant who had never studied, but had the soul of a poet, felt that those unforgettable days should be celebrated in song. Aside from its value as a document, I would never find anything so beautiful or so true.

After recalling past events, Beppe came to the core of our story, when my sister and I moved to Molino:

> ...through a close friend
> It was decided to take them
> Down to the molino
>
> A solitary place near the river
> They were closed in a small room
> From the window they could only see
> Birds flying to get a drink
>
> By a little table they sat
> Reading books they had brought
> Passing the days being closed in
> We could see they were restricted
>
> To let them breathe fresh air
> Through a path we let them go
> Even on the roof we stood on guard
> So that they could crawl to a thicket
>
> Luisa said what a nice place this is
> It's like being on the seashore

> No one sees us under the branches
> But we can see people go by...

> ...In the hot hours they loved
> Reading and studying in the little hut
> Which seemed a cavern and it was called
>   '*ripresa*'

Then he alternated idyllic and comic verses like those describing how and where "Luisa broke her umbrella," and later,

> Luisa always ahead wanted to go
> And Lia said now we must return
> Come on Luisa don't make me mad...

Beppe touched intense and pathetic moments when he wrote,

> Whenever I returned from Colle
> They asked for the newspaper right away
> And as they read about the tortures of the evil
>   ones
> We all had tears on our cheeks

> This is all truth and not invention
> I'm a small landowner, you do understand.

Peasants have a precise feeling of what is just and what is unjust. While they scrupulously respected tradition and moral laws, they sensed the wicked and arbitrary injustice of the fascist laws. Thus they had the will and pleasure of eluding them. It amused them to have us "crawl to a thicket." Besides, Beppe, being used to the countryside freedom, could not stand having us hidden and,

> passing the days being closed in
> ...could see...that we were restricted...

Whenever he was constricted at home on long rainy days, he couldn't take it. Sometimes he wove baskets. More often he mended shoes, replacing a heel or sewing up a sole again, because shoes in that place "didn't last long."

But Beppe suffered by being shut away.

He looked like a king when he worked in the field, in the open air, in the middle of a large space of green and open sky.

I would watch him from a distance. There he was, that little man who scattered seeds and helped them grow and produce fruits.

It was he who was acquainted with the eternal secrets of life, birth, and blooming.

Climbing the slope, with spade or hoe on his shoulder, with a smile on his face, his eyes bright, he looked happy.

Depending on the season, he used to show me the spikes of wheat, the olives that were almost invisible among the leaves, and the vines, which appeared dead, but, on the contrary, had been sprouting buds that only his keen eyes could detect. He pointed to cherries or plums as small as needle points and to the first small dark artichoke, still tightly closed and hidden among the thorny thistles of a beautiful blue-green color.

During our escapes, we felt somewhat like *la chèvre de Monsieur Seguin.*

Every breath of air, every blade of grass became more and more precious to us. Every moment was our own, we enjoyed it and savored it in full, as if snatched away from those who only wanted our end.

On an old blanket, with the sky above our heads and a beautiful green carpet at our feet, we were separated from the rest of the world by a light curtain made of leafy branches. We could just see the water, shining in the distance.

A breeze carried the scent of bitter almonds coming from a hedge of blooming hawthorn. A wild hazel tree, with its thin crooked trunk, was leaning out against the sky. On its branches glistened its silvery new leaves.

I had carried with me an old anthology, and turned its pages day after day. The poems seemed to absorb air and light; air and light assumed the colors invented by the poets.

We would return home after sunset, when the orange-colored moon was already rising and the evening smelled of mint and catnip. A thread of smoke arising from the chimney, appearing at a distance, in the twilight, made our hearts rejoice.

We would push open the door, and immediately see the light and hear the noise of the wheel generating it.

The peasants, like bees returning to the hive, would enter, one after the other, each carrying something, a bucket of water, a bunch of twigs...

The turning of the wheel and the coming on of the light seemed to quicken the pulse of the choral life that was renewed each night. Beppe would go back and forth between the kitchen and the stable. Tonino would take off his shoes and with a big knife scrape the mud from his soles. Grandma Evelina would poke the fire under the pot, Elvira would put dressing on the salad, and the children would set the table. Before supper, the rosary, then the steaming soup, and Beppe inviting me, "Come on, Luisa, scoop it up!" And at the end of the meal, the ritual words, "today, too, we have eaten."

After supper, everything was tidied, Elvira got busy threading the needle under the light, while the girls would come and sit down with us on one of the benches by the fireplace.

In front of us, Beppe would lay on the grey blanket, next to the blissfully snoring cat. We were five on the bench, one next to the other, close together. A little push, a nudge of the elbow, a small kick, or even the closeness itself was enough reason to joke or laugh.

Along with a gust of wind, fifteen-year-old Tonino would rush in cheerfully, his hair ruffled and his head almost disappearing under a huge bundle of dry branches.

"Shut! Shut the door!" the girls would yell at him.

But Tonino always greatly enjoyed teasing his sisters, and he would reply, "why are you yelling? If I were a girl like you, I would cherish the cold, because it makes the cheeks rosy."

He would leave the door open to upset them.

When the door was finally closed, the ashes were stirred and branches and thornbushes were put on the andirons. Immediately, flames would spread and flare up from branch to branch, flying lightly from one bush to the other, forming a handful of sparks, then lighting up into several small sharp tongues that crackled as if the fire also wanted to laugh and have fun.

Then, in the dark rear of the fireplace, a single big flame, inflated by the wind, would rise high, red, like a sail set on fire by the sun. For a second, a burning joy would flare up in me, like a lively drop of blood from such a different past.

Lucia, the youngest, would start a song and we would join in. The girls' eyes were radiant. Magic words, like "bride," "to get married," "we will get married," and "roses," were enough to make them happy.

After the song that told the story of Rosabella came the one about Ninetta. The girls had sung these songs hundreds of times, but they would always laugh joyfully, with their fresh, candid mischief.

Beppe would also participate frequently, with his *stornelli* or with some verses of his own. After having vigorously cleared his throat, he would start singing.

Other nights, the girls sewed or spun wool. On those nights, Beppe would spread the grey blanket on the bench by the fireplace and would invite Lia and me to join him. We would chit-chat in low voices.

Beppe would ask us to tell him of our experiences, our past dangers. He would listen intently. Then he would pull out a small black book, a notebook of his accounts. He would balance his accounts and would make remarks and comments, telling us the prices for calves, pigs, and eggs that were sold.

Strangely enough we became involved in all his trades. We were glad when a sheep sold well and we suffered when the cow had a bad delivery. Beppe's everyday problems became our problems too. This included all the animals on the farm, hens, pigeons, turkeys, and ducks. The black ducks, called *nane mute*, were a strong species, and we agreed with Beppe that they "were better than the rest."

The Nanninis never threw away anything.

They were like industrious bees, drawing profits and earnings from everything, not just from the produce they grew themselves. We would eat wild radicchio and asparagus, wild cherries, Chinese dates, and blackberries. We ate all sorts of mushrooms, from the most precious, like porcini, ovoli, and lardaioli, which sometimes were sold, to the more common ones, such as rosselle and spergi-famiglie. Then there were fish from the canal, frogs from the pond, snails from the fields, a badger from the woods, and once even an owl.

The wood served for warmth, the reeds for the trellis and cages, and the rushes had many uses. I remember we would braid it in the winter evenings to make baskets and hampers.

Everything came directly from the earth, like the woolen mattress and the huge sack stuffed with feathers, warm for winter; and another, filled with Indian corn shucks, cool for the summer. The sheets and tablecloths, of a large weave, were made of hemp or linen, which at first we watched budding in the field, then as it was gathered, spun, and woven.

The tools, such as scythes, hoes, and spades, lasted a long time, smoothed from frequent use. The metal became shinier, the wood became smooth as bone, and displayed the quiet splendor of antique ivory.

The black smoke from the chimney thickened on the cornmeal kettle.

The trellises on which fruit was dried were always pregnant with the fragrance of tomatoes, figs, and grapes. The terracotta pots held the aromas of broth, tomato paste, and honey. The oil crocks retained the scent of olives forever.

In the wooden table were the marks from knives, glasses, and all that served everyday living.

Things seemed destined to remain this way, to survive from generation to generation, as if they were the curators of the lives of those gone by.

Even the little that was bought seemed homemade. The green glass demijohn, the straw-covered flasks, jars, knives, and many other objects of common use, had a worn appearance, yet they were solid and genteel. Actually, they had never really looked new, since they were caressed for so long by the expert hands of the village artisan.

All things were kept religiously.

The enamel and earthenware pots that had served for years and become worn through were filled with soil for geraniums and basil.

The Nanninis were frugal, but not avaricious.

If an unexpected guest were to arrive, they would celebrate his coming and insist that he stay for lunch or dinner.

Elvira would set the table with a fresh white tablecloth. She would immediately take out a whole new loaf of bread from the kneading trough, and would say to her son, "hurry, go get a flask of wine from the cellar; mind you, a full one!" and to one of her girls, "go fetch the cheese and the prosciutto from the storage room." At the end of the meal, there were always bunches of raisins, nuts, or *Vin Santo*. And everything was offered from the heart and in great abundance.

Even for the family expenses, they would assess very carefully if something was worth or wasn't worth buying. If "it wasn't worth it," they would do without; if, however, "it was worth it," it was a splendid purchase.

When the girls from Molino were invited to some little party or dance, not only did they wear the natural ornament of their beautiful youth, but also an appropriate dress and matching shoes.

Tonino was bright and intelligent. Having finished only elementary school, Beppe decided to make him continue with school, and he gladly spent his money on books and notebooks for his son.

The Nanninis were open and sensitive to progress. Elvira was so proud of the new dentures that she had ordered from the dentist in town.

Grandma Evelina was too old for anything new, and even if "she couldn't gnaw," she had become accustomed to living on soup. She used to long for nuts. She would crack them, then grind them with a little pestle, making a mush with sugar and bread crumbs.

But Elvira was still young, and could still chew very proudly with a hearty laugh, and with her big new beautiful white teeth.

It comes to my mind, as contrast, Nunziata, who lived on a farm not too far away. She had a horselike face, was practically toothless, and had certain resolute mannerisms that made her seem like a man.

With a little black kerchief tied under her chin, and annoyed by a toothache, she once said to me, "I'm just waiting for all my teeth to go to pieces, but the pliers will never be allowed in my mouth!"

But all opinions are worthy of respect, and there was a good dose of stoicism on Nunziata's part, almost a kind of grandeur in not accepting any other possibility than that which was her "fate."

The Nanninis, however, would severely judge Nunziata's family by observing that they "let everything fall through."

Nunziata's son had run away from home on the 8th of September. He was nicknamed "Butcher-boy" because he used to tell everyone how much "butchering" he had done in the fields. But now that he had returned home, he never did anything, and would spend all day smoking an extinguished cigarette butt.

The Nanninis would even scorn *sor* Giacomo, a forty-year-old good-for-nothing, the only son of a proprietor in the neighborhood. On the other hand, his father, *sor* Pietro, was respected because he was cunning, and watched his belongings like a hawk. But *sor* Giacomo would spend the entire day behind his wife's skirts, or would sunbathe on the haystacks with his stomach in the air, getting as fat as a pig.

The Nanninis possessed many good qualities, good will, intelligence, initiative. They could understand people who would allow themselves a bit of luxury, or whims, as long as they knew how to maintain them. For example, Elia, who was single, had a peacock. Everyone knows that peacocks serve no purpose, and they are even "nasty."

Once, it assaulted Elia with its long nails. It had wounded only his head, because Elia had been quick to duck. Otherwise, the peacock would have taken out one of his eyes.

Even more than nasty, the peacock was "naughty."

Elia had the female, too, but the male "wouldn't lower himself" to the female, for he liked the younger hens instead. When he was courting, he would "do his little number" from morning till night, a powerful mating call that kept everyone wide awake. So Elia used to close him in a wire pen, even though it greatly displeased him, for when all closed up, the peacock wouldn't spread his colorful tail.

So Elia, as poor as he was, chose to endure expenses, toil, and injuries, all for the love of his useless Beauty.

Oh, the power of the "spread tail," with its fascinating oriental eye!

The Nanninis did not keep useless beasts. Every animal had to do its job, fulfill its work in order to receive food, just like any good person. Thus the donkey pulled the cart, the ox the plow, the cows gave milk, the sheep the cheese and wool, the pigs, rabbits, chickens, and pigeons their flesh.

The dog, or rather the bitch, Vespa, was the watchdog and was good for hunting.

The cat's job was to catch mice. As far as eating, he had to wait until he was given something. Woe to him if tried to steal! He had chosen the fireplace, the warmest spot in the house, as his room.

When he sauntered through the kitchen, one could recognize him by a patch of discolored fur, and by a singed patch on the side that he always turned toward the fire. He would rub himself against someone's legs, wheedling, continually, insistently, until that someone, exasperated, would turn on him with a husky voice, full of who-knows-what kind of threats, sounding like the thunder that precedes the storm.

"Stupid caaaat!!!"

Thus reprimanded, Vespa would try to become invisible, disappearing like an arrow through the opening of the door, only to reenter, sly and indifferent, after a minute or so.

But for the most part, curled up on the bench, he was ignored because he was completely camouflaged against the grey blanket.

Only when the pan of boiled meat sent its enticing aroma or the tempting fat roasted on the broiler did his eyes light up like two yellow moons, while his tail would flick in anticipation. Like a spring, he would jump from his blanket, alive again, reappearing in full form, ribs, paws, and claws.

The housewife was quick to defend the supper, but on one occasion the thief was quick enough to snatch a piece of meat.

That same evening he was paid for his actions by a solid whack with a ladle. At this, even Vespa's facial features changed. For a week his wide face was swollen and his yellow eyes were wide-open and astonished, as if he were still frightened. He was also chased from the blanket and had to stay on a low chair as punishment.

"How could you, Papa?" the tender-hearted youngest daughter dared to say almost reproachingly.

But the *capoccia* had resumed control and reinstated the laws of the house.

Every mouthful of food is the fruit of hard work and one cannot steal it or waste it. Everything had to bear fruit.

The *capoccia* was allowed to drink a raw egg in the morning, because he had to think for the whole family. Not the others, though, for the eggs were to be sold.

Drinking an entire egg would have been squandering. With two beaten eggs, mixed with some fat and some soft bread, Grandmother Evelina could scrape together supper for the whole family. When she made noodles with flour, she added water to the eggs. When the spread dough was ready, a gaudy yellow, it made us feel embarrassed.

On the subject of frugality, I remember one day when a fat little old man with short legs arrived, carrying on his bicycle all the tools of his trade: a hammer and pliers, nails, screwdrivers, and an acetylene torch. He was the welder, the knife grinder, the umbrella repairman.

He stayed at the Molino the whole day, making plans and thinking, and at night he was invited to stay for supper.

He ate slowly, like the farmers, cutting bread and cheese in small cubes with his little knife. Between one mouthful and another he calmly drank the light wine, and, without reason, started laughing to himself, with a childish grin on his round face.

He said that he had been around the world and knew French.

So Beppe responded, alluding to us, "they also know French," and the little old man pointed his finger with a suspicious frown. "Can you count to twenty?" he asked.

He prompted us, as one does with children, "*un, deux, trois, quatre...*"

Obediently we repeated, "*un, deux, trois, quatre...*"

He became very happy again and began to laugh without stopping, as if the whole thing amused him greatly.

He even told us that he had a small son who was just beginning "to peck."

"He is as fat as a cow," he said as he started to laugh again, "and he does not leave even one little crumb."

While he said this, he gathered the crusts and crumbs of the bread that were on the table, one at a time, and put them in his little mouth.

In his free time he sold truffles.

One time they met him in the forest with his dog.

"What are you doing?"

"I'm looking for the black ones," he had answered slyly, winking his little eye.

He wore a cassock the color of dried leaves, which was tied to his waist with a string. This, added to his round bald head with its small crown of hair, gave him the look of a monk.

His feet were covered by a couple of rags that perhaps at one time had been shoes.

As poor as he was, this was a merry little man.

Maybe there is some truth to the saying that a man without a shirt on his back could be happy.

Grandmother Evelina used to tell us, "in my day, one saw meat only at Christmas and Easter. One bought half a kilo of bacon from the butcher and the broth would come out nice and fat, all little stars."

But the old uncle, the *capoccia*, would say, "if one ate so well all the time, the farm would remain untilled. Any job requires a little hardship.

"Now, everything has changed," Grandmother said. "These children are used to having everything, cheese, salt pork, honey, nuts... They have all become spoiled little mouths. When I was young, and we used to take care of the sheep, we would leave in the morning before sunrise, with a piece of bran bread and a knife. For drinking there was water from the fountains. We sang the whole day like skylarks."

I said that the Nanninis were open to novelty, to progress, blessed by a spirit of initiative.

Aunt Argenta, in her youth, was lively, bold, almost a rebel in her time.

Now, she was over forty years old, but, back then, she had distinguished herself from the others girls by her intelligence and beauty.

Big and tall, with fluffy hair, she had strange eyes, the color of violets.

A born farmer, she could guide the ox cart better than any man.

Her head was always uncovered, without a kerchief. She liked to dress well, and on Fridays, at the market in town, she liked to pick out for herself a flowered skirt or a light blouse. They called her "the Parisian," and many young boys invited her to dance. More than one of them would have willingly married her.

But one day Argenta felt daring and said to her father that she was bored in the country. She wanted to go to Siena to be a nurse in the insane asylum.

"You seem to be from the insane asylum yourself," answered the *capoccia*.

But Argenta was stubborn and in the end she won.

She had been a nurse for twenty years and everyone said that she "satisfied all her whims in the city." She never lacked suitors, yet she ended up alone, and no one knew why.

She was as beautiful as always, her hair had become silver, like her name. She had a fresh face with vivid eyes. But at times those eyes seemed to veil themselves, like violets that wilt from sadness.

She came to Molino once. Her arrival was an event for the nieces and nephews, because she brought a gust of city air.

We, too, looked at her with interest, for we had already heard her tell her story.

Luckily for us, our encounters with the outside world were few. For more than two months, no one had come to disturb the peacefulness of our dinners. Beppe would lock the door after sunset, when everyone was in the house.

One evening, we heard knocking at the door. My sister and I immediately went to our room while Elvira quickly removed our bowls from the table. After a few minutes, they called us, as there was no danger.

They explained that there were two young men, who, like ourselves, had to be "on the watch" not to get caught by the Germans. They were partisans and wished to join their friends on the mountain. But that evening they would sleep in the stable. Instead of one night, they stayed there two or three more nights, hiding during the daytime as well.

We would watch the green door of the stable with curiosity, fantasizing.

Another time, a family of evacuees asked Beppe if they could settle down in the chapel. The chapel was by the roadside, not far from the house of Molino. They had brought their belongings with them. The Nanninis, however, didn't think that they were nice people.

"They aren't to be trusted," they said. In order to get out of the predicament, Beppe had a brilliant idea, saying, "what do you think, my sweet bride? At the chapel, strange noises are heard."

"I hadn't finished telling them my idea when they quickly gathered their belongings onto the cart," Beppe explained.

The Nanninis were generous.

A loaf of bread here, a bottle of oil there, a basket of fruit. Relatives and friends who lived in the town, where it was difficult to get certain things, would never leave the Nanninis home empty-handed.

Later on, during the more difficult days, more than one person would come and stay the night, sleeping on a mattress that was placed on the kitchen floor. For a long time, they put up an elderly aunt who didn't have any other family left. Aunt Rita was almost ninety years old and so hunched over from arthritis that she could no longer raise her head from her chest. She would look up at us from below, blinking her small eyes as if it were a strain for her even to lift them.

She lived in a room on the ground floor. During the daytime she disappeared to who knows where. At night she would reappear, stiff and small, from a little doorway dug out of a rock. She looked like a tiny wood-worm that goes in and out of its hole. She would come to take a bowl of soup and would not accept anything else, saying, "I'm not a glutton, you know."

Nor would she ever take a seat at the table. She would sit on a chair by the fireplace and eat in silence. Then she would get up and wash her bowl in the kitchen sink. Wishing everyone a good-night, she would disappear again through her little door.

I was once astonished to see her with a book in her hand, a third-grade reading book. "She always reads the same book," the girls would say, laughing. But, to me, it was very moving that this little wood-worm knew how to read and tended to this book with love and caring.

Speaking of books, one day, as I was skimming through the pages of an old anthology, I asked the brick-layer's elder son, who was about eleven years old, if he wanted to read some poetry or a story with me.

He was an appealing young boy, with light-colored hair and big, limpid eyes. He was less vivacious than his brothers. He had been sent to a priest seminary. Perhaps because he was so used to being cloistered there, he had developed a slow mode of doing things. He had a questioning, serious expression that contrasted with his slender body, which was meant for running and jumping.

At my question, at first he seemed bewildered, and looked at me without answering, but I realized he was listening to me when I asked him to sit down near me, and I started to read outloud. He knew how to be happy, as was natural for his age. He enjoyed repeating an old rhyme about the sparks in the fireplace:

> O little nuns so beautiful and bright
> Whose loveliness is swallowed by the black
>   night
> Flying above to see the stars alight?
> Sleep tight, little sparks, sleep tight.

Exhilarated at the words "sleep tight, little sparks, sleep tight," he repeated them with animation and enjoyment in his still infantile voice.

Watching him reminded me of another little boy, whose features resembled his a bit.

His name was David. He, too, was eleven years old, also with blond hair and a limpid, almost defenseless look. His eyes never laughed.

When I met him, he had recently lost his mother. He attended a small Hebrew school where I taught in January of 1942. The window of the classroom looked over a meager garden. There were few schoolboys. I would wait for each one behind the frozen windows. David was the youngest and weakest of the group. At the orphanage, he slept in a huge cold room, and there was little food. I'd see him arriving, dragging his swollen feet in huge felt slippers.

He was from Trieste, where his father still lived. He must have felt isolated from his classmates. They made fun of him, with that unfeeling cruelty of children. "You have chilblains," they would chant, mimicking his northern accent.

I noticed that he had been absent, so I went to visit him. He had a fever and was very pale. He was wearing the grey apron orphanage uniform, which was too large for him. Upon seeing me, he became as red as fire; he hardly spoke to me, as if we weren't friends any longer. I then regretted having gone there. But when he returned to school, he came toward me, smiling timidly.

He had trouble expressing himself. Speaking of his mother in a composition, he had written, "the death of this one has meant the ruin of our home."

I felt uneasy underlining "of this one," a literary expression, which perhaps he loved using for his dead mother.

One morning I was talking about the fjords of Norway, of those narrow, deep inlets where the sea becomes like crystal. I also read about them from a book. I was touched by the boy's luminous gaze. He seemed to be returning from a far-away place.

Another time, after reading together,

> What art thou doing, moon, in the sky?
> Tell me what – oh, silent moon,

He remained quiet for a few minutes, then said to me that those lines made him tremble. Those words came from a child's lips in response to the eternal voice of poetry. I never forgot them.

As for words never forgotten, I am reminded of a young girl named Barbara.

She was somewhat rough-mannered, but had vivacious, intelligent eyes. We were reading the *Canticle of the Creatures*." After the luminous encounters with brother sun, sister moon, the stars, and with "brother fire so beautiful, robust and strong," we finally met with the dark shadow of sister death, "from which no man could escape."

The child looked at me perplexed.

"I will also die one day," I explained to her, "as will we all." To which she answered, "I hope when the day comes that you die, I will love you less."

At Molino, the hours would fly by, one after the other. We wondered what would be waiting for us in the future. In the meantime, our hearts were brave, happy, and alive.

It was almost like the carefree attitude of those who lived in the mountains preparing to confront a snowstorm wearing only a woolen sweater.

Then we heard some news: Beppe promised us that we could go outside in the mornings before dawn.

Waking up early was always pleasing to me, especially in the countryside. But during those first few days of March, the carillon of the alarm, and the light of the little lamp were actually a prelude to a party, a party for us all.

We would sneak out of our shell while it was still dark outside. As Elvira would say to us, "come back before the sun comes up!" we each felt like Cinderella fleeing with the gift of those few enchanted hours.

The carriage of our dreams awaited us.

We crossed the bridge lightly, and a reflection of the light sparkled on the water. It was very quiet walking through the countryside. We heard only some whispers of a solitary bird in the dark bushes. The grey mist made us invisible, while at the same time hiding the scenery from us. We could hear the grumbling of the water, and the slight agitation of the poplar leaves.

We were the only ones invited to the reading of a secret book.

In that antelucan hour, things were not yet denuded of their vague costumes, of that unreal disguise in which at night they recite their comedies, farces, or dramas. Soon, those veils would disappear with the coming of the sun, when everything would return to its usual self.

The earth was waking up, the morning dewdrops wet our faces; our eyes were slowly opening to a second view.

Wild roses peeked through the hedges. Long shoots were flowering, and pollen was flying in the wind. A light blue butterfly seemed to be a piece of the sky.

The air cleared. Flitting and transparent leaves embroidered by silvery snails looked like bridal veils in the early rays of the sun. One enchanting view followed another.

Most of the time, my sister and I returned home together. But once, charmed by the morning song of a finch, I continued to go up the path alone. I went further and further up until I found myself on top of the hill.

I noticed a change in the air. As if I were in flight, I saw white shining clouds coming toward me. It took my breath away. What a miracle! Blossoming cherries, shading into the distance like a milky soft light.

Ecstatic, I stayed there, admiring. The sky cleared and, for the first time, I had forgotten that the hour to return had come.

Waking up early had become a habit. Because of this, we had the opportunity to watch another miracle, "the birth" of bread, a mysterious secret of blooming and maturation.

In the silent kitchen, the hanging lamp gave off a faint light. In the middle of the kneading trough, the flour, with the yeast, created a large foaming river about to break its embankment. The river-like flow kept swallowing up more and more flour until it finally became one compact mass, which was then divided into equal parts. The oval loaves, pale in color, much like human flesh, seemed like enormous soft seeds gently placed on a wooden board and covered with a white woolen cloth. They were kept in the warmth of the fireplace under a thick woolen blanket for many hours.

During the rising, when the dough began to break open, the pulp became softer and more swollen, and the edges began to expand. Then the loaves would touch and sometimes stick together. This was called "kissing bread."

From the long board, the loaves were shaken off onto the hot stone of the fireplace.

Elvira's face was red, and her eyes shone. We waited impatiently for the miracle. The loaves came out of the oven warm, golden-brown, like ripe fruit, and the smell was glorious.

This ritual was repeated every Tuesday. It was an appointment we joyfully waited for every time. I would always feel anxious while waiting for the miracle taking place under the blanket, the *levitation*. We had to be alert in order to capture that moment.

I saw this process as a mysterious analogy of our youth. Was it not like the desire for love hidden within my sister and myself? A levitation of life...or was it too late, and that magical instant had already passed?

With the sudden exaltation that took hold of us in the early mornings during our antelucan walks, I expected a magic, unique moment. A small flower suddenly did bloom for us, before our lives were leavened, before our seeds would be wasted.

One evening, at Castello, Lia confided to me one of her secrets. After so many years, she had invented a fable, just as she had done when she was a child. But I never believed that we could invent a fable together. Yet it was so; we invented a fable.

It was always my sister who started the story, first revealing the title, "The Story of the Snail-Godparents and the Spider-Weavers."

As soon as that was said, as a wheel starts to turn, I heard a teeming of ideas, a swarm of luminous butterflies that would light up. During her telling of the story, I would interrupt with my ideas. She would then add something, and so on. As if a series of multicolored umbrellas opened, and we could hang on them, parachuting, we let our ideas flow liberally, while travelling lightly and daringly in the world of fables.

Thus our stories were born, such as:

The Story of Rica and Rock
The Story of the Red-Bowed Princess of
the Blooming Peaches
The Story of the Midget Pillo Who Made and Sold
Soap Bubbles.

During the evenings by the fireplace, when Beppe pulled out his black accounting pad, we were very excited. We dreamt of owning a brooding hen, chicks, and a sheep, just for us. But one day, the idea of bees came up. Bees didn't need anything except a hive nearby the water, in the middle of a flower field. Bees were the perfect investment for us, considering our poetic and commercial dreams. The Virgilian memories and more recent reading of Maeterlinck's *The Life of the Bees* buzzed in our minds. We invested part of our capital in buying two hives. They were set on the knoll where we spent most of our day.

Beppe was a subscriber to *The Tuscan Beekeeper* and we read with the enthusiasm of neophytes the "Letters" column, in which questions were asked and answered. We would learn magnificent secrets about the life of the perfect bee community, their gathering of nectar and pollen, about the mysterious presence of the queen bee, the nuptial flight, and the breeding of the young.

Really extraordinary stories, more fantastic even than our fables. Little by little the boundaries of reality and dreams became confused. Did reality resemble dreams or did dreams become reality?

Springtime had come. We could stay outdoors for longer hours.

The bees came and went with their sweet continuous buzzing, holding their loads of pollen in their basket between their limbs.

One after another, they would go in, lowering their heavy loads until they penetrated the narrow doorway with their green, yellow, and red grains...an enormous gathering.

We followed the ritual carefully, as it became faster as sunset approached. By the entry, the "guards," with their wings rotating non-stop, like minuscule propellers, aired the area.

A wonderful scent of honey spread out into the air of the quiet evening. It was then that we began to tell another fable, our fable. It began like this: "This is a true fable, as true as Zippo and Mussi. It was truly last year that a frightful ogre wanted to snatch them away."

Our meeting with the farmers and the land had been providential. It even seemed to be a more pleasant way to grow older. We continued to fantasize, repeating Gozzano's lines with great delight:

> No gloomy thoughts!
> Should love not come, who cares?
> The good smell of the woods reaches the heart.

It was the beginning of April, when the earth seemed to be on hold. The miracle of creation seemed to renew itself.

Celestial days!

In Molino, down where the water flowed clear, the sheep were washed before being sheared of their white wool.

The lambs and the tender kids had already been born. Eggs were hatching, and the mother hens had their small broods of fluffy yellow chicks.

Bees flew and flew in the luminous sky, making their wings iridescent.

Our state of mind was buoyant, fresh, in tune with the colors and the atmosphere.

On just one of those days, I came across a book, Pinsker's *Autoemancipation*. I had brought it with me, but I had always been reluctant to read it.

Now, after reading the first few lines I devoured it with the voracity of a famished, thirsty person. In its pages I felt the flowing of vital fluid, like a bitter river that slowly mingled with my own blood.

How many times one looks without seeing, one listens or reads without understanding! But the word *"autoeman-*

cipation" was written in letters of fire; I couldn't ignore it any longer.

That book talked to me with an austere and forthright voice. In its infinite misery, it laid bare our condition as slaves.

For the Jew, wandering from one country to another, there would always be the rude awakening, even when human and civil rights had been granted. He would become aware of his condemnation, of his being unlike the others, different from the others. More unfortunate, more unhappy than a foreigner, who still has a distant homeland, the Jew was without a country, the eternal foreigner and the excluded one.

As I read I noticed that the bitter truth was not strange to me, did not come from outside but was a spark I had always secretly tried to cover up, to smother, because of the unconscious fear that it might spread into a fire and burn me up inside.

As if a bandage had dropped from my eyes, in another light I saw what had been the reason for my life so far, my greatest passion. History, language, Italian literature didn't belong to me, but to others.

We expected a new era in which any petty nationalism would disappear and then be transformed into a universal brotherhood. I felt that something had shattered forever.

Even if the end of the war was to be as everyone hoped, how could we repair the broken threads of our lives?

During all that time we caught a glimpse of the magic word "*Liberty*" only from a distance, like a flag in a mirage. Was it now drooping, losing its colors?

We were living in a parenthesis, we had been granted a vigil. We had fallen in love with that world and were even under the illusion that we could share the simple life of the peasants forever. But we were *without roots.* That land, that world, that life were not our land, our world, our life.

A frightful void opened wide before me.

I was afraid to question myself more deeply. I felt like a prisoner again, within a labyrinth of contrasting thoughts and feelings. Perhaps that book would offer me Ariana's thread to find my way out, but I also felt that by following it I would land in a dreadful desert.

Now that everything was going to be given back to us, were we to give up everything? Start all over again, leave for exile, voluntary exile, but no less painful...?

To abandon our country, the country where we were born, and our maternal language for the Babel language, and for different habits? That country called Palestine, about which we had heard. Would that become our country?

Those who had fled there came from countries where the ferocious anti-Semitism caused them to hate their country of origin and perhaps incited their love for a new country. But we had no hatred; all our loving ties drew us closer to the country that gave us birth.

What would we do there? Without our language, with our poor useless culture, with our weak strengths?

An answer came suddenly to my lips: *strength springs from love.*

Love was what I did not have.

We were the desperate daughters of diaspora. By force of reasoning I had reached a finish-line, but not out of love. Pinsker's passion, acting on me as a catalyst, had ignited a reaction.

I understood that the divine face of liberty could not be contemplated as a gift; but it was a conquest, a price to pay with blood and tears.

This is what "*autoemancipation*" meant.

This truth appeared to me naked and simple, and yet it disturbed my inner being.

After such a disquieting revelation, for a few days I felt very tired, as if I were not well.

I tried not to think, yet for the first time since I was in Molino I spent some restless nights. But little by little my tiredness disappeared.

Once again my mind was clear. I was anticipating something, within a tense atmosphere, like a child playing hide and seek, as when one feels a living presence behind a wall, a tree, or a hedge, even though nothing can be seen. So it was, in that excitement of mine, I knew that soon I would find what I was looking for.

One night I couldn't fall asleep; time seemed to rush by at a swift pace and I felt totally relaxed as if I had rested, until, to my great surprise, I had a glimpse of the light of dawn. I couldn't remember what my thoughts were during the night, but I did recall that I had not even said one prayer. Then I began reciting "*Scemàn*," as I had never done before, or I had forgotten to for quite a while, translating mentally each verse from Hebrew into Italian.

Scemàn Israèl Adonài Eloénu Adonài Ebàd...
Listen oh Israel, Eternal, our God, the Eternal is
one.

As I translated, the words sounded new, as if I had never heard them before, or as if someone were prompting their true meanings to me. They merged with my desire, my vow, with the prayer and beat of my heart.

> ...And thou shalt love God your Lord with all your heart, with all your soul, with all your strength...

I listened with different ears:

> ...And if thou shall obey diligently my commandments that I give you today, loving your Eternal God and serving Him with all your heart and with all your soul, I shall give rain to your land at the right time, rain in the fall and rain in the spring, and you shall gather your wheat, your must, and your oil and I shall give grass to your fields for your cattle and you shall eat and be satisfied...

I felt a wave of love enlarging into an infinite circle.

My poor Jewish brothers and sisters, whom I had not loved, who seemed to be sadly enclosed within a sterile bookish doctrine, were the descendants of the ghetto prisoners who had not seen the sun for centuries, closed inside the walls of the most dismal and unwholesome districts of the city.

Yet those wretched ones had not forgotten that they were the children of their land. They had so much faith and imagination to be able still to speak of the wonderful succession of the seasons, of autumn rain and of spring rain, of wheat and must, of oil and grass...

In their homeland, on their soil, they had been shepherds, peasants, and they still expressed themselves in that airy celestial language.

After that night, as if my eyes regained sight, I read the papers of the prayer book that Mother had given me.

Passover...the Exodus from Egypt, the country of their slavery.

History had repeated itself. Once again we were the lost Jews who lived waiting, entrusted to the grace of God.

"*Le sciana abba Ieruscialaim* – next year in Jerusalem."

During those sad centuries, in exile, the Jews had repeated that wish ad infinitum.

This was what the Holy Scriptures promised:

> Even if your Exiled were at the extremities of
> the Heavens, your Eternal God will lead you to
> the country that belonged to your fathers and
> that will belong to you.

Now the miracle was on the verge of being fulfilled. Next year to Jerusalem... For someone it was true, it would have been true.

The nostalgic song of *Tikva – Hope*:

> Our faith is not lost yet,
> O hope of a thousand years,

To return to the land of our fathers,
In the city where David was.

From one century to another, from generation to generation, in their fervent dialogue with God, the People cried
out:

Eternal God, gather all of us together,
From the four corners of the earth
As quickly as possible, in our day.
Return and live in your city.

"To return"... The secret of love unveiled itself. For
the Jews, that land, although unknown, was always the land
of their forefathers.

Was I beginning to feel that call, that love for a distant
land, for my people, for that language of which I knew only
a few words?

With new excitement, like a child who begins to read
in syllables, I started to pronounce some words:

scemesc, the sun
levrana, the moon
or, the light
laila, the night
sciamaim, the sky

I discovered that they were beautiful, as beautiful as
the words of my native tongue; they too expressed the
mystery, the infinity of Creation.

Waiting for Passover, we prepared ourselves with
sweet thoughts, nostalgic family memories, tender memories of childhood.

Supper at sunset, the brilliant setting of the table at our grandparents' house.

The youngest member present repeats in a sweet sing-song voice, with innocent wonder:

"What is there different tonight from the other nights?"
And the oldest answers:

> Moses said to the people: remember the day of your Exodus from Egypt, from slavery, because the Eternal took you from there with his power-ful hand. Do not eat leavened bread, You come out today, in the month of spring. On that day you will explain to your son...

We, too, wanted to bake unleavened bread, our *azzime*. Elvira went along with our wish.

Besides the *azzime*, we also made those small sweet *ciambelle*, tasty and golden, which Mother used to call "*egg roschette*" [spongecake].

Those were the best *azzime* of our lives.

Prepared on the spur of the moment, they had the fragrance of the good taste of toasted wheat. And the *ciambelle* smelled so good that we wanted to send some to our dear ones.

As if our thoughts had met, a peasant arrived with a letter from them.

"*Dear daughters*" Mother wrote, and she had crowded three pages with her minute but clear and slightly slanted handwriting.

She sent us a small embroidered tablecloth as a gift and ended her letter with Passover good wishes and bless-ings.

In seeing the familiar handwriting and her signature *"your very affectionate mother, Margherita,"* we felt her close to us more than ever.

Papa, too, had added a few lines.

We were happy to reciprocate by sending them a jar of honey, two *azzime* and a small basket of *ciambelle*.

Another little basket was prepared for Uccio. We had had no news about him, although he was nearby. The basket contained this message:

> To our "prisoner" cousin, Greetings and best
> wishes for the ancient Passover!

At sunset we were sitting at our small table. Lia lit the candles. In that golden glow, our unleavened bread shone on the embroidered table cloth.

We stood up for the blessing.

> Blessed are thou, oh Lord, our God,
> King of the World,
> Who ordered us to eat unleavened bread.

This was our first true Passover.

No answer from Uccio.

Elvira, who had brought the small basket, did not get to talk to him. She had asked him what message he wanted to send to his cousins. But they sent her off, saying only "he's lying down."

So there was a wall of silence between us.

"He's lying down." It could mean laziness, a gloomy mood, but also, I thought with relief, a surrender to daydreaming and the world of dreams.

I imagined him stretched out, with his eyes half closed in a grey-green drowsiness. Maybe, behind those pupils, in which the walls reflected without him seeing them, the four walls of the room where he lived as a prisoner, passed other images – images of life, of freedom.

I wanted so much to see him again. Suddenly, I decided to go to him. Beppe gave his permission, providing it was evening, and dark outside. Tonino, his son, would escort me. Through the paths and the shortcuts, our brief trip was completed without any problems. An adventure like this, in that starry night, had excited me a little; I felt serene and happy going to see my cousin after we had been so far apart for more than six months.

Yet when the house was in view, my heartbeat suddenly quickened.

The peasants had been warned and the housewife did not show any surprise at seeing me and the boy who was with me. However, after she motioned us into the house, she closed the door with a certain amount of suspicion. Tonino took leave and I stayed seated on a small bench waiting to see Uccio.

I had expected to meet him immediately, to find him waiting for me, to hug him.

The peasants, maybe to be tactful, had left the room and I was left there alone on that small bench, with a sense of anxiety, a vague uneasiness, like when you make yourself at home before being introduced to a stranger in whose presence you feel shy or intimidated.

Intimidated, shy!?

But I was waiting for Uccio! Why was he late? A door opened and I rushed into my cousin's arms.

"Uccio, Uccio!" I could not say anything else as I embraced him.

I felt that it was he, but I could not see his face while I was hugging him. I was struck, instead, by the sound of the voice, which did not seem to be his.

"Isa," he said, "why did you come? It's dangerous for you and for me, too. Where is your common sense?"

Was this Uccio who was talking like this? I pulled away from him.

His face was pale, like someone who has not been in the sun for a long time. His eyes were sunken, his hair had grown long behind his ears, and his cheeks were unshaven.

He seemed older, yet at the same time to have receded to the ungrateful years of adolescence.

I remembered him as I had seen him once, after he had been sick, suddenly grown so different, with something unpleasant, discordant, with his legs that were too long, his skinny arms, his pale face, part of which was dark from his first beard.

Meanwhile the peasants had come back into the kitchen. I felt relieved by their presence. Aunt Freda did not come out at all; Uccio said that she had a headache. We exchanged news. My sister, my parents... But after two or three strained sentences, it seemed that there was nothing else to say.

The *capoccia* proposed that we play a little bingo. I heard the numbers being called out and dazedly marked them on the game card. It was like part of a strange dream or a nightmare.

After bingo, Uccio started another "game," weaving a string between his hands and persisting childishly to undo the knots. But he was so serious, so gloomy, as if it were a matter of life or death, as if he had made a bet and his destiny depended upon the outcome of the game.

When he became exhausted, he gave up and threw away the string, and I felt an absurd pity.

While going to bed, I said goodbye to him; the next morning I would be leaving before dawn.

I slept badly that night.

To my astonishment, the next morning, while it was still dark, Uccio appeared before me like a spirit in the silent kitchen.

"I wanted to see you again, Isa," he said, with a special, strange seriousness in his voice.

"Uccio," I answered, "Uccio...what happened to you?"

"Nothing, Isa, *nothing ever happens to me.*"

I trembled. I heard behind those words a deep darkness that frightened me.

I said to him again, "maybe you're too lonely. Can't you even draw or paint here?"

"I tried," he answered, "but it's useless. Not even that Signora, the 'Muse,' has deigned to keep me company anymore... I am really *alone* now. *Addio*, Zippo."

When he called me that, I felt an echo of the affection from long ago, and I saw in his eyes a glimpse of the old light.

After I closed the kitchen door behind me, I set out for the hidden path in the high grass. The sun was already starting to rise, so I had to hurry. The road was downhill, and I started to run, and I felt my blood flow.

Days became longer and we spent more time outside on the bee knoll. The wild cherry tree was dressed in new leaves; the canal water was tinted with green reflections. The sun was warmer.

Drowsy from the long time spent outside, we would retire to our little room, and close the shutters in order to dim the light. The total afternoon silence invited us inside to rest. One time, we suddenly heard splashes, laughter, and guttural voices. We peeked through the narrow opening of the shutters: *the Germans!*

There were five of them. They were standing on the rock almost naked, laughing and egging each other on to plunge into the water.

Without their stiff military uniforms, unarmed, their skin rosy-white like skinned rabbits, they seemed harmless, but to see them actually there, alive, a few feet away from us, made us shiver.

What if they had come into the house! Luckily, as soon as they had bathed, they left.

The next day they were there again. Closed in our room, we felt disgusted at the thought that they were making the water of the Molino filthy. We stopped peeking: we knew they were there. We held our breath, eagerly awaiting the end of their splashes, and their laughing voices.

On the third day two of them came inside. Elvira rushed to advise us not to leave the room: "They are in the kitchen," she said. "They want to eat."

With our hearts in our throats, we huddled together under the bed, waiting.

Finally, they left and Elvira came up to free us.

It became dangerous even to stay inside. All day we would hide in the bushes. We squatted on the dirt step; our arms and legs felt numb, our bones aching, our throats parched.

The countryside appeared sadder as we stared at it for long hours as if it were a picture where only the light changed from dawn to sunset. The wheat stalks were turning yellow and dying.

To all these real fears others were added: we were told of incidents of violence and arrogance.

How were our parents coping with the difficulties all alone?

Fear became blacker and blacker for us: we, who could not group with others. That solitary private danger, within all of the other dangers, seemed to us unbearable.

Meanwhile, everybody tried to hide their belongings. The majority hid them in hollow walls, behind a wardrobe, in hiding places more and more secretive. It was known, however, that the Germans, and not only they, had learned to tap their knuckles on the walls to feel if they were hollow.

A story was going around that in a neighboring villa, they took away a leather bag crammed with jewels. How could people keep jewels in a bag!

The peasants, instead, would save their small quantity of gold in a sock or perhaps an old shoe. Peasants' houses were always crowded with dirty old shoes while the shoes of the Germans were good and made of strong hide.

How clever, the idea of the sock! Perhaps we, too... But then we decided to save a few brooches, two rings and a chain inside a cold-cream jar buried at the foot of our wild cherry tree. In doing this, the fable-like atmosphere somewhat lifted our spirits. Would it end as it did with Pinocchio and his golden coins hidden in the miracle fields?

A theft occurred at the Molino also. A German soldier simply walked into the house where we were staying and took two or three round forms of pecorino cheese from the pantry.

"He cleaned me out," Beppe screamed furiously. "He cleaned me out!"

Elvira and the children tried to calm him. They tugged at his sleeves, keeping him from leaving the kitchen.

Beppe was not stingy. He was anything but stingy. Whoever was in need would go to him and he would give away even what he had worked hard for. But he couldn't take being robbed. This made his blood boil, so that he didn't even think of the danger of confronting the German soldier.

Tranquility was lost.

What if we had to run away from here, too!? And if the Germans... And if...?

Books we had read about invasions came to mind.

The peasant girls were afraid. No one got undressed for bed at night.

Whenever a plane formation approached, we could hear everybody shouting, "the planes, the planes!!!" And they would run and throw themselves on the ground, over-come with panic. The hissing and the crash were heard...

But my sister and I were not afraid of the bombings. We were afraid of other dangers.

All of us stayed indoors longer. When someone went out the rest would worry. Elvira didn't want her girls to go into town, but she herself would bike there, if necessary.

Isa and I were inseparable now. Whatever happened we wanted to be together. But we worried about our parents; would we ever see them again?

We heard about atrocities *later*, such as of someone whom the Germans had pushed in a truck while a close rel-ative was pushed in another or left dead on the ground. Brother separated from brother, mother from son... We were told of a poor woman in Siena, old and stooped, who was kicked as she tried to get near a truck that was taking away all her loved ones.

"They've blown up the bridges... The Germans are retreating!"

Michele came to see us; his eyes were bright with joy, his large face beamed. He said: "Be happy, signorine, the suffering is practically over. You, too, can come out now. The Germans have other things to think about."

The towns nearby had been "freed"; it was just a question of days, perhaps of hours.

A breath of new life!

"In this hollow you are safe. Besides, the grotto in this boulder makes a built-in shelter."

Thus all the peasants from the neighborhood suddenly came to the Molino. Many of them were complete strangers, others barely acquaintances.

To our surprise, we noticed that our presence was known to them. God only knows how they "knew."

Everyone smiled at us, willingly exchanged a few words with us, even though times were still hard. There was a lively atmosphere of expectancy, almost a festive air, a need to help each other.

Elvira was always busy.

The house seemed like a camp ground: mattresses and blankets were strewn all about. More than twenty people slept there.

The Molino had become like a little town. The peasants even brought their animals.

To the right of the house the stable was completely filled; two cows were kept under a shed. Some peasants milked in the open. A donkey was tied to the trunk of a walnut tree, grazing on the small patch of grass.

To the left of the house stood the boulder that formed a sort of natural stone grotto, where the two-wheeled cart and tools were usually kept. Now it served as shelter for the night as did the cellar.

In the center stood the house, like a warm heart, where everybody came and went for food and solace. The open space in front of the house was like a stage where all the actors performed close up. My sister and I were among the actors, happy to be able to mingle with the others at last.

War was a serious thing, the danger had not ended. The *front line* was yet to pass. However, the mood had changed: no longer did the people talk about the raids, the dead, the horrible cruelties and robberies. Instead, they talked about the imminent arrival of the Allies, the end of fear, the abundance that was to return to their homes.

Human beings forget their troubles quickly, or at least they delude themselves, opening their souls to hope like sails spread out against the wind.

Hours went by as we lived all together. We received fresh news: maybe tonight the Allies would arrive!

One, two, three nights went by.

Some remained in the house: the sickest, the eldest, the laziest, and those who were indifferent. Others went down into the cellar, mostly women, girls, and children, where they felt more secure. Others felt suffocated being "tightly closed in," so they chose the grotto, where air circulated. This is where we stayed too.

Tonight is *the night*! Yesterday booms and bangs, hissings and crashes were heard nearer and nearer, but tonight more than ever... Like a crescendo.

During pauses, through the half-open cellar door, came sounds of old women lamenting, young girls sobbing, children crying.

Many of us were in the grotto, mostly men, squeezed any which way – some at the head of the mattress, some at the foot, some crosswise – in order to utilize all the space.

Snuggled in a grey blanket, Lia and I breathed its smell as well as that of the night, while holding each other tightly.

Beyond two big peasants' shoes I could see a slice of the sky and a branch of the walnut tree. During the brief pauses of the cataclysm, there was total silence, like a vacuum crowded with human presence: nobody moved, nobody slept, nobody dared breathe. One could only hear water dripping like a friendly discreet sound. I looked up at the sky, which had momentarily cleared.

Suddenly I was no longer afraid. I had a sense of great peace, a perfect peace, almost physical, which I breathed in along with the night air.

The *Psalm* words came to my lips:

> The Lord is my shepherd; I shall not want.
> He maketh me to lie down in green pastures;
> He leadeth me beside still waters.
> Though I walk through the valley
>   of the shadow of death,
> I will fear no evil...

Faces of my loved ones came to mind: Mother, Father, Uccio, Aunt Iginia.

I hadn't thought of Aunt Iginia for years, as if I had forgotten her, yet that night thoughts of her came to keep me company.

When I was a child, I adored her.

Sometimes "the others" would scold me, but not Aunt Iginia. She had come to this world to bring joy to others.

I had been taught never to ask anything of anyone, but I could ask Aunt Iginia with a sort of secret complicity, as if she were as little as I and yet big enough to dispose and give inexhaustible riches, hidden treasures.

"Ninia, Ninia... Sugar!" I would impatiently whisper while pulling her skirt unbeknownst to my mother. And Aunt "Ninia" would laugh and caress me, giving me a crystal-like sugar cube.

She was the one who introduced me to chalk. With it in my hand, I would draw on the blackboard long white roads and houses with roofs covered with white snow.

Unlike my grandmother and other aunts, who wore dark-colored clothing, Aunt Iginia always wore a turquoise or green apron scattered with minute yellow and red flowers. I hugged her, pointing my tiny finger at her bosom: feeling as if I were in a meadow covered with flowers that I could pick to make a bouquet.

Perhaps I dozed off. I felt light and happy in my dream.

I liked to be with the peasants; it gave me new strength to be among them, sharing the same destiny, waiting for life or death, as if standing on a threshold.

There was silence in the grotto. Then someone moved, coughed, broke the silence:

"Is the war really over?"

"Are we safe?"

An old man sat up and began to tell a story:

"One morning I was alone in the house. In comes a German with a rabbit dangling from his hand. It was dead all right, but not skinned, because skinning was not to his liking. I had never skinned rabbits either. Well, you know, it's women's work. But how could I explain this to a German? He simply pointed his gun at me. He sure made me understand, believe you me! And that's how I learned to skin rabbits!"

Everyone laughed. They were all sitting in a circle, as if at a party.

They kept talking about the Germans who could eat a whole omelette of a dozen eggs apiece, adding to it anything at all, such as sugar and fatty meat. "True pigs that they were! Worse than those dear little creatures, with all due respect!"

The story of the "guzzling Germans" and the stories told the night before were all becoming past history, almost legends.

Finally we got up to go back to our little room.

We leaned from the window, breathing the fresh air as if it were for the first and last time.

"What a historic night," my sister said aloud.

We lay on the bed silent, in a sort of lucid delirium.

How long did we sleep? Perhaps a few hours or only a few minutes, since we fell asleep when the sky brightened and we woke up to find that it was scarcely dawn.

We washed our faces, combed our hair, and changed from wrinkled dresses into fresh ones. Suddenly we heard happy, breathless voices calling at our door:

"Come, come! They are arriving!"

Should I live a thousand years I would never forget the encounter with the French; those were intense moments, when our souls opened to joy and hope.
They filed in front of the house in their armored trucks and stopped. To our wondering eyes and excited hearts, they were indeed '*the liberators*,' our first friendly soldiers.
It was a miracle to see them right there, at the Molino, a place so out of the way. They seemed to come from a legendary world, from an old print. The legendary knights of France and the musketeers flashed through our minds. But these were living soldiers, in modern dress, in grey-green military uniforms. They had been fighting, yet they looked fresh and lively. This also was a miracle! They were clean-shaven, healthy and tanned, young and well-proportioned, with clear eyes.
Their strength was gentle, sustained by an ideal. What impressed me most was their pride, without arrogance, an enlightened, vigilant authority, not blind and passive.
It was pure joy not to hear the detested guttural German, but to hear French, a Latin language so familiar and sweet to our ears and hearts. The French soldiers also seemed glad to find someone who could understand and answer them.
"*Parlez-vous Français?*"
"*Bien!*"
"*Bon!*"
They smiled at us.
We dared to speak to them in our scholastic French. We carried on friendly conversations, and we told them a bit of our story.
We felt ourselves women again, young, and above all, legitimate members of society.

The peasants looked at us with surprise, most probably disapprovingly. As a rule, they never trust foreign soldiers, and they understood the difference only to a certain degree.

Some of the officers knew a little Italian.

"Bello Molino del Sasso," an officer repeated, half closing his eyes in the morning sun.

For the time being, the officers established their headquarters precisely at Molino. They probably chose it because of its location at the crossing of many roads, yet isolated and protected by the big boulder, situated in a hollow so that the house couldn't be seen from a distance, as if it were camouflaged.

Naturally, our enthusiasm was great. My sister wore the blue pullover she had been knitting for months, with a white collar and a velvet skirt. She put on the silk stockings she had guarded religiously, and high-heeled shoes. I noticed she had a new, perky hairdo, with a strand of hair falling on one side of her forehead.

I did my best, too.

The officers gave Beppe two big cases full of food and goodies, including champagne. In fact, they invited Lina and me to drink with them. We stood around the rustic table where soup had been scooped up every evening, lit only by the weak light bulb. What a difference, with those elegant young officers joking and laughing while pouring champagne in the glasses. And there we were with them, as if we were onstage. We were asked to join them in the kitchen for one or two waltzes. Our shyness had completely disappeared – perhaps the champagne helped. We felt uninhibited, free and young.

Standing in groups outside the door, the peasants watched. More than once I caught a hostile look from the girls – I'll never know whether for secret envy or plain disapproval.

After dancing, we stayed up late talking. The French language flowed back to my lips as if roused from an oblivion, as if I were continuing a conversation begun in Lausanne years before.

In memory of that date and that evening, a lieutenant gave us an issue of *Le Monde*. One of them wrote two lines on the front page and all the rest signed. One of the captains' names was Francois Mauriac, just like the author. He added under his signature, "*un grand nom.*"

We sang together:

> "*J'ai deux amours*
> *Mon pays et Paris*"

and also:

> "*Auprès de ma blonde*
> *Qu'il fait bon, fait bon, fait bon!*
> *Auprès de ma blonde*
> *Qu'il fait bon coucher...*"

We felt too warm, so we went outside to breathe the night air. The Molino had an unusual look: here and there small lanterns had been lit. By those flickering lights one could see the silhouettes, the faces, the dark gleaming eyes, and the very white teeth of the Moroccan soldiers.

They were seated on the ground, cross-legged, at the outskirts around the courtyard in front of the house. They were so still they seemed unreal, like a strange, exotic wreath encircling the familiar scene of the Molino. They were kept in check by the officers' presence.

That evening we regarded them only as a curiosity, without any fear or disgust: we had not yet heard the horrible stories about them.

During the next two days, an officers' mess hall was set up.

Elvira and her daughters kept busy.

A few roosters' necks were twisted, some black ducks were sacrificed, small new potatoes were fried, and early tomatoes from the garden were fixed for salad. Beppe fetched two or three flasks of wine from the cellar. Lina and I set the table with our good embroidered tablecloth, our silver, and a crystal vase with a bunch of yellow broom flowers.

Nothing seemed to us good enough to honor them. We were sorry it was not our own home so that we could offer them more luxury.

For the first time we disagreed with the peasants, who, as usual, were thrifty, reserved, and self-contained.

The two cases of food that the officers had given them contained provisions for a month. In fact, even after they left, like a ship's wake marking their passage, cans of cheese, jars of milk, tea and coffee, candies and chocolates were put out on the table every day.

There were also cigarettes, which the peasants kept, but didn't smoke.

We two were ecstatic over all the city delicacies, tastes that we had forgotten and now found again. That wonderful thick hot chocolate, just like the food of the gods!

We were captivated by the fragrance of roses from the tea and the incomparable aroma of the coffee that was lighter than ours.

To our great surprise, the peasants, curious at first, showed no emotion. In fact, they were indifferent, even hostile in front of such delights. They didn't throw anything away, being thrifty by nature. While in the morning we had cappuccino now, the peasants continued to eat cornmeal, or sliced bread with cheese or onions. Beef and pork in tin containers were greatly appreciated at first. The French had left a lot behind. After tasting it, the peasants passed judgment: "we'll stick with our own soup." The meat, masked with local beans and homemade bread, became more acceptable to their palates.

Fears, past dangers, all seemed forgotten. Life returned to the usual routine. Many things had to be attended to; the wheat stalks were turning yellow in the furrows.

We still lived in the atmosphere of the days just past. We were fascinated to be making new contacts, to mingle again with people, to experience these extraordinary moments. We were living in historic times, while adding new pages to the novel of our lives.

We couldn't bear staying inside the house, so we would use any pretext to leave it, to mingle with the others, to listen to other people's stories.

People continued to arrive at Molino: each one had something to tell.

I remember one refugee, a little woman with a black kerchief on her head, with charcoal-black eyes, who came to ask for tomatoes to make *ragù*. She was a Sicilian who happened to be in our area – God knows how. She was not so much involved in the collective upheaval of war as much as with her own private affairs. A daughter of hers had gotten married only a few days before. For months they had lived crowded into a sort of chicken coop. The daughter had become involved with a young man from another family living in the same hut, and the "inevitable" had happened. To repair the damage, a proper marriage had hastily taken place.

Every five minutes the mother would mention this daughter, underlining emphatically her present, legitimate condition and status: "my daughter, the bride," she would say with her Sicilian accent.

The woman told of a Frenchman giving her a loaf of bread. "A whi-i-te bread," she said, and "oh-oh, what a brea-d!" Actually, it was a loaf of white sliced bread, soft and somewhat insipid, that was nothing to compare with the tasteful country bread. She opened her eyes and mouth wide in amazement: "A whi-i-te bread! Oh-oh, what a brea-d!"

Later she told us about an incident that happened to her daughter, "the bride." She was doing laundry at the small, outdoor spigot when a soldier came up to her asking for a drink of water. His eyes shone with unmistakable desire. In his hand he had what, unfortunately, in those sad, sinful days was considered an irresistible merchandise for exchange: a bar of chocolate. Realizing that the soldier "was thirsty for something else," the daughter heroically refused the chocolate, and managed to run away.

"Butcherboy," the young peasant living next to us, told another story.

...A soldier had run after a housewife who lived in an isolated house on top of a small plateau. She was an enormous woman, already middle-aged and past fifty.

She, who had understood and had not taken it too seriously, yelled at him: "Me? Are you out of your mind? I'm old; I could be your grandma!"

The soldier, who knew a little Italian, answered quite seriously: "*No... No... E abastansa.* You'll suffice, Terzilia. Don't be discouraged, you are still..."

In telling the story, "Butcherboy" laughed his head off. The peasant girls winked at each other and laughed, while reproaching "Butcherboy" for being so shameless.

"The bees! The bees!"

Elvira came rushing to tell us, "They smashed everything."

We ran to the knoll. The hives were uncovered, the honey-combs wrecked, the bees all over the place just like groups of unemployed workers gathered to threaten or to plot a strike. In the air, a revolt, a civil war was brewing.

What had happened?

Without a doubt, some Moroccan had assaulted the bees' homes. We had heard they were gluttons for honey.

"Those black-faced rogues are like beasts!" Beppe said. "Their skin is tough; they don't even mind being stung and for sure the bees gave them a taste of their poison."

Then, seeing how upset we were, he picked up his big hat and the blower and helped us to put back the roof and the trays into the hives. His children called him, "hey, Papa, come inside! What are you doing? Are you crazy?" but he ignored them.

As a matter of fact, it was quite dangerous to stay in the open on the knoll. Reconnaissance planes flew overhead; to stay outside was like tempting the gods. But we didn't worry about it either; we had to hurry in order to save the bees. "Perhaps it's all for nothing, anyway, and the bees will die just the same!" We were then suddenly overcome by discouragement and sadness. The profaned beehives seemed to us a symbol of so many of the houses that had been violated and destroyed.

But we were far from imagining what was going to happen the next day, the terrible night of the Moroccans, the worst night of our lives.

Up to that time, danger had been terrifying, but somewhat invisible, like a nightmare, almost unreal.

That night, however, we encountered it, we saw it; for the first time we came face-to-face with it. And those faces were truly frightful, those brutal faces of the Moroccans.

As usual we went to bed fully dressed. That evening, having taken a small pointed kitchen knife upstairs, I put it under my pillow. "In case the Germans should still show up," (some were disbanded here and there). "We'll defend ourselves." So saying, we laughed, brandishing the little knife usually used to cut cheese and onions.

From the bed next to ours we could hear the girls' breathing: they were already asleep. My sister and I, however, were awake, eyes wide open in the dark.

All of a sudden, behind the closed door, after a strange incomprehensible muttering, we clearly heard Beppe's words: "No, no, not there. There are no Germans hiding; the children are asleep upstairs and they would get scared!"

Then someone kicked the door wide open.

Two shadows entered; in the darkness a search light shone.

The light came toward our bed, toward our faces.

In reconstructing the event, I see that I have no sense of time. A sequence of emotions followed one after another, upsetting us as though we were going through an endless agony... Perhaps it only lasted a few minutes – from the moment we were bathed in the light of the lantern and a hand reached out as if grabbing us, to which we responded with screams – to the moment when we could hardly believe they had really gone away, away for good, leaving us alone in our room, our faces swollen from the beating, our eyes still fixed on a horrendous vision.

I was trembling and I was still frightened, trembling with a fear that lasted for many days after.

After that terrible ordeal, the girls and we two sisters left the Molino temporarily and were taken in by some peasant friends whose house was less secluded and less isolated.

From there we could see the French camp. To console and reassure us, the peasants told us to look out the windows at the soldiers, Moroccans included, with their women – a small *harem* – that traveled with them as the front line moved.

Half hidden behind the shutters, with the giggling children of our new family, we observed some women with dark faces. Their colorful striped gowns were enough for us to identify their sex. If some wore pants, the girls would say: "Hey, don't you see their breasts? and their buttocks sticking out in back?"

There was absolutely nothing to fear anymore.

We were also told that we should go to the military headquarters to seek redress. If "*those ugly beasts*" – they couldn't call them humans – could be recognized, they would have been shot.

But, how to recognize those we had caught only a glimpse of, for a few moments, in the uncertain light of a search light, with all our senses blunted, not knowing whether we were dead or alive? And suppose we had an innocent man condemned?

Meanwhile, everybody makes a fuss over us; we are the protagonists and they want us to tell them about the incident.

"But what happened?" they ask. "What happened?"

And I talk and talk, with my voice still hoarse from the screams, words running into one another as in a turbulent sea. Some vivid details surge to the forefront, my audience incites me to go on; again they want to know "of the moment when the Moroccan fired the gun in the darkness."

"My sister Lia and the other girls had succeeded in running away, but she knew I was alone with those two soldiers and heard me scream, so she came back into the room. Right at that moment one of the two fires the gun and I cry: 'Lia, are you dead?' with a voice that doesn't seem like mine, as if coming from another world.

"Imprisoned between the two extended arms of a Moroccan, I was thrown down on my back on the bed. Suddenly his head is bent closely over me and I grab his helmet. He raises up his face and at that very moment I hit him on the nose with his hard helmet."

...Blood dripping from his nose... Blood stains were found on my dress and on the wall, and the bullet was found as well...

...Light coming on suddenly in the room...

"Most likely it was Elvira's doing that saved us. That brave little woman, with extraordinary presence of mind, had gone down to the cellar to start the water wheel that controlled the house light, and shouted, 'the Commanding Officers are here! The Commanding Officers are here!'

"At that point the Moroccans backed up toward the exit with the gun pointed, the same gun that a moment earlier was aimed at Beppe, who was unable to defend us because two more Moroccans held his arms while a third watched the door. Hearing our desperate cries, Beppe could only say, 'Poor little ones, poor little ones!'"

...The gunshot in the darkness... The blood, the sudden light... The episode, the way we told it, always had a telling effect.

But not on our parents, poor dears.

When mother heard the beginning of our story, she grew so pale, as if she might faint, that we did not have the heart to continue. We only said that "nothing happened." She held us tightly as if to protect us now, thanking God for our safety.

She didn't know that in those horrifying moments, even from far away, she had protected me. The image of her sweet face had helped me: I felt her near me, and I found the strength not to faint, but to resist, while one Moroccan was hitting me on my head trying to knock me unconscious.

The horrible thought going through my brain at first was: "This is life in its reality, everything else has been useless, a sadistic mockery, an insult to your malevolent destiny: your greatest suffering coming straight from your *Liberators!*" This lucid thought was immediately followed by another one: "No, it can't be true, it can't end this way, it won't end this way!"

Meantime, in desperation, my heart offered a strong prayer of abiding faith.

The episode of the Moroccans by now was in our memory like a legend, a tale. It seemed as if it had never happened. What's more, to us it sounded almost improbable, as it must have sounded to the people who had heard about it.

I remember that once, while telling the incident to an acquaintance of ours, met by chance in Siena at the "Trattoria del Partigiano," at the high point of the narration:

There was a gun shot in the dark...
And blood began dripping..."

A gentleman nearby overheard, his fork with the entwined spaghetti remained in mid-air, but the expression on his face was incredulous, like somebody listening to an incredible adventure, absolutely unreal.

Meanwhile, we began to come out of the hole, like snails after a storm. There was so much to look at, so varied, different, unusual and interesting.

After the French and the Moroccans, the English and the Indians, then the Americans and the Blacks arrived.

They seemed figures who stepped out of a scholastic atlas; they intermingled with the memory we had of their distant lands: India, a triangle; America, with a somewhat crooked tail...

But what stupefied us most was to see them moving and living within such a different setting, within our familiar landscape of Tuscan countryside, and even of our Molino.

We could hardly tear our gaze from a group of Indians. They were naked down to the waist, with a white cloth wrapped around their hips, with long greasy hair that they continually combed after immersing the comb in the spring water. Then they braided the hair into thick dark plaits. The pupils of their eyes – luminous and almost black – ran into the black of the iris, which stood out on the white sky-blue cornea.

Looking at those eyes, at those large mouths, at the amber complexion, the novel *Rain* came to mind, in which the author defined a European face *an anemic mush*, as opposed to the outstanding liveliness of an East Indian face.

Enchanted, we listened to the Canadians laugh with their childlike laughter. They wore the military beret tilted over one ear, and their faces were young and fresh, with clear innocent eyes, their shirts open on their chest, the sleeves rolled up.

They gave away mounds of candies and chewing gum.

Then there were the incredibly black faces of the Blacks. They were really frightening, even more than the Moroccans! But, it wasn't true. The Negroes revealed themselves to be much better and more civilized people.

Once, but only in their enthusiastic desire to help as they were riding in a jeep, one of them threw a hard "bullet," almost hitting our heads: a can of meat and vegetables.

We started to use our bicycles again, always taking longer and longer trips. We met innumerable army trucks; often we had to dismount, and move to one side to let them pass.

One day, on the road to Siena...

Our hearts stopped for a moment, then started again, beating faster. Hypnotized, we stared at a car parked on the side of the road.

The star of David!

The sky-blue and white colors, the gentle colors of the tallith, the prayer shawl, were waving before our eyes; we ourselves were uncertain whether to smile or to weep at the sight.

A soldier got out of the car; he looked at us with steely grey eyes. We were so moved that we dared not approach him or speak to him. Everything unfolded as in a dream, extraordinary, and at the same time natural.

"*Shalom*," he greeted us.

"*Shalom*," we replied.

The ancient greeting, in the ancient language.

Any timidity was overcome by a wave of affection, by a sudden trust, like finding a brother.

Shalom – Peace! The mournful sigh of all peoples at that time; but invoked with more soulful longing by our people in a perpetually deluded and ongoing hope spanning thousands of years.

We got into the car and sat next to him, listening to new words:

kibbutz, mosciav, haluzim...

His name was Sammy. He also knew a little Italian.

"Which is the most beautiful country in the world?" I asked him.

"Our home is...our land," he answered.

Meanwhile, he took out his wallet and showed us pictures of his wife, and of the children born in *Erez Israel*, and those of his parents deported by the Germans.

"This...our house," in Austria, a little house surrounded by a garden. In front of the small gate, two old people smiling: his father and mother.

"Here, *Kibbutz*." An extension of huts, all exactly alike, surrounded by the desert. At a window, a young woman, at the door, a little boy, the sun shining on his light hair.

"These two, happy..." he said, pointing to the old people.

"He is very good," pointing to the boy, as if the living and the dead were together in one and the same reality, outside the dimensions of space and time.

And I felt it was beautiful and right to speak that way.

In the course of our lives we travel only an infinitesimal part of the way; we live only an instant in time. However, our individual destiny belongs to another design, more vast, eternal, in which we are all equally present.

Now, ahead of us, ways were opening up again.

Like white ribbons that unfold endlessly, seeming to join countries and peoples all over the world.

It's enough to go out our front door, enter upon a familiar pathway and keep going.

But at times, ways take a turn or come to a fork. When we are young, each choice seems the only one possible. Afterward, with the passing of years, the horizon recedes. As we near the end of our journey, we shall encounter another fork, another turn.

We know, however, that whatever our choice may be, our goal, our true homeland will never be found here on earth.

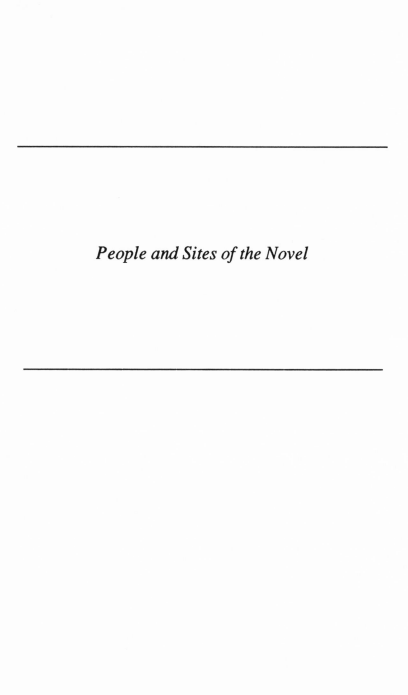

People and Sites of the Novel

FIRENZE **O**

MOLINO DEL SASSO

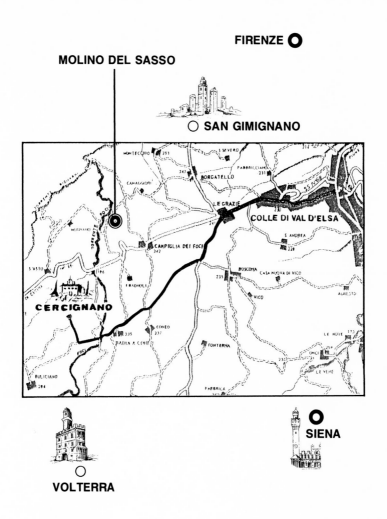

O SAN GIMIGNANO

VOLTERRA

O

O
SIENA

The sites in this novel, in the countryside near Colle Val d'Elsa.

The little church of Our Lady of Grace, outside the wall of Colle which stands on the country road leading to Poggio (Cercignano).

On opposite page, the crenellated walls of Colle; *below*, driver Michele (Ciro Cardinali) from Colle, with his son, taken at the time of this story.

Above, the Albieris' farm house.

On opposite page, the "Palazzo," as the villa in Poggio was called, and a detail of the facade with the entrance door and the stone benches.

Pietro, the *capoccia* of the Mannozzi family, and his wife Corinna (Amelia).

Above, on the opposite page, the "young master" of Poggio, the cousin Uccio (Giulio), photographed the way he liked, in the meadow. Below, Isa, the narrator of the story, at age 14.

Lia (Lina), Isa's sister, at the time of her doctorate.

One of the protagonists of the story, cousin Annalena (Vittorina), with her bicycle.

Taken by a noted photographer of Leghorn, Bruno Miniati, this photo portrays Isa, the author and protagonist, at the time of this story.

Isa, as a little girl not yet two and a half years old, when everyone called her "Zippo."

Isa and Lia's parents at the time of their wedding.

Above, the pathway from the house of Molino del Sasso, nestled "in the hollow." One of Beppe's daughters, Rosalba (Maretta), is leading the sheep to the grazing site.

To the right, Beppe, *capoccia* of the Molino family, with one of his daughters.

On opposite page, Castello (San Gimignano) in silhouette. After the death of Signorina Gentileschi (Andreina Messeri), Edonide burned all her papers and photographs.

Beppe and Elvira
(Amelia) on their wed-
ding day.

The Nannini family
(Anichini) of Molino
del Sasso.   Beppe's
parents are in the cen-
ter between their son
and his wife Elvira.

Rolando, one of the young men who hid in the stable at Molino del Sasso for three days in order to escape from the Germans.

Tonino (Marino), Beppe's son, at the time of our story.

Uncle Ugo, Uccio's father and brother of Isa and Lia's mother. He was the first to fall in love with the Sienese countryside and bought the villa and the estate of Poggio (Cercignano). Without him, this story would have taken a different turn, and *Beside Still Waters* could not have been written.